MASTER ● THE
Basics
Second Edition

Marcel Danesi, P.h.D.

ITALIAN

BARRON'S

Contents

Parts of Speech   64

Special Topics 204

A READING AND GRAMMAR BRUSH-UP

PREFACE

After having gone through the experience of studying a language for the first time, one invariably feels the need to do it all over again—to brush up one's grammar. Actually, this is a crucial stage in the process of learning another language. It gives you the opportunity to reflect upon what you know, to reinforce your skills, to fill in the gaps, to clarify difficult points—in sum, to help you build a more solid linguistic foundation.

This text is intended to give you the chance to brush up your Italian. It is written in a nontechnical, easy-to-read style. In fact, even the beginning learner would be able to work through the book without too much difficulty.

To find out how to use this book, just read ahead!

HOW TO USE THIS BOOK

This book can be used for both self-study and classroom learning. The first thing to do is to try the test provided for you in the "Find Out What You Know" part. This will give you not only the opportunity to "get into the action" right away, but it will also point out those areas where you are strong and those that need more study. At the end of the test there is a diagnostic summary that relates the questions to the chapters of this book.

After a brief introduction to grammatical terms with examples, this book is divided into four main parts: *The Basics* (chapters 1–3), *Parts of Speech* (chapters 4–12), *Special Topics* (chapters 13–20), and *A Reading and Writing Brush-Up* (chapters 21–22). Each part is subdivided as follows.

- The *Basics* part is made up of three chapters (1–3) containing a nontechnical and easy-to-follow discussion of Italian sounds, spelling conventions, word-order patterns, and the basic words and expressions needed to carry out common conversations. If you are using this book for self-study, we suggest that you go through this part as though you were reading a story. The story in this case is the Italian language. This part provides you with the main "storyline" or "plot" of our language story.

- The *Parts of Speech* part (chapters 4–12) introduces the "main characters" of our story—the nouns, articles, pronouns, etc. that make up the Italian language.

- The *Special Topics* part (chapters 13–20) describes the "supporting characters"—idiomatic expressions, numbers, synonyms, antonyms, etc. that allow us to complete our narrative. Incidentally, at the end of the book you will find the *Verb Charts* section containing irregular verbs—the "evil characters" of our story.

- The *Reading and Writing Brush-Up* is made up of two chapters (21–22) that give you insights on how to read and write in Italian. This is your chance to be a "critic" or "creative writer" of your own story.

Some chapters are longer than others and require both more time and more effort to learn. But never become discouraged! The explanations have been made as simple as possible. There are many charts and diagrams to help you "see" what is involved. And there are plenty of examples that illustrate each point. Only common vocabulary has been used throughout this book, and it is repeated frequently so that you will have a better opportunity to reinforce it. The topics in each chapter are numbered in order. This will allow you to go backward and forward in the book, and to relate grammatical points to each other. The numerical reference system for each section can be found at the start of the section.

You will find an *Exercise Set* after the *Basics, Parts of Speech, Special Topics,* and *Reading and Writing* parts. Each set contains exercises and activities that allow you to practice what you have just learned and/or reviewed in the part.

The final part of this book is *Let's Review.* This contains exercises and activities that will allow you to review the whole course. The questions are keyed to the numerical reference system in the *Answers* section. The exercise and review sections contain puzzles and humorous activities to help make the learning process as enjoyable as possible.

If you are using this book as a classroom text, the procedure just described is also applicable. However, your teacher undoubtedly will want to give you more chances to practice your Italian through other kinds of exercises and activities. Moreover, your teacher will certainly want to help you learn "the story of Italian" by elaborating upon and amplifying the book's explanations.

Now, let the story begin!

FIND OUT WHAT YOU KNOW

Let's get started with a test to help you pinpoint those areas in which you are strong and those in which you need some review. The following seventy questions correspond to the three main sections of this book.

- There are fifteen questions on the basics: the sounds, spelling conventions, word-order patterns, and basic vocabulary of Italian.

- There are thirty questions on the parts of speech: the nouns, articles, pronouns, etc. of Italian.

- There are twenty questions that will allow you to find out how much you remember about such topics as telling time and counting in Italian.

- Finally, there are five questions that test your ability to read and write Italian.

At the end of the test, you will find the answers and an indication of where to go in this book to review and strengthen your weaker areas.

Test Yourself

THE BASICS

Each of the following four sentences contains one error. See if you can find the error, and then correct it.

1. Giovanni mangia tanta choccolata. _____
2. A jugno partiremo per l'Italia. _____
3. Mia madre è stanca e ha sono. _____
4. Andiamo al cinema ogni Mercoledì. _____

In the next two sentences there is one word that does not belong. Can you find the two extra words?

5. Maria aspetta per l'autobus. _____
6. Ogni sera mio padre ascolta a un programma italiano alla radio. _____

The next four sentences have something wrong with them. Rewrite each sentence correctly.

7. Il professore telefona suoi studenti.

_____

8. Maria ha non scritto quella lettera.

_____

9. Guida tua madre una FIAT?

_____

10. La ragazza è italiana che legge il giornale.

_____

In each of the next five questions there is one word that does not belong. Can you find the five "odd" words?

10a. padre, madre, amica, sorella, fratello
10b. italiano, inglese, spagnolo, lingua, francese
10c. verde, albero, rosso, giallo, marrone
10d. simpatico, gamba, naso, testa, orecchio
10e. Francia, Italia, Giappone, Germania, Roma

Test your ability to form the plural of nouns. Which is the correct plural form for each of the following nouns?

PARTS OF SPEECH

11. ragazzo
    ragazzi ☐
    ragazze ☐
    both ☐
12. artista
    artisti ☐
    artiste ☐
    both ☐
13. automobile
    automobile ☐
    automobili ☐
    both ☐
14. città
    città ☐
    cittè ☐
    both ☐
15. uomo
    uomi ☐
    uomini ☐
    both ☐

Match each definite article in the left column with an appropriate noun in the right column.

16. lo   figlio
    l'   studentessa
    gli   amici
    il   amiche
    i   amico
    la   studente
    le   libri

Now match each indefinite article with the appropriate noun.

17. uno   automobile
    una   specchio
    un'   occhio
    un   donna

Here's one more! Match each demonstrative with the appropriate noun.

18. quegli	entrata
quell'	uscite
questi	ragazzo
quel	ragazzi
questa	sbagli
queste	penna

Now check the appropriate partitive plural for each of the following nouns.

19. uno zio
    degli zii ☐
    alcuni zii ☐
    both ☐
20. un'amica
    delle amiche ☐
    qualche amica ☐
    both ☐

The adjectives in the following sentences do not have their endings. Can you supply them?

21. Qual _____ libri hai comprato?
22. Quei ragazzi sono frances _____.
23. Anche quelle ragazze sono frances _____.
24. La lor _____ professoressa è italian _____.
25. Tutt _____ le studentesse in questa classe sono
    american _____.

The following pronouns are missing from sentences 26–31. Can you put each one in its appropriate slot?

PRONOUNS: si, la, le, quella, il mio, chi
---

26. Il tuo orologio è bello, ma anche _____ è bello.
27. _____ ha mangiato tutti gli spaghetti?
28. Quale penna vuoi, questa o _____?
29. Hai chiamato Maria? Sì, _____ ho già chiamata.
30. Hai telefonato a Maria? Sì, _____ ho già telefonato.
31. Quei turisti _____ sono divertiti in Italia.

Can you match each subject pronoun with its verb?

32. io	avete dormito
tu	mangiavano
lei	capisco
noi	dovrebbe studiare
voi	siamo arrivati
loro	scriverai

The following verbs are missing from the passage. Can you put them in their appropriate slots?

> VERBS: avesse, sembrava, comprare, siamo andati,
> abbiamo comprato, conosceva

33. Ieri _____ ad un negozio a _____ delle
    scarpe nuove. Il commesso ci _____. Era un vec-
    chio amico di scuola. Benché _____ quarant'anni,
    _____ ancora molto giovane. _____ due paia
    di scarpe italiane.

Here are three adjectives. Check their corresponding
adverbs.

34. sincero
    sincermente ☐
    sinceramente ☐
35. facile
    facilmente ☐
    facilemente ☐
36. elegante
    elegantmente ☐
    elegantemente ☐

The following prepositions are missing from the passage.
Put them in their appropriate slots.

> PREPOSITIONS: fra, all', negli, del, di

37. Il figlio _____ signor Bianchi ha ventidue anni.
    Studia _____ università _____ Bologna.
    _____ due anni tornerà _____ Stati Uniti.

Check the appropriate answer to each question.

38. Giovanni, conosci qualcuno in questa città?
    No, non conosco nessuno. ☐
    No, non conosco niente. ☐
39. Dove sono i miei libri?
    Ci sono i tuoi libri. ☐
    Ecco i tuoi libri. ☐
40. Hai fatto lavare i piatti a tuo fratello?
    Sì, glieli ho fatti lavare. ☐
    Sì, li lava. ☐

**COMMUNI-
CATION
TOPICS**

Put *piace* and *piacciono* into the appropriate slots.

41. Non mi _____ quel programma televisivo. Mi _____
    solo i film. Anche a te _____, non è vero?

There is an incorrect expression in each of the following two
groups. Which ones are they?

42. Maria ha fame. ☐
    Giovanni ha sete. ☐
    Il signore fa il biglietto. ☐
    Marco fa freddo. ☐
43. Il professore è torto. ☐
    Il fumo mi dà fastidio. ☐
    Abbiamo bisogno di dormire. ☐
    Signora Binni, come sta? ☐

Fill in the missing parts.

44. 2.456 = due _____ quattro _____ cinquanta _____
45. Questa è la ventitr _____ volta che ti telefono!

Write out the following times.

46. 8:24 P.M. = _____.
47. 9:55 A.M. = _____.

Complete each sentence with the appropriate expression.

> EXPRESSIONS: il tre febbraio, maggio, autunno, fa
> freddo

48. Nel nord d'Italia il bel tempo non comincia prima
    di _____.
49. Le foglie degli alberi cadono ogni _____.
50. D'inverno _____.
51. Che data è oggi? _____.

Check the appropriate "conversation strategy."

52. It is the afternoon, and you meet someone. You might
    say:
    Buona notte ☐
    Buona sera ☐
    Buon giorno ☐
53. When answering the phone, you first say:
    Ciao. ☐
    Chi parla? ☐
    Pronto. ☐
54. To say "good-bye" to a friend, you might say:
    Ciao. ☐
    ArrivederLa. ☐
    Buon giorno. ☐

Can you match the synonyms in each column?

55. strada   sfortunatamente
    purtroppo   via
    uguale   lo stesso
    perciò   quindi

Now can you match the antonyms?

56. alto   pieno
    fuori   basso
    vuoto   dentro
    ricco   povero

How good are you at translating? Try the following words. But be careful! There are some tricks in the sentences.

57. (*This nation*) _____ è molto bella.
58. (*My parents*) _____ abitano in Italia.
59. Devo andare (*to the library*) _____ per studiare un po'.
60. Ho già letto (*that magazine*) _____.

READING AND WRITING

Read the following passage; then indicate if the three statements are *vero* (true) or *falso* (false).

> *Ieri ho visto il mio amico. Non era tanto contento. Marco è sempre triste quando fa brutto tempo. Allora io l'ho invitato a prendere un caffè. Dopo un caffè e una breve conversazione, ha perso la sua tristezza.*

60a. Ieri faceva brutto tempo.
    Vero   ☐
    Falso   ☐
60b. Alla fine, Marco era ancora triste.
    Vero   ☐
    Falso   ☐
60c. I due amici hanno conversato per un po'.
    Vero   ☐
    Falso   ☐

Following are two letter salutations (an example of a salutation is "Dear John…"). Can you supply the missing word from each?

60d. _____ Maria
60e. _____ signor Marchi

Answers

1. cioccolata
2. giugno
3. sonno
4. mercoledì
   (*not capitalized*)
5. per

6. a
7. Il professore telefona *ai* suoi studenti.
8. Maria non ha scritto quella lettera.
9. Tua madre guida una FIAT?/Guida una FIAT, tua madre?
10. La ragazza che legge il giornale è italiana.
10a. amica *(all the others are words designating family members)*
10b. lingua *(all the others are actual names of languages or nationalities)*
10c. albero *(all the others are color adjectives)*
10d. simpatico *(all the others are words designating body parts)*
10e. Roma *(all the others are the names of countries)*
11. ragazzi
12. both
13. automobili
14. città
15. uomini
16. lo studente
l'amico
gli amici
il figlio
i libri
la studentessa
le amiche
17. uno specchio
una donna
un'automobile
un occhio
18. quegli sbagli
quell'entrata

questi ragazzi
quel ragazzo
questa penna
queste uscite
19. both
20. both
21. Quali
22. francesi
23. francesi
24. loro/italiana
25. Tutte/americane
26. il mio
27. Chi
28. quella
29. la
30. le
31. si
32. io capisco
tu scriverai
lei dovrebbe studiare
noi siamo arrivati
voi avete dormito
loro mangiavano
33. siamo andati; comprare; conosceva; avesse; sembrava; Abbiamo comprato
34. sinceramente
35. facilmente
36. elegantemente
37. *del* signor Bianchi; *all'* università *di* Bologna; *Fra* due anni; *negli* Stati Uniti.
38. No, non conosco nessuno.
39. Ecco i tuoi libri.
40. Sì, glieli ho fatti lavare.
41. Non mi *piace* quel programma televisivo. Mi *piacciono* solo i film. Anche a te *piacciono*, non è vero?
42. "Marco fa freddo".
43. "Il professore è torto."
44. due*mila* quattro*cento* cinquanta*sei*

45. ventit*reesima*
46. le otto e ventiquattro di sera / le venti e ventiquattro
47. le dieci meno cinque / le nove e cinquantacinque
48. maggio
49. autunno
50. fa freddo
51. Il tre febbraio.
52. Buona sera.
53. Pronto.
54. Ciao.
55. strada — via
    purtroppo — sfortunatamente
    uguale — lo stesso
    perciò — quindi

56. alto — basso
    fuori — dentro
    vuoto — pieno
    ricco — povero
57. Questa nazione
58. I miei genitori
59. alla biblioteca
60. quella rivista
60a. Vero
60b. Falso
60c. Vero
60d. Cara/Carissima
60e. Gentile/Egregio

Diagnostic Analysis

Section	Question numbers	Number of Answers	
		Right	**Wrong**
THE BASICS			
1. Italian Sounds and Spelling	1, 2, 3, 4		
2. Elements of an Italian Sentence	5, 6, 7, 8, 9, 10		
3. Basic Italian Vocabulary	10a, 10b, 10c, 10d, 10e		
THE PARTS OF SPEECH			
4. Nouns	11, 12, 13, 14, 15		
5. Articles	16, 17, 18		
6. Partitives	19, 20		

Section	Question numbers	Number of Answers	
		Right	Wrong
THE BASICS			
7. Adjectives	21, 22, 23, 24, 25		
8. Pronouns	26, 27, 28, 29, 30, 31		
9. Verbs	32, 33		
10. Adverbs	34, 35, 36		
11. Prepositions	37		
12. Negatives and Other Grammatical Points	38, 39, 40		
COMMUNICATION TOPICS			
13. The Verb "Piacere"	41		
14. Idioms	42, 43		
15. Numbers	44, 45		
16. Telling Time	46, 47		
17. Days, Months, Seasons, Dates, Weather	48, 49, 50, 51		
18. Common Conversation Techniques	52, 53, 54		
19. Synonyms and Antonyms	55, 56		
20. Cognates	57, 58, 59, 60		
READING AND WRITING			
21. Reading	60a, 60b, 60c		
22. Writing	60d, 60e		
TOTAL QUESTIONS	70		

Use the following scale to see how you did.

60 to 70 right:	**Excellent**
55 to 59 right:	**Very Good**
50 to 54 right:	**Average**
45 to 49 right:	**Below Average**
Fewer than 45 right:	**Unsatisfactory**

A GRAMMAR BRUSH-UP
The Basics

BASIC GRAMMATICAL TERMS WITH EXAMPLES

The study of grammar is as old as civilization itself. The word *grammar* comes from the Ancient Greek word for "letters," becoming, eventually, the technical term for the study of language—a use that has survived throughout the ages!

Before starting your review of Italian grammar, it is useful to go over the most important grammatical terms—even though the concepts associated with such terms are presented in clear language throughout the text.

active voice   *la voce attiva*
the form of the verb indicating that the subject of the sentence performs the action.

EXAMPLE: Mark <u>eats</u> pizza all the time. / *Marco <u>mangia</u> sempre la pizza.*
['Mark' is performing the action of eating.]

adjective   *l'aggettivo*
any word that describes, limits, or qualifies a noun.

EXAMPLE: What a <u>pretty</u> hat! / *Che <u>bel</u> cappello!*
['Pretty' describes 'hat,' the noun.]

adverb   *l'avverbio*
any word that modifies the meaning of a verb, adjective, or other adverb with regard to time, place, manner, cause, degree, and so on.

EXAMPLES: Mary did it <u>gladly</u>. / *Maria l'ha fatto <u>volentieri</u>.*
['Gladly' tells you the 'manner' in which Mary did something.]
Mary did it <u>yesterday</u>./ *Maria l'ha fatto <u>ieri</u>.*
['Yesterday' tells you the 'time' when Mary did something.]

affirmative   *affermativo*
a word, expression, or sentence that indicates assent (that the fact is so).

EXAMPLE: <u>Yes</u>, I agree. / *<u>Sì</u>, sono d'accordo.*
['Yes' conveys affirmation or consent.]

agreement of   *l'accordo tra*
adjective and noun   *l'aggettivo e il nome*
an adjective corresponds in person, number, case, and/or gender with the noun it modifies.

EXAMPLES: This boy speaks Italian. / *Questo ragazzo parla*
italiano.
['This' is the singular form of the demonstrative adjective agreeing with the singular form of the noun, 'boy.']
These boys speak Italian. / *Questi ragazzi parlano*
italiano.
['These' is the corresponding plural form agreeing with 'boys.']

auxiliary verb   *il verbo ausiliare*
a verb that helps the main verb express tense, mood, etc.

EXAMPLE: She has gone already. / *Lei è andata già via.*
['Has' helps the verb 'to go' express the past tense.]

cardinal number   *il numero cardinale*
any number that expresses the actual objects or units being considered.

EXAMPLE: I need two dollars. / *Ho bisogno di due dollari.*
['Two' expresses exactly how many dollars are needed.]

causative   *il causativo*
a form of the verb that expresses causation (the act of causing).

EXAMPLE: You made me do it! / *Me l'ho hai fatto fare!*
[This form of the verb expresses the fact that some-one caused you to do something.]

clause   *la proposizione*
a group of words in a sentence that contain a subject and predicate.

EXAMPLE: The woman who is drinking the espresso is not
Italian. / *La donna che sta bevendo l'espresso non è*
italiana.
['Who is drinking the espresso' is a clause in the sentence; it has a subject 'who' and a predicate 'is drinking the espresso.']

comparative   *il comparativo*
adjective   *dell'aggettivo*
the form of an adjective that expresses degree ('more,' 'less,' '(same) as'), thus allowing for comparison with some-thing or someone.

EXAMPLE: Mary is <u>taller</u> than John. / *Maria è <u>più alta</u> di Giovanni.*
[‘Taller’ is the form of ‘tall’ that expresses a higher degree of ‘tallness.’]

comparative   *il comparativo*
adverb   *dell’avverbio*

the form of an adverb that expresses degree (‘more,’ ‘less,’ ‘(same) as’), thus allowing for comparison.

EXAMPLE: She walks <u>more quickly</u> than I do. / *Lei cammina <u>più lentamente</u> di me.*
[‘More quickly’ expresses a higher degree of ‘quickness.’]

complex sentence   *il periodo complesso*

a sentence consisting of an independent clause and one or more dependent (subordinate) clauses.

EXAMPLE: I knew that he was coming. / *Sapevo che veniva.*
[This sentence consists of the independent clause ‘I knew’ and the dependent clause ‘that he was coming.’]

compound sentence   *il periodo complesso*

a sentence consisting of two or more independent clauses, usually connected by a semicolon or conjunction.

EXAMPLE: I like pizza but I don’t like panzerotti. / *Mi piace la pizza ma non mi piacciono i panzerotti.*
[This sentence consists of two independent clauses, ‘I like pizza’ and ‘I don’t like panzerotti,’ connected by the conjunction ‘but.’]

compound verb   *il verbo composto*

a verb consisting of an auxiliary verb and the past participle of the main verb.

EXAMPLE: I <u>have</u> <u>eaten</u> already. / *<u>Ho</u> <u>mangiato</u> già.*
[The verb consists of an auxiliary verb ‘have’ and the past participle ‘eaten.’]

conditional mood   *il modo condizionale*

the form of a verb expressing a condition.

EXAMPLE: I <u>would</u> <u>do</u> it, but I can’t. / *Lo <u>farei</u>, ma non posso.*
[‘Would do’ implies a condition.]

conjugation   *la coniugazione*

the changing of the forms of a verb to indicate a change in person, number, tense, mood, voice, and so on.

EXAMPLE: I <u>am</u>, she <u>is</u>. / *io <u>sono</u> lei <u>è</u>.*
[The forms 'am' and 'is' are part of the present indicative conjugation of the verb 'to be.']

conjunction   *la congiunzione*

a word used to connect words, phrases, clauses, etc.

EXAMPLE: Mary <u>and</u> Bill are good friends. / *Maria <u>e</u> Guglielmo sono buoni amici.*
['And' connects the two subject nouns 'Mary,' 'Bill.']

declarative sentence   *il periodo dichiarativo*

a sentence that makes a declaration or statement.

EXAMPLE: They are right!. / *Loro hanno ragione!*
[This sentence makes a clear declaration.]

definite article   *l'articolo determinativo*

the article, *the*, which particularizes or specifies the noun.

EXAMPLE: <u>The</u> woman I married is just not anyone. / <u>La</u> *donna che ho sposato non è una qualsiasi.*
['The' specifies 'woman' as being one particular person.]

demonstrative adjective   *l'aggettivo dimostrativo*

the adjective that serves to demonstrate or point out something or someone.

EXAMPLE: I want <u>this</u> book, not <u>that</u> book. / *Voglio <u>questo</u> libro, non <u>quel</u> libro.*
['This' and 'that' serve the function of demonstrating or pointing out the books referred to in the sentence.]

demonstrative pronoun   *il pronome dimostrativo*

the pronoun that stands for a corresponding demonstrative adjective; i.e., the pronoun that directly points out its antecedents.

EXAMPLE: I want <u>this</u> one, not <u>that</u> one. / *Voglio <u>questo</u>, non <u>quello</u>.*
['This one' and 'that one' refer to antecedents such as 'this book' and 'that book.']

dependent clause — *la proposizione dipendente*

a clause that functions as a subject, object, or modifier in a sentence (also called *subordinate clause*).

EXAMPLE: The person <u>who just got up</u> is my grandson. /
La persona <u>che si è appena alzata</u> è il mio nipotino.
['Who just got up' is a clause modifying the noun 'person.']

descriptive adjective — *l'aggettivo qualificativo*

an adjective that describes a noun in some way.

EXAMPLE: She's an <u>intelligent</u> person. / Lei è una persona <u>intelligente</u>.
['Intelligent' describes the 'person' in terms of her mental abilities.]

direct object (noun) — *il complemento oggetto*

a noun or noun phrase that receives the direct action of the verb.

EXAMPLE: He gave her <u>the pie</u>. / Le ha dato <u>la torta</u>.
['The pie' is the noun phrase that receives the direct action.]

direct object pronoun — *il pronome di complemento oggetto*

a pronoun that stands for a direct object.

EXAMPLE: He gave <u>it</u> to Michael. / <u>Lo</u> ha dato a Michele.
['It' is the pronoun form that stands for a direct object like 'the cake.']

disjunctive pronoun — *il pronome disgiuntivo*

a pronoun that is used separately—'disjoined'—from the verb; in Italian the forms *mi, ti,* etc. are put next to the verb (or in some cases attached to it), whereas *me, te,* etc. are not.

EXAMPLE: He comes with <u>me</u>. / Lui viene con <u>me</u>.

ending of a verb — *la desinenza di un verbo*

the last sound or sequence of sounds on a verb form that designates person, number, etc.

EXAMPLE: She sings well. / *Lei canta bene.*
[The final 's' of 'sings' tells you that the subject is in the third person.]

feminine *femminile*

the category of noun, adjective, etc. that indicates feminine gender (as opposed to masculine), and often the female sex.

EXAMPLE: She is always right. / *Lei ha sempre ragione.*
['She' is the feminine form of the third person subject pronoun that refers to a female.]

gender *il genere*

the category of noun, adjective, etc. used to keep references distinct as *masculine, feminine,* or *neuter.*

EXAMPLE: She is right; he is wrong. / *Lei ha ragione; lui ha torto.*
['She' is a pronoun in the feminine gender, while 'he' is a pronoun in the masculine gender.]

gerund *il gerundio*

the form of the verb made up with *-ing* in English.

EXAMPLE: I am eating. / *Io sto mangiando.*
['Eating' is the gerund form of 'to eat.']

imperative (command) *l'imperativo*

the form (mood) of the verb used to express commands, requests, exhortations, etc.

EXAMPLE: Sit down please! / *Si sieda per favore!*
[The form 'sit' expresses a command.]

indefinite article *l'articolo indeterminativo*

the articles, *a, an*, which do not specify the noun.

EXAMPLE: A woman called for you. / *Una donna ti ha chiamato.*
['A' does not identify 'woman' as being one definite person.]

indefinite pronoun *il pronome indefinito*

a pronoun which does not specify anything or anyone in particular.

EXAMPLE: Everyone knows that. / *Tutti lo sanno.*
['Everyone' does not refer to specific people, but to a group of people in general.]

independent clause   *la proposizione indipendente*

a clause that can stand alone as a simple sentence or combine with other clauses to form complex sentences (also called *main clause, principal clause*).

EXAMPLE: He already knew what you told him. / *Sapeva già quello che gli hai detto.*
[The clause 'he already knew' can stand alone as a sentence.]

indicative mood   *il modo indicativo*

the mood of the verb used for stating or indicating facts, information, actions, etc.

EXAMPLE: I know that he is right. / *So che lui ha ragione.*
[The forms 'know' and 'is' are in the present indicative.]

indirect object (noun)   *il complemento di termine*

a noun or noun phrase that receives the secondary action of the verb.

EXAMPLE: He gave the pie to Mary / *Ha dato la torta a Maria.*
['To Mary' is the noun phrase that receives the secondary action of the verb.]

indirect object pronoun   *il pronome di complemento di termine*

a pronoun that stands for an indirect object.

EXAMPLE: He gave the cake to him. / *Gli ha dato la torta.*
['To him' is the pronoun form that stands for an indirect object like 'to Michael.']

infinitive   *l'infinito*

the form of the verb, used often with *to* (*to go, to say,* etc.), that is unconjugated for person, tense, mood, etc.

EXAMPLE: She also wants to go. / *Anche lei vuole andare.*
[The verb form 'to go' is not specified as to person, number tense, mood, etc.]

interjection   *l'interiezione*

a word expressing emotion or exclamation.

EXAMPLE: Alas!. / *Meno male!*
['Alas' is an interjection implying an emotional state.]

interrogative adjective — *l'aggettivo interrogativo*

an adjective that allows one to express a specific kind of question.

EXAMPLE: <u>Which</u> glass is yours? / *<u>Quale</u> bicchiere è tuo?*
['Which' is an adjective that allows you to ask a specific kind of question.]

interrogative pronoun — *il pronome interrogativo*

a pronoun that introduces a specific kind of question.

EXAMPLE: <u>Who</u> is it?. / *<u>Chi</u> è?*
['Who' is a pronoun that introduces a specific kind of question.]

interrogative sentence — *il periodo interrogativo*

a sentence that allows you to express a specific kind of question.

EXAMPLE: Is that yours? / *E' tuo?*
[This sentence asks the kind of question that can be answered with either 'yes' or 'no'.]

intransitive verb — *il verbo intransitivo*

a verb that does not take a direct object.

EXAMPLE: John <u>goes</u> to school. / *Giovanni <u>va</u> alla scuola.*
[The verb 'to go' cannot take a direct object.]

irregular verb — *il verbo irregolare*

a verb that does not conform to a regular pattern of conjugation.

EXAMPLE: I <u>am</u> Italian. / *<u>Sono</u> italiano.*
[The form 'am' of the verb 'to be' is irregular; compare it with 'I <u>speak</u> Italian' which reflects a regular form of the present indicative of 'to speak.']

main clause — *la proposizione principale*

a synonym for *independent clause*.

masculine — *maschile*

the category of a noun, adjective, etc. that indicates masculine gender, and often the male sex.

EXAMPLE: He is always right. / *Lui ha sempre ragione.*
['He' is the form of the third person subject pronoun that refers to a male.]

mood of a verb   *il modo di un verbo*

the forms of a verb showing the attitude, point of view, state of mind, etc. of the speaker regarding the action expressed.

EXAMPLE: I would go if I had time. / *Ci andrei se avessi tempo.*
[This form of the verb 'to go' reveals that the speaker envisions the action expressed in terms of a specific condition.]

negative   *il negativo*

a word, expression, or sentence that indicates negation, denial, or refusal.

EXAMPLE: No, I do not agree. / *No, non sono d'accordo.*
[This sentence expresses negation.]

noun   *il nome*

a word referring to a thing, quality, person, or idea.

EXAMPLE: That book is mine. / *Quel libro è mio.*
['Book' is a noun referring to a thing.]

number   *il numero*

the form of a word indicating that it is singular or plural.

EXAMPLE: Those books are hers. / *Quei libri sono suoi.*
[The form 'books' is the plural form of 'book.']

ordinal number   *il numero ordinale*

a number denoting the order, ranking, position, etc. of something or someone in a series as first, second, third, etc.

EXAMPLE: She is the first in her class. / *E' la prima della sua classe.*
['First' indicates the position of the subject with respect to her class.]

orthographical changes in verb forms   *le modifiche ortografiche alle forme del verbo*

changes in the spelling of verbs that are often predictable.

EXAMPLE: You always pay. / *Tu paghi sempre.*
[In Italian the form *'paghi'*, with an *h* is spelled this way when the *g* is before an *i* to indicate that its hard sound is to be retained.]

partitive   *il partitivo*
a word or form denoting a part as distinct from the whole.

EXAMPLE: Give me <u>some</u> fruit. / *Dammi <u>della</u> frutta.*
['Some' denotes a part of something.]

passive voice   *la voce passiva*
the form of the verb indicating that the subject of the sentence is receiving the action.

EXAMPLE: Caesar <u>was</u> <u>killed</u> by Brutus. / *Cesare <u>è stato ucciso</u>*
da Bruto.
[Compare this sentence with its corresponding active form: 'Brutus <u>killed</u> Caesar.']

past participle   *il participio passato*
the form of the verb which indicates a past action.

EXAMPLE: She has <u>gone</u> home already. / *E' <u>andata</u> già a casa.*
['Gone' is the past participle of the verb 'to go.']

person   *la persona*
the form of a pronoun or verb that identifies the person or persons speaking (first person), spoken to (second person), or spoken of (third person).

EXAMPLE: <u>I</u> said it, not <u>they</u>. / *L'ho detto <u>io</u>, non <u>loro.</u>*
['I' is the first person singular subject pronoun; 'they' the third person plural.]

phrase   *la frase*
a group of two or more associated words, not containing a subject and a predicate (like a clause).

EXAMPLE: They live <u>in the suburbs</u>. / *Loro abitano <u>in periferia</u>.*
['In the suburbs' is an adverbial phrase, i.e., a phrase that functions like an adverb.]

plural   *il plurale*
the form of a word indicating that it is not singular (i.e., that it is more than one).

EXAMPLE: Those <u>books</u> are yours. / *Quei <u>libri</u> sono tuoi.*
[The form 'books' is the plural of 'book.']

possessive adjective   *l'aggettivo possessivo*
an adjective denoting possession.

EXAMPLE: Where's <u>my</u> hat? / *Dov'è <u>il mio</u> cappello?*
['My' indicates to whom the hat belongs.]

possessive *il pronome*
pronoun *possessivo*
a pronoun denoting possession.

EXAMPLE: Where's mine? / Dov'è il mio?
['Mine' denotes that something belongs to the speaker.]

predicate *il predicato*
the verb of a sentence or clause together with its objects, adverbs, phrases, etc.

EXAMPLE: I love pizza. / Io amo la pizza.

preposition *la preposizione*
a word such as *in, of, to,* etc. introducing a phrase.

EXAMPLE: I live in an apartment. / Abito in un appartamento.
['In' introduces the adverbial phrase 'in an apartment.']

pronoun *il pronome*
a word that replaces a noun or noun phrase.

EXAMPLE: He lives downtown. / Lui abita in centro.
['He' replaces a noun phrase such as 'that man,' 'my brother,' etc.]

reflexive pronoun *il pronome riflessivo*
a pronoun that reflects (is the same as) the subject.

EXAMPLE: I wash myself twice daily. / Mi lavo due volte al
giorno.
['Myself' is the same as 'I.']

reflexive verb *il verbo riflessivo*
a verb conjugated with reflexive pronouns; i.e., a verb having an object identical to the subject.

EXAMPLE: He dresses himself. / Lui si veste (da solo).
[The object of the verb 'himself' is identical to the subject 'he.']

regular verb *il verbo regolare*
a verb that conforms to a regular pattern of conjugation.

EXAMPLE: She speaks Italian. / Lei parla italiano.
[The verb 'to speak' is a regular verb, with the predictable form 'speaks' for the third person singular of the present indicative.]

relative pronoun *il pronome relativo*
a pronoun that refers to an antecedent and introduces a dependent clause.

EXAMPLE: The cake <u>that</u> I am eating is too sweet. / La torta <u>che</u> sto mangiando è troppo dolce.
['That' refers to the antecedent 'cake' and introduces the clause 'that I am eating.']

simple sentence *il periodo semplice*
a sentence consisting of a subject and a predicate, without dependent clauses.

EXAMPLE: I love Italian. / *Io amo l'italiano.*

singular *il singolare*
the form of a word indicating that it is not plural (i.e., that it denotes one of something).

EXAMPLE: That <u>book</u> is mine. / *Quel <u>libro</u> è mio.*
[The form 'book' refers to one book.]

stem of a verb *il tema del verbo*
the part of the verb that does not vary in a conjugation.

EXAMPLE: I speak, you speak. / *io parlo, tu parli.*
[In the Italian examples, note that *parl-* does not vary as the verb is being conjugated in the present indicative; this is the stem of the verb.]

subject *il soggetto*
the word, phrase, or clause of a sentence (or clause) about which something is stated or asked in the predicate.

EXAMPLE: <u>That person</u> speaks well. / *<u>Quella persona</u> parla bene.*
['That person' is the subject noun phrase of the sentence.]

subject pronoun *il pronome soggetto*
the pronoun standing for a subject noun or noun phrase.

EXAMPLE: <u>She</u> is Italian. / *<u>Lei</u> è italiana.*
['She' stands for a noun phrase such as 'the woman,' 'the girl,' etc.]

subjunctive mood *il congiuntivo*
the mood of the verb that does not convey facts, statements, assertions, etc., but rather, doubts, beliefs, etc.

EXAMPLE: It is necessary that he <u>come</u>. / *E' necessario che lui <u>venga</u>.*

[The form 'come' rather than 'comes' is subjunctive, conveying the notion of necessity.]

subordinate clause   *la proposizione subordinata*

a synonym for *dependent clause*.

superlative adjective   *l'aggettivo superlativo*

the highest degree of comparison of the adjective.

EXAMPLE: Alexander is the <u>tallest</u> student in his class. / *Alessandro è lo studente <u>più</u> alto della sua classe.*

['Tallest' expresses the highest degree of 'tallness.']

superlative adverb   *l'avverbio superlativo*

the highest degree of comparison of the adverb.

EXAMPLE: He speaks <u>the best</u> of all. / *Lui parla <u>il meglio</u> di tutti.*

['The best' expresses the highest degree of 'well.']

tense of the verb   *il tempo del verbo*

the feature of the verb that relates it to time.

EXAMPLE: I eat, I ate. / *io <u>mangio</u>, io <u>ho mangiato</u>.*

[The form 'eat' relates the verb to the present time; the form 'ate,' on the other hand, to the past.]

transitive verb   *il verbo transitivo*

a verb that can take a direct object.

EXAMPLE: Alexander <u>loves</u> school. / *Alessandro <u>ama</u> la scuola.*

[The verb 'to love' can take a direct object such as 'school.']

verb   *il verbo*

the part of the sentence that expresses existence, action, occurrence, thought, and other activities.

EXAMPLE: I <u>speak</u> Italian. / *Io <u>parlo</u> italiano.*

[The word 'speak' expresses the action of the sentence.]

§1.

Guide to Italian Sounds and Spelling

§1.1
WHAT ARE VOWELS AND CONSO- NANTS?

There are two kinds of sounds in any language.

- *Vowels* are produced by air passing out through the mouth without being blocked. The letters that represent these sounds are: *a, e, i, o, u.*

- *Consonants,* on the other hand, are produced by blockage (partial or complete) of the air. The remaining alphabet letters are used to represent consonant sounds: *b, c, d,* etc.

§1.2
VOWELS

Italian vowels should not cause you any problems.

Alphabet Letters	Sounds	Examples
a	Similar to the *a* sound in "father," or to the excla- mation "ah!"	casa/ house acqua/ water
e	Similar to the *e* sound in "bet," or to the exclama- tion "eh!"	bene/well esame/ exam
i	Similar to the *i* sound in machine	vini/wines indirizzi/ addresses
o	Similar to the *o* sound in "sorry," or to the excla- mation "oh!"	otto/eight oro/gold
u	Similar to the *oo* sound in "boot," or to the excla- mation "ooh!"	uva/ grapes gusto/ taste

- Speakers in various parts of Italy pronounce *e* and *o* differently. In some parts, these vowels are pronounced with the mouth relatively more open. In others, they are pronounced with the mouth relatively more closed. In many areas, however, *both* pronunciations are used.

- To get an idea of what this means, consider how the *a* in "tomato" is pronounced in North America. In some areas, it is pronounced like the *a* in "father." In other areas, it is pronounced like the *a* in "pay." However, whether it is pronounced one way or the other, no one will have much difficulty understanding that the word is "tomato." This is exactly what happens in the case of Italian *e* and *o*.

- The letter *i* stands for the semivowel sounds similar to those represented by the *y* in "yes" and "say."

Words Pronounced Like "yes"	Words Pronounced Like "say"
ieri/yesterday	*mai*/ever, never
piatto/plate	*poi*/then

- This pronunciation feature occurs when the *i* is next to another vowel and both are pronounced rapidly together. If there is a slight pause between the two vowels, then pronounce *i* in its normal way as in the word *zio* (uncle).

- Similarly, the letter *u* stands for the semivowel sounds represented by the *w* in "*w*ay" and "ho*w*."

Words Pronounced Like "way"	Words Pronounced Like "how"
uomo/man	*causa*/cause
buono/good	*laurea*/degree (university)

- Once again, this feature occurs when the *u* is next to another vowel and both are pronounced rapidly together.

§1.3 CONSO- NANTS

The following Italian consonants should cause you few problems

Alphabet Letters	Sounds	Examples
b	Identical to the *b* sound in "*b*oy."	*bello*/beautiful *bravo*/good
d	Identical to the *d* sound in "*d*ay." This is true even when followed by *r*; in English, the tongue is raised a bit more: "*dr*op."	*dopo*/after *ladro*/thief

Alphabet Letters	Sounds	Examples
f	Identical to the *f* sound in "*f*un."	*f*orte/strong *f*rutta/fruit
l	Identical to the *l* sound in "*l*ove." This is true even when it comes at the end of a word or syllable; in English, the back of the tongue is raised a bit more: "bi*ll*."	*l*atte/milk a*l*to/tall
m	Identical to the *m* sound in "*m*ore."	*m*atita/pencil *m*ondo/world
n	Identical to the *n* sound in "*n*ose."	*n*aso/nose *n*ono/ninth
p	Identical to the *p* sound in "*p*rice."	*p*orta/door *p*rezzo/price
q	Identical to the *q* sound in "*q*uick." It is always followed by *u*.	*qu*anto/how much *qu*into/fifth
r	Like a "rolled" *r* sound (as in some Scottish dialects). Pronounced with flip of tongue against the upper gums.	*r*osso/red *r*aro/rare
t	Like the *t* sound in "fa*t*" (with the tongue against the upper teeth).	*t*ardi/late *t*u/you
v	Identical to the *v* sound in "*v*ine."	*v*ino/wine

The following consonants are pronounced in different ways, as explained in the chart:

Alphabet Letters	Sounds	Examples
c	Represents the *k* sound in "*k*it" and "*c*at." Used in front of *a, o, u,* and any consonant.	Before *a, o, u:* *c*ane/dog *c*ome/how *cu*ore/heart Before any consonant: *c*lasse/class *c*ravatta/tie

Alphabet Letters	Sounds	Examples
ch	Represents the same *k* sound. Used in front of *e* and *i*.	*ch*e/what *ch*i/who *ch*iesa/church
c	Represents the *ch* sound in "*ch*urch" when used in front of *e* and *i*.	*c*ena/dinner *c*inema/movies
ci	Represents the *ch* sound when used in front of *a, o, u*.	*ci*ao/hi, bye *ci*occolata/chocolate
g	Represents the *g* sound in "*g*ood." Used in front of *a, o, u,* and any consonant.	Before a, o, u: *g*atto/cat *g*ola/throat *g*uanto/glove Before any consonant: *g*loria/glory *g*rande/big, large
gh	Represents the same *g* sound. Used in front of *e* and *o*.	spa*gh*etti/spaghetti *gh*iaccio/ice
g	Represents the *j* sound in "*j*ust." Used in front of *e* and *i*.	*g*ente/people *g*iro/turn, tour
gi	Represents the same *j* sound. Used in front of *a, o, u*.	*gi*acca/jacket *gi*orno/day *gi*ugno/June
sc	Represents the sound sequence *sk* in front of *a, o, u,* or any consonant.	*sc*ala/staircase *sc*opa/broom *sc*uola/school *sc*rivere/to write
sch	Represents the same *sk* sequence in front of *e* and *i*.	*sch*erzo/prank *sch*ifo/disgust
sc	Represents the *sh* sound in front of *e* and *i*.	*sc*ena/scene
sci	Represents the same *sh* sound in front of *a, o, u*.	*sci*opero/labor strike *sci*upare/to waste

● The sound represented by *gli* is similar to the *lli* in "million":

> fi*gli*o / son
> lu*gli*o / July

● The sound represented by *gn* is similar to the *ny* of "canyon":

> so*gn*o / dream
> giu*gn*o / June

● The letter *s* can stand for both the *s* sound in "sip" or the *z* sound in "zip." The *z* sound occurs before *b, d, g, l, m, n, r, v;* otherwise, the *s* sound is used.

EXAMPLES

s-sound	z-sound
sapone / soap	*sbaglio* / mistake
stanco / tired	*smettere* / to stop
sete / thirst	*svegliarsi* / to wake up
specchio / mirror	*slittare* / to slide

● When *s* occurs between vowels, either sound may be used.

> *casa* / house
> s   z

● The letter *z* stands for the *ts* sound in "ca*ts*" or the *ds* sound in "la*ds*":

> *zio* / uncle
> ts   ds

● The letter *h* does not represent any sound. It is like the silent *h* of "*h*our": *ho* (I have) (pronounced "oh!").

● Any one of these consonants can have a corresponding double consonant. The pronunciation of double consonants simply lasts twice as long as the corresponding single consonant.

EXAMPLES

Single Consonant	Corresponding Double
fato / fate	*fatto* / fact
caro / dear	*carro* / cart
pala / shovel	*palla* / ball
sono / I am	*sonno* / sleep

§1.4 STRESS

Knowing where to put the stress, or main accent, on an Italian word is not always easy, but you can always look up a word you are unsure of in a dictionary that indicates stress.
Here are some general guidelines:

- In many words, the stress falls on the next-to-last syllable. You can identify most syllables easily because they contain a vowel.

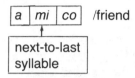

- But be careful! This is not always the case.

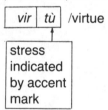

- Some words show an accent mark on the final vowel. This is, of course, where you put the stress.

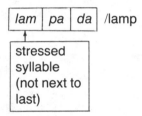

- The accent mark in Italian can always be made to slant to the left (à). However, in words ending in -ché, it normally slants to the right:

EXAMPLES
    perché (OR *perchè*)   why, because
    benché (OR *benchè*)   although

§1.5 SPELLING CONVENTIONS

To spell Italian words, just follow the guidelines described in the previous sections. Italian also uses the same punctuation marks as English.
The Italian alphabet does not have the letters *j, k, w, x,* and *y.* These are found, however, in words that Italian has borrowed from other languages, primarily English.

EXAMPLES

il karatè	karate
il jazz	jazz
il weekend	weekend
lo yacht	yacht

Like English, capital letters are used at the beginning of sentences and with proper nouns (see §4.1). However, there are a few conventions worth noting.

- The pronoun *io*/I is not capitalized (unless it is the first word of a sentence).

    Vengo anche io.   I'm coming too.

- Titles are not usually capitalized.

    il professor Verdi   Professor Verdi
    la dottoressa Martini   Dr. Martini

- Adjectives and nouns referring to languages and nationality are not capitalized.

    È un italiano. / He is an Italian.
    La lingua spagnola è interessante. / The Spanish language is
    interesting.

- Names of the seasons, months of the year, and days of the week also are not capitalized.

    la primavera   spring
    mercoledì   Tuesday
    maggio   May

§2.

Summaries of Word Order in an Italian Sentence

A *sentence* is an organized series of words that allows us to make a statement, ask a question, express a thought, offer an opinion, etc. In writing, a sentence is easily identified because it starts with a capitalized word and ends with either a period, a question mark, or an exclamation mark.

EXAMPLES

Quella donna è italiana. / That woman is Italian. (statement)
È italiana, quella donna? / Is that woman Italian? (question)
Penso che quella donna sia italiana. / I think that woman is Italian. (thought/opinion)

- Notice that the way in which a sentence is organized is related to what you intend to say and how you are going to say it. You cannot put words in just any order!

    donna è italiana quella   Quella donna è italiana.

Sentences have two basic parts: a *subject* and a *predicate*.

- A *subject* is "who" or "what" the sentence is about. It is often the first element in a simple sentence.

EXAMPLES

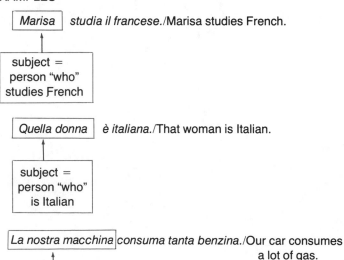

| Marisa | *studia il francese.*/Marisa studies French. |

subject =
person "who"
studies French

| Quella donna | *è italiana.*/That woman is Italian. |

subject =
person "who"
is Italian

| La nostra macchina | *consuma tanta benzina.*/Our car consumes a lot of gas. |

subject =
"what" consumes
too much gas

- But be careful! The subject is not always the first element.

  EXAMPLES

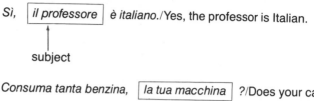

  Sì, │ *il professore* │ *è italiano.*/Yes, the professor is Italian.

  subject

  Consuma tanta benzina, │ *la tua macchina* │ ?/Does your car consume a lot of gas?

  subject

- A *predicate* is the remaining part of the sentence that expresses what is said about the subject. In many simple sentences, you will find it after the subject.

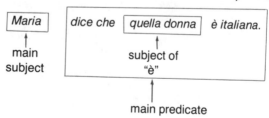

  Sentence

  │ subject │   │ predicate │

  Marisa   *studia il francese.*
  Quella donna   *è italiana.*
  La nostra macchina   *consuma tanta benzina.*

- A main subject will, of course, have a main predicate.

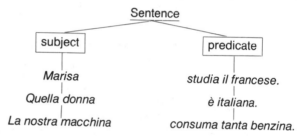

  │ *Maria* │   *dice che* │ *quella donna* │ *è italiana.*

  main subject   subject of "è"

  main predicate

- A subject must contain a noun (see Chapter 4) or pronoun (see Chapter 8); a predicate must include a verb (see Chapter 9). The parts of speech that make up the subject and predicate are defined and discussed in Chapters 4 to 12.

§2.2
SENTENCES
BY FUNCTION

§2.2 – 1
Affirmative

This type of sentence states or affirms something in a positive way.

EXAMPLES

Subject	Predicate
Giovanni	*è italiano.*/John is Italian.
Quella bambina	*suona il violino.*/That little girl plays the violin.
Tutti i nostri parenti	*abitano in Italia.*/All our relatives live in Italy.

- The predicate of such sentences may or may not have an object. An *object* is the noun or noun phrase that receives the action, and normally follows a verb. A *noun phrase* consists of a noun accompanied by an article and, possibly, an adjective. An object can also be a pronoun that replaces the noun or noun phrase.

- There are two types of objects: *direct* and *indirect*. These can be identified very easily as follows:

> A noun, or noun phrase, that directly follows the verb is a *direct object*.

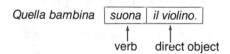

Quella bambina | *suona* | *il violino.*
     verb direct object

> A noun, or noun phrase, that follows the verb but is introduced by the preposition *a* (to, at) is an *indirect object*.

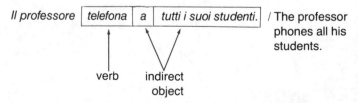

Il professore | *telefona* | *a* | *tutti i suoi studenti.* | / The professor phones all his students.
     verb indirect object

- Whether an object is direct or indirect depends on the verb. Some verbs must be followed only by one type of object or the other. Fortunately, most verbs in Italian match their English equivalents when it comes to whether or not a direct or indirect object should follow.

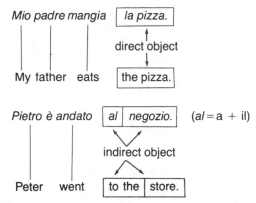

- However, there are some special cases! Here are the most important ones.

Verbs Requiring a Direct Object
ascoltare/to listen (to) *Mia madre ascolta la radio ogni sera.*/My mother listens to the radio every evening.
aspettare/to wait (for) *Maria aspetta l'autobus.*/Mary is waiting for the bus.
cercare/to search, look (for) *Tina cerca la sua borsa.*/Tina is looking for her purse.

- One way to remember these differences is to view the Italian verb as "containing" the preposition.

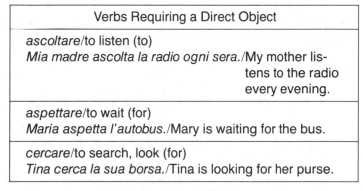

Verbs Requiring an Indirect Object
chiedere/*domandare (a)*/to ask (someone) *Gino chiede al professore di venire alla festa.*/ Gino asks the professor to come to the party.
telefonare (a)/to phone *Gina telefona a sua madre.*/Gina phones her mother.
rispondere (a)/to answer *La studentessa risponde alla domanda.*/The student answers the question.

- Some verbs can take both kinds of objects.

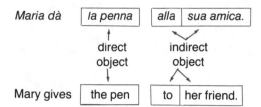

- As mentioned earlier, it is not always necessary to have an object in a sentence.

Il bambino dorme.	The child is sleeping.
Loro partono domani.	They are leaving tomorrow.

§2.2 – 2 Negative

To make any sentence negative in Italian, just put *non* before the predicate.

EXAMPLES

Affirmative	Negative
Maria aspetta l'autobus. / Mary is waiting for the bus.	*Maria non aspetta l'autobus.* / Mary is not waiting for the bus.
Il bambino dorme. / The child is sleeping.	*Il bambino non dorme.* / The child is not sleeping.
Maria mi dà la mela. / Mary gives me the apple.	*Maria non mi dà la mela.* / Mary does not give me the apple.

- Notice that the pronoun *mi*, which is still part of the predicate, comes before the verb, (see §8.3–1).

- And do not forget to say "yes" and "no."

si/yes *Sì, Gina aspetta il suo amico.*/Yes, Gina is waiting for her friend.
no/no *No, Gina non aspetta il suo amico.*/No, Gina is not waiting for her friend.

- Other negatives are discussed in Chapter 12.

§2.2 – 3 Interrogative

An interrogative sentence allows you to ask a question. In writing, it always has a question mark at the end. In Italian the two most common methods of turning an affirmative sentence into an interrogative one are:

> Simply put a question mark at the end. In speaking, the voice goes up at the end of the sentence as in English.

EXAMPLES

Affirmative	Interrogative
Anna cerca il gatto. /	*Anna cerca il gatto?* /
Ann is looking for the cat.	Ann is looking for the cat?
Il bambino dorme. /	*Il bambino dorme?* /
The child is sleeping.	The child is sleeping?

> Put the subject at the end of the sentence, adding a question mark.

EXAMPLES

subject

Marco   *ascolta la musica.*/Mark is listening to the music.

Ascolta la musica   Marco   ?/Is Mark listening to the music?

subject

Il bambino   *dorme.*/The child is sleeping.

Dorme   il bambino   ?/Is the child sleeping?

Interrogative sentences can also be formed by using interrogative adjectives (see §7.4–2) or pronouns (see §8.2). These allow you to ask "what?," "when?," "where?," etc.

EXAMPLES

Quale macchina preferisci? /	Which car do you prefer?
Come va? /	How's it going?

More will be said about these in the appropriate chapters. Use either *no?, vero?,* or *non è vero?* to express the following:

Giovanni è italiano, { *no?* / *vero?* / *non è vero?* }

John is Italian,   isn't he?

Tua madre guida una macchina sportiva, { *no?* / *vero?* / *non è vero?* }

Your mother drives a sports car,   doesn't she?

§2.2 – 4
Emphatic

To put emphasis on the subject of a sentence, all you have to do is put the subject at the end. In writing you must, of course, add an exclamation mark.

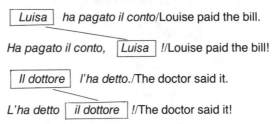

Luisa *ha pagato il conto*/Louise paid the bill.

Ha pagato il conto, *Luisa* *!*/Louise paid the bill!

Il dottore *l'ha detto.*/The doctor said it.

L'ha detto *il dottore* *!*/The doctor said it!

The imperative forms of the verb also are used for adding emphasis (see §9.3).

Anna, paga il conto! / Ann, pay the bill!

§2.3
SENTENCES BY STRUCTURE

§2.3 – 1
Simple

A simple sentence has only *one* (main) subject and *one* (main) predicate.

§2.3 – 2
Complex

A complex sentence has one main clause and at least one subordinate, or dependent, clause. It still has a main subject and predicate.

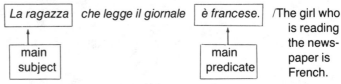

La ragazza *che legge il giornale* *è francese.* /The girl who is reading the newspaper is French.

main
subject

main
predicate

(a) Relative Clauses
A *clause* is a group of related words that contains a subject and predicate and is part of the main sentence. A *relative clause* is a dependent clause introduced by a relative pronoun. (see §8.4).

Main sentence: *La ragazza è italiana.*/The girl is Italian.
Sentence to be changed into a clause:

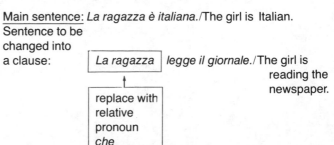

La ragazza *legge il giornale.*/The girl is reading the newspaper.

replace with
relative
pronoun
che

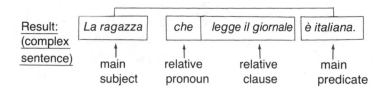

Result: (complex sentence)	*La ragazza*	*che*	*legge il giornale*	*è italiana.*
	↑ main subject	↑ relative pronoun	↑ relative clause	↑ main predicate

(b) Temporal Clauses

Temporal clauses are introduced by subordinating conjunctions. A *conjunction* is a word that connects words, phrases, and clauses. Temporal means that it expresses a time relationship. The main subordinating conjunctions are:

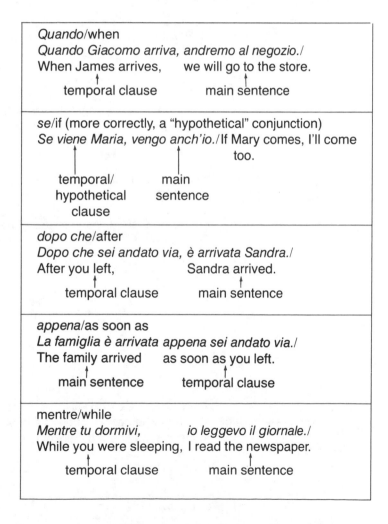

Quando/when
Quando Giacomo arriva, andremo al negozio./
When James arrives,   we will go to the store.
            ↑   ↑
    temporal clause   main sentence

se/if (more correctly, a "hypothetical" conjunction)
Se viene Maria, vengo anch'io./If Mary comes, I'll come
                                            too.
        ↑   ↑
    temporal/   main
    hypothetical   sentence
    clause

dopo che/after
Dopo che sei andato via, è arrivata Sandra./
After you left,   Sandra arrived.
            ↑   ↑
    temporal clause   main sentence

appena/as soon as
La famiglia è arrivata appena sei andato via./
The family arrived   as soon as you left.
        ↑   ↑
    main sentence   temporal clause

mentre/while
Mentre tu dormivi,   io leggevo il giornale./
While you were sleeping, I read the newspaper.
            ↑   ↑
    temporal clause   main sentence

Notice that these have exact equivalents in English.

(c) Other Types of Conjunctions
Other kinds of conjunctions can also introduce
clauses into sentences.

Benché piova, esco lo stesso./Although it is raining, I'm going
out just the same.

conjunction

A number of these require the *subjunctive* form of the
verb, and thus will be discussed in the sections dealing
with the subjunctive (see §9.5).
To join two sentences, two clauses, two words, etc.,
simply use the conjunctions *e*/and or *o*/or.

EXAMPLES

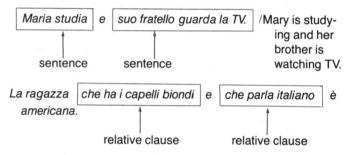

Maria studia e *suo fratello guarda la TV.* /Mary is studying and her
brother is
watching TV.

sentence   sentence

La ragazza *che ha i capelli biondi* e *che parla italiano* è
americana.

relative clause   relative clause

The girl who has blonde hair and who speaks Italian is
American.

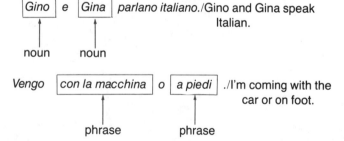

Gino e *Gina* *parlano italiano.*/Gino and Gina speak
Italian.

noun   noun

Vengo *con la macchina* o *a piedi* ./I'm coming with the
car or on foot.

phrase   phrase

§2.4
INCOMPLETE
SENTENCES

When we speak, we don't always use complete sentences,
that is, a sentence with a subject and predicate. Either part
of a sentence may be left out when it is clearly implied.

Complete Sentence   Incomplete Sentence

Come stai?/How are you?

Sto bene, grazie. / I am well, thanks.←→ *Bene, grazie.* / Well, thanks.

> *Chi è arrivato in ritardo?*/Who arrived late?

Mio padre è arrivato in ritardo./ ←——————→ *Mio padre.*/My father.
My father arrived late.

> *Quando sei andato al teatro?*/When did you go to the
> theater?

Ieri sono andato al teatro./ ←——————→ *Ieri.*/Yesterday.
Yesterday I went to the
theater.

§2.5 ACTIVE VERSUS PASSIVE SENTENCES

All the sentences used so far are *active* sentences — the verb always expresses the action performed by the subject. But for many active sentences there are corresponding *passive* ones in which the action is performed *on* the subject. (The passive voice, however, is found less frequently in the Italian than in English.)

Active	Passive
Maria legge il libro. / Mary reads the book.	*Il libro è letto da Maria.* / The book is read by Mary.

You will learn how to change active sentences into passive ones in Section §9.8.

§2.6 DIRECT AND INDIRECT SENTENCES

Sentences can be subdivided into two general categories: direct speech and indirect speech. *Direct* speech occurs when talking directly to someone. *Indirect* speech occurs when talking about someone or something. Notice that there are differences between the two forms of speech (e.g. the "article" is dropped in direct speech).

Indirect	Direct
Carlo dice che i ragazzi sono italiani.	*Carlo chiede, "Ragazzi, siete italiani?"*
Carlo says that the boys are Italian.	Carlo asks, "Boys, are you Italian?"

§3.

Basic Vocabulary

The words and expressions that make up a language form the "materials" with which to communicate ideas, thoughts, feelings, and so on. The aggregate of words and phrases in a language is called its *vocabulary*.

A basic vocabulary will contain the words and expressions that are most useful for carrying out routine conversations. The basic vocabulary to be covered in this chapter will allow you to talk in general about *people*, *places*, and common *things*.

§3.2
PEOPLE

§3.2 – 1
Family
Members

Knowing the words for referring to the members of one's family and to one's relatives is obviously basic vocabulary. Here are the most common ones:

Italian		English	
Masculine	**Feminine**	**Masculine**	**Feminine**
il babbo/ il papà	*la mamma*	dad	mom
il bisnonno	*la bisnonna*	great grandfather	great grandmother
il cognato	*la cognata*	brother-in-law	sister-in-law
il cugino	*la cugina*	cousin	cousin
il figlio	*la figlia*	son	daughter
il fratellastro	*la sorellastra*	half brother; stepbrother	half sister; stepsister
il fratello	*la sorella*	brother	sister
il gemello	*la gemella*	twin	twin
il genero	*la nuora*	son-in-law	daughter-in-law

Italian		English	
Masculine	**Feminine**	**Masculine**	**Feminine**
il marito	*la moglie*	husband	wife
il nipote	*la nipote*	grandchild/ nephew	grandchild/ niece
il nonno	*la nonna*	grandfather	grandmother
il padre	*la madre*	mother	father
il patrigno	*la matrigna*	stepfather	stepmother
il suocero	*la suocera*	father-in-law	mother-in-law
lo zio	*la zia*	uncle	aunt

**§3.2 – 2
The Body**

Words referring to parts of the body are also to be included in a basic vocabulary of Italian.

Italian	English
l'anca	hip
i baffi	mustache
la barba	beard
la bocca	mouth
il braccio	arm
i capelli	hair
la caviglia	ankle
il cervello	brain
il ciglio	eyelash
il collo	neck
il corpo	body
la coscia	thigh

Italian	English
il cuore	heart
il dito	finger
la faccia/il viso	face
la fronte	forehead
il ginocchio	knee
la gola	throat
il gomito	elbow
la guancia	cheek
il labbro	lip .
la lingua	tongue
la mano	hand
il mento	chin
il muscolo	muscle
la narice	nostril
il naso	nose
la nocca	knuckle
l'occhio	eye
l'orecchio	ear
l'osso	bone
la palpebra	eyelid
la pelle	skin
il petto	chest

il piede	foot
il polmone	lung
il polso	wrist
il sangue	blood
il sopracciglio	eyebrow
la spalla	shoulder
lo stomaco/la pancia	stomach
la testa	head
l'unghia	fingernail
la vita	life

**§3.2 – 3
Physical and
Social Traits**

Knowing how to describe people physically and socially is yet another basic vocabulary skill. The most common words and phrases for talking about people are as follows. For information on agreement patterns associated with descriptive adjectives, see §7.4–1:

Appearance		Age and Personal Information	
alto	tall	*l'adulto*	adult
attraente	attractive	*l'adolescente*	adolescent
bello	beautiful	*il bambino*	child
brutto	ugly	*il/la ragazzo/a*	boy/girl
la donna	woman	*vecchio*	old
elegante	elegant	*giovane*	young
la femmina	female	*l'anziano*	elderly person

Appearance		Age & Personal Information	
forte	strong	il compleanno	birthday
grande	big	l'anno	year
grasso	fat	il nome	name
magro	skinny, thin	il cognome	surname
il maschio	male	l'indirizzo	address
piccolo	small	Mr.	signore
l' uomo	man	Mrs., Ms./Miss	signora/ signorina

Characteristics and Social Traits			
aggressivo	aggressive	arrabbiato	angry
avaro	greedy	cattivo	bad
calmo	calm	coraggioso	courageous
cortese	courteous	pazzo	crazy
creativo	creative	colto	cultured, educated
energico	energetic	invidioso	envious
sciocco	foolish, silly	amichevole	friendly
meticoloso	fussy	buono/bravo	good
felice/allegro	happy	onesto	honest
umile	humble	ingenuo	naive
intelligente	intelligent	geloso	jealous
pigro	lazy	malizioso	malicious
capriccioso	mischievous	simpatico	nice

Characteristics and Social Traits			
antipatico	odious	*pignolo*	picky
povero	poor	*fiero*	proud
ricco	rich	*maleducato*	rude
triste	sad	*sensibile*	sensitive
furbo	shrewd	*testardo*	stubborn
educato	well-mannered	*altezzoso*	snobbish

§3.3
PLACES

Nouns referring to places are known technically as *toponyms*.

§3.3 – 1
Countries

Toponyms are treated like regular nouns. So, they are classified as either masculine or feminine (see §4.2). Here are some common country and continent toponyms:

Italian	English
l'Africa	Africa
l'America	America
l'Asia	Asia
l'Australia	Australia
l'Austria	Austria
il Belgio	Belgium
il Brasile	Brazil
il Canada	Canada
la Cina	China
la Danimarca	Denmark
l'Egitto	Egypt

Italian	English
l'Europa	Europe
la Francia	France
la Germania	Germany
il Giappone	Japan
la Grecia	Greece
l'Inghilterra	England
l'Irlanda	Ireland
Israele	Israel
l'Italia	Italy
il Messico	Mexico
la Norvegia	Norway
l'Olanda	Holland
la Polonia	Poland
il Portogallo	Portugal
la Russia	Russia
la Spagna	Spain
gli Stati Uniti	United States
la Svezia	Sweden
la Svizzera	Switzerland

§3.3 – 2 Languages and Nationalities

Words referring to languages are nouns (§4) and those referring to nationalities are adjectives (§7.4–1).

Nationality		Language	
americano	American	*l'inglese*	English
arabo	Arabic	*l'arabo*	Arabic
australiano	Australian	*l'inglese*	English
belga	Belgian	*il fiammingo/ il francese*	Flemish/ French
brasiliano	Brazilian	*il portoghese*	Portuguese
canadese	Canadian	*l'inglese/ il francese*	English/ French
cinese	Chinese	*il cinese*	Chinese
danese	Danish	*il danese*	Danish
ebreo	Hebrew	*l'ebreo*	Hebrew
francese	French	*il francese*	French
greco	Greek	*il greco*	Greek
inglese	English	*l'inglese*	English
irlandese	Irish	*l'inglese*	English
italiano	Italian	*l'italiano*	Italian
polacco	Polish	*il polacco*	Polish
portoghese	Portuguese	*il portoghese*	Portuguese
russo	Russian	*il russo*	Russian
spagnolo	Spanish	*lo spagnolo*	Spanish
svedese	Swedish	*lo svedese*	Swedish
tedesco	German	*il tedesco*	German

§3.4
THINGS

§3.4 – 1
Colors

Basic color adjectives are treated like descriptive adjectives (see §7.4–1), unless they are invariable. The invariable ones are identified with an asterisk (*):

Italian	English
arancione*	orange
argento*	silver
azzurro	blue
bianco	white
blu*	dark blue
celeste	light blue
giallo	yellow
grigio	gray
marrone*	brown
nero	black
oro*	gold
rosa*	pink
rosso	red
verde	green
viola*	purple

§3.4 – 2
Foods

The following words referring to foods and eating are nouns (see §4).

Italian	English
gli affettati	cold cuts
l'agnello	lamb

Italian	English
l'albicocca	apricot
l'anatra	duck
l'aragosta	lobster
l'arancia	orange
i broccoli	broccoli
la carne	meat
la carota	carrot
il cavolfiore	cauliflower
il cavolo	cabbage
la cena	dinner
il cetriolo	cucumber
il cibo	food
la ciliegia	cherry
la cipolla	onion
la colazione	breakfast
le cozze	mussels
i fagiolino	string bean
il fagiolo	bean
il fico	fig
la fragola	strawberry
i frutti di mare	seafood
il fungo	mushroom

Italian	English
il gambero	shrimp
il limone	lemon
il maiale	pork
la mela	apple
la melanzana	eggplant
il mirtillo	blueberry
l'oliva	olive
il pasto	meal
la patata	potato
la pera	pear
la pesca	peach
il pesce	fish
il pisello	pea
il pollo	chicken
il pomodoro	tomato
il pompelmo	grapefruit
il pranzo	lunch
il prosciutto	ham
il sedano	celery
il tacchino	turkey
il tonno	tuna
la trota	trout

Italian	English
l'uva	grapes
la verdura	vegetables
il vitello	veal
la vongola	clam

**§3.4 – 3
Travel**

Here are some common words and expressions associated with the vocabulary theme of traveling:

Italian	English
l'aeroporto	airport
l'albergo	hotel
l'arrivo	arrival
l'assistente di volo	flight attendant
l'atterraggio	landing
l'autobus/il pullman	bus
l'automobile/la macchina	car
il bagaglio	luggage
il biglietto	ticket
la camera	hotel room
la carta d'identità	identification (paper)
la cintura di sicurezza	seat belt
il corridoio	aisle
il decollo	take-off
la dogana	customs
il finestrino	window

Italian	English
l'imbarco	boarding
la metropolitana	subway
la partenza	departure
il passaporto	passport
il passeggero	passenger
il posto	seat
la prenotazione	reservation
la sala d'aspetto	waiting room
la stazione ferroviaria	train station
il tassì	taxi
il treno	train
l'uscita	gate
la valigia	suitcase
il volo	flight

§3.4 – 4
Emergencies

Finally, here are some common words and expressions associated with the vocabulary theme of emergencies and common ailments:

Italian	English
l'aggressione	assault
l'allergia	allergy
la bronchite	bronchitis
il delitto/il crimine	crime
il/la dentista	dentist

Italian	English
il dolore	pain
la febbre	fever, temperature
la ferita	wound
il fumo	smoke
il fuoco/l'incendio	fire
gonfio	swollen
l'incidente	accident
l'indigestione	indigestion
l'infezione	infection
l'influenza	flu
il mal di denti	toothache
il mal di gola	sore throat
il mal di schiena	sore back
il mal di stomaco	stomachache
il mal di testa	headache
la malattia	sickness
l'osso rotto	broken bone
la pasticca	tablet
la polmonite	pneumonia
la pressione del sangue	blood pressure
il pronto soccorso	first aid
il raffreddore	cold

Italian	English
i raggi X	X-rays
la rapina	robbery
lo scontro	collision
le tonsille	tonsils
la tosse	cough
la violenza	violence
vomitare	throw up, vomit

Exercise Set 1

The following passage is about *La Famiglia Tozzi*. However, the words referring to family members are missing their vowels. Can you supply them? (§1.2 and §3.2–1).

1.   *La Famiglia Tozzi*

La famiglia Tozzi consiste di tante persone. C'è il n___nn__, che si chiama Mario. Poi c'è sua m___glie, che si chiama Maria. La loro f__gli___ si chiama Franca. Suo m__rit__, che sarebbe il loro g__n__r__, si chiama Giorgio.

    Franca e Giorgio hanno quattro f__gli. Pino è un b__mb__n__ molto bravo. Ama molto sua m__dr__ e suo p__dr__. Sua s__r__ll__, Claudia, suo fr__t__ll__ Gianni, e la sua altra s__r__ll__ Santina sono anche molto bravi. Claudia e Santina sono g__m__lle.

    Rino Marchi è lo zi__ dei bambini e il c__gn__t__ di Franca; Laura Franceschi è la zi__ dei bambini e la c__gn__t__ di Giorgio. La f__gli__ di Rino è la c__g__n__ dei bambini, e la n__p__t__ di Franca e Giorgio, e il figlio di Laura è il c__g__n__o dei bambini e il n__p__t__ dei loro genitori.

Unscramble the following letters and you will get words referring to family members and colors (§1.2, 1.3, 3.2–1, and 3.4–1).

2. OILAV _____ VREDE _____
UOCSORE _____ RSSOO _____ SROA _____
SCUOERA _____ ROO _____ REON _____
PANOTRIG _____ RIGNATAM _____
RAUON _____ RRONMAE _____
GIOGRI _____ SOREASTRALL _____
FRAASTROTELL _____ ALLOGI _____
SIBNONNO _____ NONBISNA _____
LESTECE _____ LUB _____ NCOBIA _____
BBBAO _____ AAMMM _____ AÀPP _____
ZZRRUOA _____ CIONEARAN _____
GENTOAR _____

Missing from the following words are the alphabet characters *c, ch, ci, g, gh, gi, s, z, gli, gn, sc, sch, sci.* Can you supply them (§1.3)? The words chosen for this exercise are taken from §3.2–2 and 3.2–3. They are words referring to or describing body parts and people.

3. an____a ____pelli ____aviglia ____ervello ci___o
____rpo co____a ____uore ____inocchio ____omito
guan____a mu____olo nari____e na____o ____angue
____tomaco pan____a te____ta un____ia ele____ante
co____ome an____iano pi____olo ami____evole
si____ore adole____ente ma____io ____ovane ____occo

Missing from the following words are double consonants. Can you supply them (§1.3)? Once again, the words chosen for this exercise are taken from §3.2–2 and 3.2–3.

4. ba____i bo____a bra____io co____o fa____ia
la____ ro no____a o____hio ore____hio o____o
pe____e pe____o sopra____iglio spa____a raga____o
indiri____o a____o complea____o a____ressivo
alte____oso inte____igente cora____ioso pa____o

Can you find the words referring to body parts (§3.2–2) in the word-search puzzle? There are 13 words in all.

5. Word-search puzzle

b	a	r	b	a	b	n	o	d	i	t	o	v	q
b	n	f	r	o	n	t	e	t	g	o	p	i	e
m	l	i	n	g	u	a	n	m	o	a	m	s	i
p	i	l	o	p	o	l	t	n	l	n	a	o	n
o	m	e	n	t	o	l	l	t	a	t	n	t	p
l	o	t	r	e	s	b	b	m	m	o	o	n	i
s	p	a	l	p	e	b	r	a	n	m	o	l	e
o	m	o	l	p	o	i	u	y	t	r	e	r	d
n	m	l	p	o	p	o	l	m	o	n	e	n	e
v	i	t	a	m	p	o	l	k	m	t	r	n	v

> Can you supply the word with the opposite meaning (§3.2—2)?

6. Opposites

Word	Opposite
bello, attraente	
basso	
donna	
femmina	
magro	
piccolo	
adulto	
vecchio	
maleducato	
furbo	
triste	
ricco	
simpatico	
cattivo	

> Each of the following sentences has at least one spelling error. Rewrite each sentence with the correct spelling (§1.4 and 1.5).

7. Spelling errors.
   a. quel ragazo è malizioso.
   b. Non capiscio perche non sei venuto ieri.

c. Vengo anch'Io al cinema.
d. Maria non è Francese, ma vive in francia.
e. Ogni Giovedì o una lezione d'Italiano.

Put the words in each question together to make a complete sentence (§2.2–1, 2.2–2, 2.2–4, 2.3–1, 2.3–2). Some of the vocabulary used refers to foods (§3.4–2) and/or emergencies (§3.4–4).

---

8. Making sentences.
   a. scontro / uno / ha / fatto / ieri / Maria
   b. Marco / di / denti / mal / un / ha / telefonato / perché / al / dentista / aveva
   c. mal / di / ha / un / stomaco / perché / Maria / non / la / carne / mangia
   d. mal / mio / di / testa / figlio / ha / un / e / un / forte / raffreddore
   e. non / il / pesce / preferiscano / generalmente / benché / mangeranno / trota / la

---

Form an appropriate question for each of the following statements (§2.2–2). You are interviewing Mr. Marco Signorelli. Use polite verb forms throughout.

---

9. a. Mi chiamo Marco Signorelli.
   b. Ho 48 anni.
   c. Abito a New York.
   d. Sì, studio l'italiano.
   e. Esercito la professione di medico (*esercitare una profesione:* to practice a profession)

10. Crossword puzzle (§3.3–1, 3.3–2, 3.4–2, 3.4–3, 3.4–4).

Across
1. to vomit
4. allergy
5. celery
6. German
8. meal
9. pea
11. olive
13. a little

Down
1. violence
2. subway
3. cough
7. Poland
10. tomato
12. ticket
13. fish

Pick out the word or expression that does not belong (§3.3).

11. a. Africa America Asia Australia Austria
    b. Belgio francese Brasile Canada Cina Israele
    c. belga polacco americano canadese brasiliano irlandese
    d. Danimarca Egitto Europa Francia Germania Norvegia
    e. Grecia Inghilterra Giappone Irlanda Italia Olanda
    f. Stati Uniti Svizzera Svezia Spagna Portogallo Russia Polonia

Finally, each of the following words/phrases is misspelled. Correct each one (§1.5, 3.3–2, 3.4–3).

12. a. Spagnolo   b. portogese   c. grecho   d. chinese
e. arabbo   f. albergho   g. arivo   h. autobusso
i. bigletto   j. chintura di sicurezza   k. decolo   l. ushita

Answers

1. nonno   moglie   figlia   marito   genero   figli   bambino
madre   padre   sorella   fratello   sorella   gemelle   zio
cognato   zia   cognata   figlia   cugina   nipote   cugino
nipote

2. viola   verde   scuocero   rosso   rosa   suocera   oro
nero   patrigno   matrigna   nuora   marrone   grigio
sorellastra   fratellastro   giallo   bisnonno   bisnonna
celeste   blu   bianco   babbo   mamma   papà   azzurro
arancione   argento

3. anca   capelli   caviglia   cervello   ciglio   corpo   cuore
ginocchio   gomito   guancia   muscolo   narice   naso
sangue   stomaco   pancia   testa   unghia   elegante
cognome   anziano   pignolo   amichevole   signore
adolescente   maschio   giovane   sciocco

4. bocca   braccio   collo   faccia   labbro   nocca   occhio
orecchio   osso   pelle   petto   sopracciglio   spalla
ragazzo   indirizzo   anno   compleanno   aggressivo
altezzoso   intelligente   coraggioso   pozzo

5.

b	a	r	b	a	b	n	o	d	i	t	o	v	q
b	n	f	r	o	n	t	e	t	g	o	p	i	e
m	l	i	n	g	u	a	n	m	o	a	m	s	i
p	i	l	o	p	o	l	t	n	l	n	a	o	n
o	m	e	n	t	o	l	l	t	a	t	n	t	p
l	o	t	r	e	s	b	b	m	m	o	o	n	i
s	p	a	l	p	e	b	r	a	n	m	o	l	e
o	m	o	l	p	o	i	u	y	t	r	e	r	d
n	m	l	p	o	p	o	l	m	o	n	e	n	e
v	i	t	a	m	p	o	l	k	m	t	r	n	v

6. brutto
alto
uomo
maschio
grasso
grande
bambino
giovane
educato/cortese/colto
ingenuo
felice/allegro
povero
antipatico
buono/bravo

7. a. Quel ragazzo è malizioso.
   b. Non capisco perché non sei venuto ieri.
   c. Vengo anch'io al cinema.
   d. Maria non è francese, ma vive in Francia.
   e. Ogni giovedì ho una lezione d'italiano.

8. a. Ieri Maria ha fatto uno scontro/Maria ha fatto uno scontro ieri.
   b. Marco ha telefonato al dentista perché aveva un mal di denti.
   c. Maria non mangia la carne perché ha un mal di stomaco.
   d. Mio figlio ha un raffreddore e un forte mal di testa/Mio figlio ha un forte raffreddore e un mal di testa.

e. Mangeranno la trota benché generalmente non preferiscano il pesce/Mangeranno la trota benché non preferiscano il persce generalmente.

9. a. Come si chiama (Lei)?
   b. Quanti anni ha (Lei)?
   c. Dove abita (Lei)?
   d. Studia l'italiano?
   e. Che/Quale professione esercita (Lei)?

10.

11. a. Austria (a country / all the others are continents)
    b. francese (a language / all the others are countries)
    c. polacco (a language and nationality / all the others are only nationalities)
    d. Egitto (the only toponym ending in -o / all the others end in -a)
    e. Giappone (the only toponym ending in -e / all the others end in -a)
    f. Stati Uniti (the only plural toponym / all the others are singular in form)

12. a. spagnolo   b. portoghese   c. greco   d. cinese
   e. arabo   f. albergo   g. arrivo   h. autobus   i. biglietto
   j. cintura di sicurezza   k. decollo   l. uscita

Parts of Speech

§4.

NOUNS

§4.1
WHAT ARE
NOUNS?

Nouns are words that allow us to name and label the persons, objects, places, concepts, etc., that make up our world. In Italian, a noun generally can be recognized by its vowel ending, which indicates the gender (see §4.2) and number (see §4.3) of the noun.

EXAMPLES

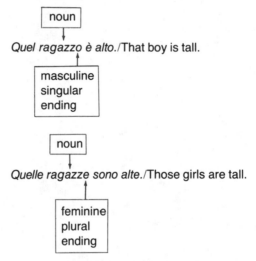

There are two main types of nouns:

- *Proper* nouns are the names given to people and places. They are always capitalized.

EXAMPLES

Il signor Rossi è simpatico./Mr. Rossi is pleasant.

Maria è felice./Mary is happy.

```
┌────────┐
│ proper │
│ noun   │
└────────┘
    │
```

L'Italia è bella./Italy is beautiful.

- *Common* nouns are all the other kinds of nouns used in a language. These can be "count" or "noncount."

- Count nouns refer to persons, things, etc., that can be counted. They have both a singular and plural form.

  EXAMPLES

Singular	Plural
il libro / the book	*i libri* / the books
la penna / the pen	*le penne* / the pens

- Noncount nouns refer to persons, things, etc., that cannot be counted, and therefore normally have only a singular form.

  EXAMPLES

  l'acqua / water
  lo zucchero / sugar
  il pane / bread

- Some noncount nouns can, of course, be used in a figurative way in the same manner as count nouns.

  EXAMPLE

  le acque del mare / the waters of the sea

- Common nouns are not capitalized unless they occur at the beginning of a sentence. Nouns referring to languages, speakers of a language, or inhabitants of an area normally are not capitalized.

  EXAMPLES

  L'italiano è una bella lingua. / Italian is a beautiful language.
  Ci sono tanti spagnoli in quella città. / There are lots of Spaniards in that city.

However, there is a tendency now to imitate the English practice of capitalizing such nouns.

To summarize:

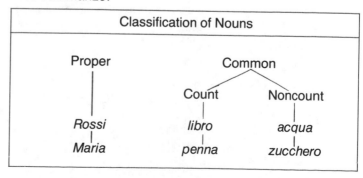

Classification of Nouns

§4.2
GENDER

Italian nouns have two genders: masculine and feminine. More will be said about genders in the next section (see §3.2–1). For now, it is important to know that this system of classification determines the form of both the articles (see Chapter 4) and adjectives (see Chapter 6) that accompany nouns in speech.

The ending of a noun gives us an important clue as to its gender.

● Nouns ending with the vowel -*o* are normally masculine.

EXAMPLES
il ragazzo / the boy
il giorno / the day
l'aeroporto / the airport
Carlo / Charles
Belgio / Belgium

● Nouns ending with the vowel -*a* are normally feminine.

EXAMPLES
la ragazza / the girl
la carta / the paper
la valigia / the suitcase
Carla / Carla
l'Italia / Italy

● Nouns ending with the vowel -*e* are either masculine or feminine. To be sure about the gender of a specific noun ending in -*e*, you will have to consult a dictionary.

EXAMPLES

Masculine	Feminine
dottore / doctor	*gente* / people
padre / father	*madre* / mother
nome / name	*televisione* / television
Giuseppe / Joseph	*notte* / night

● In normal speech, the gender of a common noun often can be determined by the form of its modifiers.

il giornale italiano/the Italian newspaper

masculine
singular
forms

la notte lunga/the long night

feminine
singular
forms

Nouns that have the above characteristics are referred to as regular nouns.

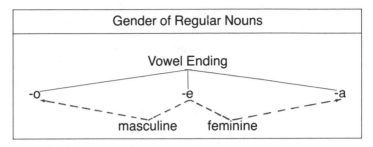

Gender of Regular Nouns

§4.2 – 1
Some Gender Patterns

The assigning of genders to nouns, especially those referring to an object or concept, is arbitrary, so it is not always possible, on the basis of the noun's meaning, to determine whether it will have a masculine or feminine ending. Noun endings, however, do reflect biological gender (i.e., sex). In general, male beings are designated by nouns ending in -o or -e (masculine endings); and female beings are designated by nouns ending in -a or -e (feminine endings).

EXAMPLES

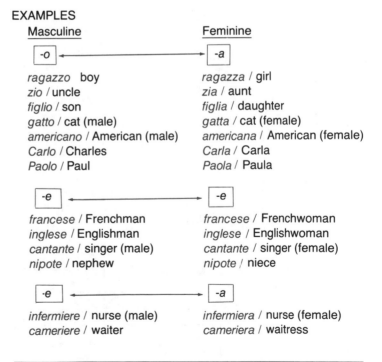

Masculine	Feminine
-o	-a
ragazzo boy	*ragazza* / girl
zio / uncle	*zia* / aunt
figlio / son	*figlia* / daughter
gatto / cat (male)	*gatta* / cat (female)
americano / American (male)	*americana* / American (female)
Carlo / Charles	*Carla* / Carla
Paolo / Paul	*Paola* / Paula
-e	-e
francese / Frenchman	*francese* / Frenchwoman
inglese / Englishman	*inglese* / Englishwoman
cantante / singer (male)	*cantante* / singer (female)
nipote / nephew	*nipote* / niece
-e	-a
infermiere / nurse (male)	*infermiera* / nurse (female)
cameriere / waiter	*cameriera* / waitress

EXCEPTION: *Il soprano* is a masculine noun referring to a female person.

Following are some other interesting patterns.

● In general, the names of trees are masculine, whereas the fruit they bear is feminine.

EXAMPLES

Masculine	Feminine
melo / apple tree	*mela* / apple
arancio / orange tree	*arancia* / orange
pesco / peach tree	*pesca* / peach
pero / pear tree	*pera* / pear
ciliegio / cherry tree	*ciliegia* / cherry

> EXCEPTIONS: *Limone* (lemon), *fico* (fig), and *mandarino* (mandarin) refer to both the tree and the fruit.

● Masculine nouns ending in *-tore* referring to male persons often have corresponding feminine nouns ending in *-trice* referring to female persons.

Masculine	Feminine	Translation
genitore	*genitrice*	parent
pittore	*pittrice*	painter
autore	*autrice*	author
attore	*attrice*	actor/actress
scultore	*scultrice*	sculptor/sculptress

● Some masculine nouns referring to male beings have corresponding feminine nouns ending in *-essa* referring to female beings.

Masculine	Feminine	Translation
dottore	*dottoressa*	doctor
professore	*professoressa*	professor
avvocato	*avvocatessa*	lawyer
elefante	*elefantessa*	elephant

§4.2 – 2
Nouns Ending in -*ista*

These nouns generally refer to professional persons. They can be either masculine (even if they end in -*a*) or feminine, according to whether they designate a male or female person.

Masculine	Feminine	Translation
il dentista	*la dentista*	dentist
il pianista	*la pianista*	pianist
il farmacista	*la farmacista*	pharmacist
il violinista	*la violinista*	violinist

§4.2 – 3
Nouns Ending in an Accented Vowel

A few Italian nouns end in an accented vowel. In general, those nouns ending in -*à* and -*ù* are feminine; the others are masculine.

EXAMPLES

Masculine	Feminine
il tè / the tea	*la città* / the city
il caffè / the coffee	*l'università* / the university
il lunedì / Monday	*la gioventù* / the youth
il tassì / the taxi	*la virtù* / virtue

> EXCEPTIONS: There are several exceptions to this pattern, notably *il papà* (father/dad) (= masculine).

§4.2 – 4
Borrowed Nouns

These are nouns that have been borrowed from other languages, primarily English. Unless they refer to a female being (e.g., *hostess*), they are all treated as masculine nouns.

EXAMPLES
lo sport / sport
il tram / streetcar
il computer / computer
il clacson / car horn
il tennis / tennis
l'autobus / bus

§4.2 – 5
Nouns Ending in -*ema* and -*amma*

These nouns correspond to English nouns ending in -*em* and -*am*, and are of Greek origin. They all are masculine, even if they end in -*a*.

EXAMPLES

il problema / the problem
il teorema / the theorem
il programma / the program
il telegramma / the telegram
il diagramma / the diagram

§4.2 – 6 Nouns Ending in -si

These nouns correspond to English nouns ending in *-sis*, and also are of Greek origin. They all are feminine.

la crisi / the crisis
la tesi / the thesis
l'analisi / the analysis
l'ipotesi / the hypothesis

> EXCEPTION: *Il brindisi* ([drinking] toast) is masculine and is of Germanic origin.

§4.3 NUMBER

Number means that a word can be *singular* (= referring to one person, thing, etc.) or *plural* (= referring to more than one). Recall that noncount nouns (see §4.1) have only a singular form.

EXAMPLES

l'acqua / water
il pane / bread
la fame / hunger
la sete / thirst
il pepe / pepper
il sale / salt

A few nouns occur only in the plural form. They refer to things made up of more than one part.

EXAMPLES

le forbici / scissors
gli occhiali / (eye)glasses
i pantaloni / pants
le mutande / underwear
i baffi / moustache

§4.3 – 1 Plural of Regular Nouns

Common count nouns have both a singular and plural form. Regular Italian nouns (see §4.2) are put into the plural by making the following changes to the vowel endings.

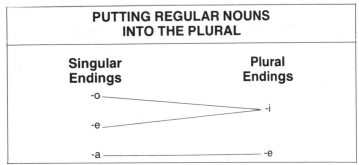

**PUTTING REGULAR NOUNS
INTO THE PLURAL**

Singular Endings	Plural Endings
-o	-i
-e	-i
-a	-e

EXAMPLES

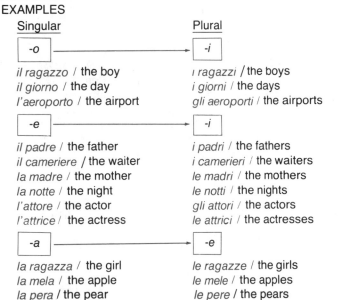

Singular	Plural

-o → -i

il ragazzo / the boy	*i ragazzi* / the boys
il giorno / the day	*i giorni* / the days
l'aeroporto / the airport	*gli aeroporti* / the airports

-e → -i

il padre / the father	*i padri* / the fathers
il cameriere / the waiter	*i camerieri* / the waiters
la madre / the mother	*le madri* / the mothers
la notte / the night	*le notti* / the nights
l'attore / the actor	*gli attori* / the actors
l'attrice / the actress	*le attrici* / the actresses

-a → -e

la ragazza / the girl	*le ragazze* / the girls
la mela / the apple	*le mele* / the apples
la pera / the pear	*le pere* / the pears

- Be careful! The noun *gente* (people) is singular in Italian.

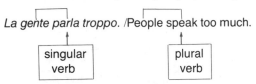

La gente parla troppo. /People speak too much.

singular verb	plural verb

- Note that the plural ending *-i* is used when the noun refers to both male *and* female beings.

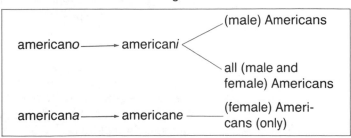

americano → americani	(male) Americans
	all (male and female) Americans
americana → americane	(female) Americans (only)

§4.3 – 2 Plural of Nouns Ending in -*ista*, -*ema*, and -*amma*

Nouns ending in -*ista* are either masculine or feminine (see §3.2–2). The plural of such nouns is obtained as follows:

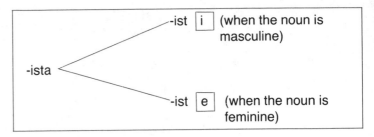

EXAMPLES

Singular	Plural
il dentist the (male) dentist	*i dentisti* the (male) dentists
la dentista the (female) dentist	*le dentiste* the (female) dentists
il turista the (male) tourist	*i turisti* the (male) tourists
la turista the (female) tourist	*le turiste* the (male) tourists

- Note that in this case as well, the plural ending -*i* is used to designate both male and female beings.

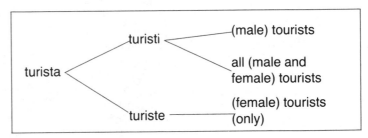

All nouns ending in -*ema* and -*amma* are masculine (see §3.2–5). The plural of such nouns is obtained as follows.

EXAMPLES

Singular	Plural
il problema / the problem	*i problemi* / the problems
il programma / the program	*i programmi* / the programs
il diagramma / the diagram	*i diagrammi* / the diagrams

§4.3 – 3 Plural of Other Nouns

Nouns ending in -*si* (see §4.2–6) and in an accented vowel (see §3.2–3), as wel as borrowed nouns (see §4.2–4) (and all nouns ending in a consonant), do *not* undergo any changes in the plural.

EXAMPLES

Singular	Plural
la città / the city	*le città* / the cities
il computer / the computer	*i computer* / the computers
la crisi / the crisis	*le crisi* / the crises

§4.3 – 4 Spelling Peculiarities

When putting nouns that end in *-co, -go, -ca, -ga, -cio, -gio, -cia, -gia,* and *-io* into the plural, follow the patterns given below.

● Nouns ending in *-co* are pluralized as follows:

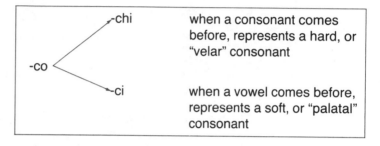

-chi — when a consonant comes before, represents a hard, or "velar" consonant

-co

-ci — when a vowel comes before, represents a soft, or "palatal" consonant

EXAMPLES

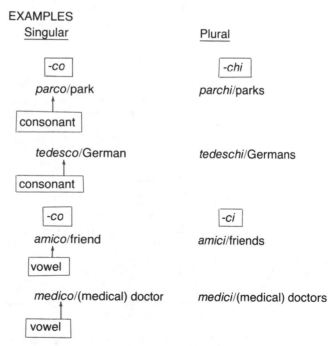

Singular	Plural
-co	-chi
parco/park	*parchi*/parks
consonant	
tedesco/German	*tedeschi*/Germans
consonant	
-co	-ci
amico/friend	*amici*/friends
vowel	
medico/(medical) doctor	*medici*/(medical) doctors
vowel	

EXCEPTIONS: *Porco* (pig), *fuoco* (fire), *fico* (fig), and *buco* (hole) have the following plural forms: por*ci*, fuo*chi*, fi*chi*, bu*chi*.

● Nouns ending in *-go* are pluralized as follows:

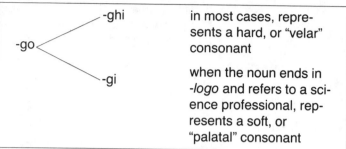

EXAMPLES

Singular	Plural

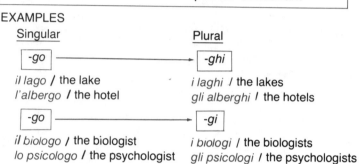

il lago / the lake	*i laghi* / the lakes
l'albergo / the hotel	*gli alberghi* / the hotels
il biologo / the biologist	*i biologi* / the biologists
lo psicologo / the psychologist	*gli psicologi* / the psychologists

● But be careful! Not all nouns ending in *-logo* refer to scientists of some kind. In such cases, the *-go* becomes *-ghi* in the plural.

EXAMPLES

Singular	Plural
il catalogo / the catalog	*i cataloghi* / the catalogs
il dialogo / the dialogue	*i dialoghi* / the dialogues

● The above rules are to be considered only as guidelines.

● Nouns ending in *-ca* and *-ga* always retain the hard (velar) sound in the plural.

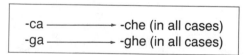

EXAMPLES

Singular	Plural
l'amica / (female) friend	*le amiche* / (female) friends
la paga / pay (check)	*le paghe* / pay (checks)

● Nouns ending in *-cio*, *-gio*, *-cia*, *-gia*, and *-io* are pluralized as follows:

If the *i* is stressed in the singular, then it is retained in the plural.

EXAMPLES

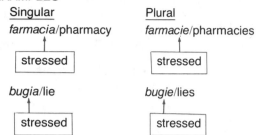

Singular	Plural
farmacia/pharmacy	*farmacie*/pharmacies
↑ stressed	↑ stressed
bugia/lie	*bugie*/lies
↑ stressed	↑ stressed

> If the *i* is not pronounced (as in English *social* and *Belgium*), it is not kept in the plural. In masculine nouns, this means that only one *i* is used.

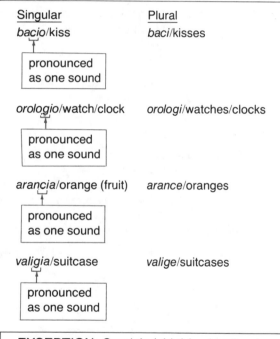

Singular	Plural
bacio/kiss	*baci*/kisses
↑ pronounced as one sound	
orologio/watch/clock	*orologi*/watches/clocks
↑ pronounced as one sound	
arancia/orange (fruit)	*arance*/oranges
↑ pronounced as one sound	
valigia/suitcase	*valige*/suitcases
↑ pronounced as one sound	

> **EXCEPTION:** *Camicia* (shirt) is pluralized as *camicie* although the second *i* is not stressed.

- A similar pattern applies to nouns ending in *-io*.

EXAMPLES

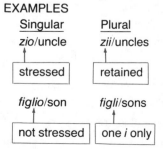

Singular	Plural
zio/uncle	*zii*/uncles
↑ stressed	↑ retained
figlio/son	*figli*/sons
↑ not stressed	↑ one *i* only

§4.3 – 5
Neuter Plurals

Like the English words "memorandum" and "compendium," which are pluralized by replacing the -*um* with -*a*, Italian also has a few plural forms in -*a*. These can be traced back to the Latin neuter forms that were pluralized in this way.

- Notice that in Italian, nouns pluralized in this way are masculine in the singular but feminine in the plural!

EXAMPLES

Singular	Plural
il dito / the finger	*le dita* / the fingers
il labbro / the lip	*le labbra* / the lips
il paio / the pair	*le paia* / the pairs
il miglio / the mile	*le miglia* / the miles

- There are not too many of these nouns, and most refer to parts of the human body.

§4.3 – 6
Miscellaneous Irregularities

Some nouns are abbreviations, and therefore do not change in the plural:

EXAMPLES

Singular	Plural
l'auto / the car	*le auto* / the cars
(from: *l'automobile*)	*le auto(mobili)*
il cinema / the movies	*i cinema* / the movie theaters
(from: *il cinematografo*)	*i cinema(tografi)*
la foto / the photo	*le foto* / the photos
(from: *la fotografia*)	*le foto(grafie)*

Some common nouns that are completely irregular are:

Singular	Plural
la mano / the hand (*f.*)	*le mani* / the hands
l'uomo / the man (*m.*)	*gli uomini* / the men
la radio / the radio (*f.*)	*le radio* / the radios

§4.4
TITLES

Be sure to drop the final -*e* of a masculine title when it comes before a name.

EXAMPLES

Masculine Title	Used Before a Name
il signore / the gentleman	*il signor Rossi* / Mr. Rossi
il professore / the professor	*il professor Verdi* / Professor Verdi
il dottore / the doctor	*il dottor Bianchi* / Dr. Bianchi
But retain the -*o*:	
l'avvocato/the lawyer	*l'avvocato Tozzi*/The lawyer Tozzi

Corresponding Feminine Titles

la signora / the lady	*la signora Rossi* / Mrs. Rossi
la professoressa / the professor	*la professoressa Verdi* / Professor Verdi
la dottoressa / the doctor	*la dottoressa Bianchi* / Dr. Bianchi
l'avvocatessa / the lawyer	*l'avvocatessa Tozzi* / the lawyer Tozzi

§4.5 NOUN SUFFIXES

In some cases, you can change the meaning of a noun by adding a suffix such as the following:

● *-ino/-ina* to add the meaning of "little" or "small" to the noun.

EXAMPLES

il ragazzo ──────────────→ *il ragazzino* / the little boy
la ragazza ──────────────→ *la ragazzina* / the little girl

● *-one/-ona* to add the meaning of "big" or "large" to the noun.

EXAMPLES

il ragazzo ──────────────→ *il ragazzone* / the big boy
la ragazza ──────────────→ *la ragazzona* / the big girl

● *-accio/-accia* to add the meaning of "bad" to the noun.

EXAMPLES

il ragazzo ──────────────→ *il ragazzaccio* / the bad boy
la ragazza ──────────────→ *la ragazzaccia* / the bad girl

● Be very careful when using these suffixes! They have many shades of meaning and can be used incorrectly. To avoid offending anyone, be absolutely sure of the meaning.

§4.6 COMPOUND NOUNS

Compound nouns are made up of two parts of speech:

Compound Noun

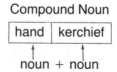

noun + noun

To form the plural of such nouns in Italian, observe the following guidelines:

● Most compound nouns are pluralized in the normal fashion (see §3.3–1).

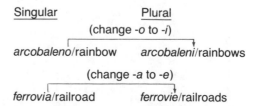

Singular	Plural
(change *-o* to *-i*)	
arcobaleno/rainbow	*arcobaleni*/rainbows
(change *-a* to *-e*)	
ferrovia/railroad	*ferrovie*/railroads

● Some change both parts of the compound noun.

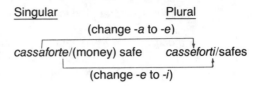

● Other compound nouns, especially those that contain a verb, do not change.

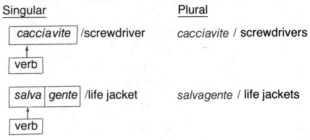

● As you can see, pluralizing compound nouns can be a complicated task. Like most Italians, check a dictionary to be sure you have pluralized the noun correctly.

§5.

Articles

§5.1
WHAT ARE ARTICLES?

Articles are words placed before nouns (or their modifying adjectives), in both English and Italian, that allow us to specify the nouns in some way.

Specific	Nonspecific
il libro / the book	*un libro* / a book

The article that allows us to speak of persons, objects, etc., in a specific way is called the *definite* article. The article that is used to designate nonspecific persons, objects, etc., is called the *indefinite* article.

Demonstratives will be included in this chapter, even though you will probably find them listed as adjectives in most grammars. They are included here because they too have the function of specifying a noun in some way. More precisely, demonstratives allow us to specify whether someone or something is relatively near or far.

Near	Far
questo libro / this book	*quel libro* / that book

§5.2
FORMS

Definite and indefinite articles, as well as demonstratives, vary according to the noun's gender, number, and initial sound.

§5.2 – 1
The Definite Article (Italian equivalent of "the")

The forms of the definite article are:

BEFORE MASCULINE NOUNS		
	Singular	**Plural**
Beginning with *z*, or *s* + consonant	lo	gli
Beginning with any vowel	l'	gli
Beginning with any other consonant	il ——— i	
BEFORE FEMININE NOUNS		
Beginning with any consonant	la	le
Beginning with any vowel	l'	le

EXAMPLES

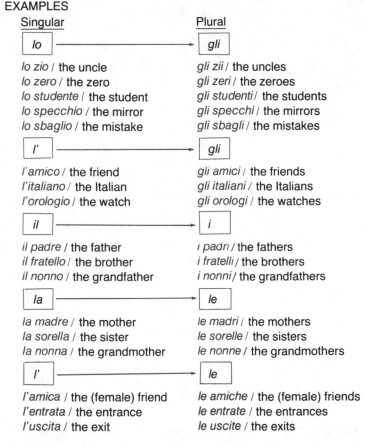

Singular	Plural
lo	*gli*

lo zio / the uncle
lo zero / the zero
lo studente / the student
lo specchio / the mirror
lo sbaglio / the mistake

gli zii / the uncles
gli zeri / the zeroes
gli studenti / the students
gli specchi / the mirrors
gli sbagli / the mistakes

| *l'* | *gli* |

l'amico / the friend
l'italiano / the Italian
l'orologio / the watch

gli amici / the friends
gli italiani / the Italians
gli orologi / the watches

| *il* | *i* |

il padre / the father
il fratello / the brother
il nonno / the grandfather

i padri / the fathers
i fratelli / the brothers
i nonni / the grandfathers

| *la* | *le* |

la madre / the mother
la sorella / the sister
la nonna / the grandmother

le madri / the mothers
le sorelle / the sisters
le nonne / the grandmothers

| *l'* | *le* |

l'amica / the (female) friend
l'entrata / the entrance
l'uscita / the exit

le amiche / the (female) friends
le entrate / the entrances
le uscite / the exits

- Be careful! With feminine nouns beginning with *z*, or *s* + consonant, you still use *la*: *la zia* (the aunt), *la scuola* (the school).

- The masculine form *lo* (plural *gli*) is also used in front of nouns beginning with *ps* or *gn* (and a few other unusual initial sounds).

EXAMPLES

lo psicologo / the psychologist	*gli psicologi* / the psychologists
lo gnocco / the dumpling	*gli gnocchi* / the dumplings

- Note, however, that there are only a few such nouns.

- Be careful! When an adjective precedes the noun, you will have to adjust the definite article according to its beginning sound.

la zia/the aunt

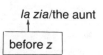

before *z*

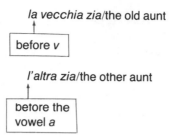

la vecchia zia/the old aunt

↑

before *v*

l'altra zia/the other aunt

↑

before the
vowel *a*

The forms of the indefinite article in the singular are as follows. Pluralization of the indefinite article is discussed in Chapter 6.

§5.2 – 2
The Indefinite Article (Italian equivalent of "a/an")

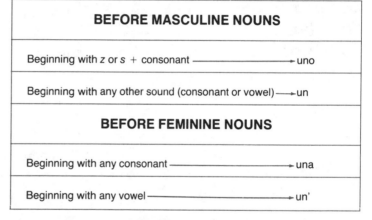

BEFORE MASCULINE NOUNS	
Beginning with *z* or *s* + consonant ──────────→ uno	
Beginning with any other sound (consonant or vowel)──→ un	
BEFORE FEMININE NOUNS	
Beginning with any consonant ──────────→ una	
Beginning with any vowel ──────────→ un'	

- Note that the apostrophe (*un'*) is used only when the indefinite article is in front of a feminine noun beginning with a vowel.

- As in the case of the definite article (see §5.2–1), the form *uno* also is used in front of nouns beginning with *ps* and *gn*.

EXAMPLES

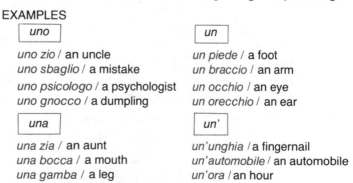

uno	un
uno zio / an uncle	*un piede* / a foot
uno sbaglio / a mistake	*un braccio* / an arm
uno psicologo / a psychologist	*un occhio* / an eye
uno gnocco / a dumpling	*un orecchio* / an ear

una	un'
una zia / an aunt	*un'unghia* / a fingernail
una bocca / a mouth	*un'automobile* / an automobile
una gamba / a leg	*un'ora* / an hour

- Don't forget! When an adjective precedes the noun, you will have to adjust the indefinite article according to the beginning sound.

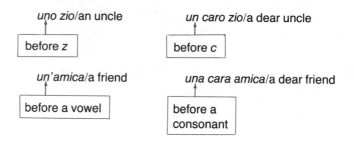

§5.2 – 3 The Demonstratives ("this/these, that/those" in Italian)

The forms of the demonstrative are:

DEMONSTRATIVE INDICATING "NEARNESS"	
Before Masculine Nouns	
Singular	Plural
quest $\boxed{\text{o}}$	quest $\boxed{\text{i}}$
Before Feminine Nouns	
quest $\boxed{\text{a}}$	quest $\boxed{\text{e}}$

EXAMPLES

$\boxed{\textit{questo}}$ ⟶ $\boxed{\textit{questi}}$

questo sbaglio / this mistake
questo giornale / this newspaper
questo esercizio / this exercise

questi sbagli / these mistakes
questi giornali / these newspapers
questi esercizi / these exercises

$\boxed{\textit{questa}}$ ⟶ $\boxed{\textit{queste}}$

questa stanza / this room
questa ora / this hour

queste stanze / these rooms
queste ore / these hours

- The form *quest'* is often used before singular nouns (or modifying adjectives) beginning with a vowel.

Singular	Plural
questo	
quest'	questi

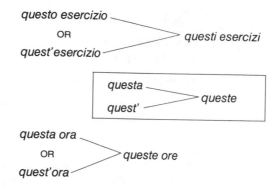

questo esercizio
OR
quest'esercizio

→ *questi esercizi*

questa
quest'

→ *queste*

questa ora
OR
quest'ora

→ *queste ore*

DEMONSTRATIVE INDICATING "FARTHER AWAY"		
Before Masculine Nouns		
	Singular	Plural
Beginning with *z* or *s* + consonant	quello	
Beginning with any vowel	quell'	quegli
Beginning with any other consonant	quel	quei
Before Feminine Nouns		
Beginning with any consonant	quella	
Beginning with any vowel	quell'	quelle

As with articles (see §5.2–1 and §5.2–2), the form *quello* (plural *quegli*) is also used before those few nouns beginning with *ps* and *gn*.

EXAMPLES

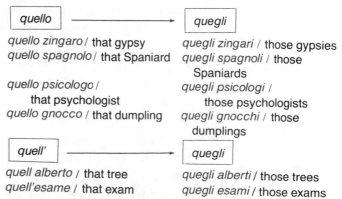

| *quello* | → | *quegli* |

quello zingaro / that gypsy
quello spagnolo / that Spaniard

quello psicologo /
   that psychologist
quello gnocco / that dumpling

quegli zingari / those gypsies
quegli spagnoli / those
   Spaniards
quegli psicologi /
   those psychologists
quegli gnocchi / those
   dumplings

| *quell'* | → | *quegli* |

quell alberto / that tree
quell'esame / that exam

quegli alberti / those trees
quegli esami / those exams

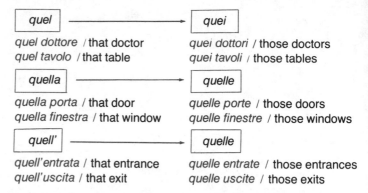

- Be careful! As with articles, when an adjective precedes a noun, you will have to change the demonstrative according to the adjective's initial sound.

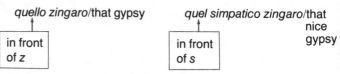

- If you look very closely, you will see that this demonstrative is exactly like the definite article.

§5.3 USES

Articles and demonstratives are used in ways similar to English. Note, however, the following differences:

- In Italian the definite article is used in front of noncount nouns (see §4.1) used as subjects (normally at the start of a sentence).

EXAMPLES
L'acqua è un liquido. Water is a liquid.
Il cibo è necessario per vivere. / Food is necessary to live.
La pazienza è una virtù. / Patience is a virtue.

- This is true even in the case of count nouns used in the plural to express generalizations.

EXAMPLES
Gli italiani sono simpatici. / Italians are nice.
I libri ci aiutano a capire. / Books help us understand.

- As a guideline, just remember that you *cannot* start an Italian sentence with a noun without its article.

- Needless to say, you do not use an indefinite article with noncount nouns ("a hunger," "a water").

- The definite article is used in front of geographical names (continents, countries, states, rivers, islands, mountains, etc.), *except* cities.

  EXAMPLES

  l'Italia / Italy

  gli Stati Uniti / the United States

  la California / California

  il Belgio / Belgium

  la Sicilia / Sicily

  il Tevere / the Tiber

  il Mediterraneo / the Mediterranean

  le Alpi / the Alps

  il Piemonte / Piedmont

  But:

  Roma / Rome
  Washington / Washington
  Parigi / Paris

- Notice that the gender of a geographical noun is determined in the usual fashion by its ending (see §4.2). If you are in doubt, consult a dictionary.

- The definite article is usually dropped after the preposition *in* and before an unmodified geographical noun.

  EXAMPLES
  Vado in Italia. / I'm going to Italy.
  Abito in Francia. / I live in France.

  But when the noun is modified:

  Vado nell'Italia centrale. / I'm going to central Italy.
  Abito nella Francia meridionale. / I live in southern France.

- The definite article is used with *dates*.

  EXAMPLES
  Il 1492 è un anno importante. / 1492 is an important year.
  Oggi è il tre novembre. / Today is November third.

  (Note that the *il* form is used).

- The definite article is commonly used in place of possessive adjectives (see §7.4–3) when referring to family members (singular only), parts of the body, and clothing.

  Oggi vado in centro con la zia. / Today I'm going downtown with my aunt.
  Mi fa male la gamba. / My leg hurts.
  Mario non si mette mai la giacca. / Mario never puts his jacket on.

- The definite article is used with the days of the week to indicate an habitual action.

EXAMPLES
Il lunedì gioco a tennis. / On Mondays I play tennis.
La domenica vado in chiesa. / On Sundays I go to church.

● Note that the days of the week, except Sunday, are masculine.

● The definite article is not used when a specific day is intended.

Il lunedì gioco a tennis, ma lunedì vado via. / On Mondays I play tennis, but Monday I'm going away.

● The definite article is used with titles, unless you are speaking *directly* to the person mentioned.

EXAMPLES

Speaking about	Speaking to
Il dottor Verdi è italiano. / Dr. Verdi is Italian.	*Buon giorno, dottor Verdi.* / Hello, Dr. Verdi.
La professoressa Bianchi è molto intelligente. / Professor Bianchi is very intelligent.	*Professoressa Bianchi, dove abita?* / Professor Bianchi, where do you live?

● A similar pattern occurs in English.

Il dottore è malato. / The doctor is ill.
Dottore, è malato? / Doctor, are you ill?

● The definite article is used before names of languages and school subjects (except with the verb *parlare*).

EXAMPLES
Impariamo lo spagnolo. / We are learning Spanish.
Studio la matematica. / I am studying mathematics.
Parlo italiano / I speak Italian.

● It is dropped with the prepositions *di* and *in*.

EXAMPLES
Ecco il libro di spagnolo. / Here is the Spanish book.
Sono bravo in matematica. / I'm good in math.

● The definite article is used with *scorso* (last) and *prossimo* (next) in time expressions.

EXAMPLES
la settimana scorsa / last week
il mese prossimo / next month

- Note that the definite article is not used in many common expressions, such as:

    a destra / to the right
    a sinistra / to the left
    a casa / at home

- The indefinite article also translates the number "one:"
  un'arancia = an orange OR one orange

- The indefinite article is not used in exclamations starting with *Che . . . !*

    EXAMPLES
    Che film! / What a film!
    Che bel vestito! / What a beautiful dress!

- Finally, remember to repeat the articles and demonstratives before every noun.

    un ragazzo e una ragazza / a boy and girl
    il ragazzo e la ragazza / the boy and girl
    questo ragazzo e questa ragazza / this boy and girl
    quel ragazzo e quella ragazza / that boy and girl

§6.

Partitives

§6.1
WHAT ARE PARTITIVES?

Partitives are words placed before Italian nouns that express the notion of "some" or "any," i.e., they refer to a *part* of something.

dell'acqua / some water   degli esami / some tests

§6.2
WITH COUNT NOUNS

Before count nouns (see §4.1), the partitive can be considered the plural of the indefinite article (see §5.2–2). The most commonly used partitive in this case is the preposition *di* + the plural forms of the definite article (as they occur normally in front of nouns).

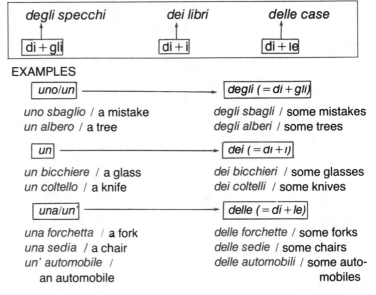

EXAMPLES

uno sbaglio / a mistake   degli sbagli / some mistakes
un albero / a tree   degli alberi / some trees

un bicchiere / a glass   dei bicchieri / some glasses
un coltello / a knife   dei coltelli / some knives

una forchetta / a fork   delle forchette / some forks
una sedia / a chair   delle sedie / some chairs
un' automobile /   delle automobili / some auto-
  an automobile   mobiles

- The partitive pronouns *alcuni* (m.) and *alcune* (f.) are often used to express the idea of "some." They are used only in the plural.

> *degli* zii OR *alcuni* zii
> *dei* bicchieri OR *alcuni* bicchieri
> *delle* forchette OR *alcune* forchette
> *delle* amiche OR *alcune* amiche (f.)

- Actually, these two types can be used together in expressions such as:

- A third type of partitive used with count nouns is the invariable pronoun *qualche*. But be careful with this one! It must be followed by a *singular* noun, even though the meaning is plural!

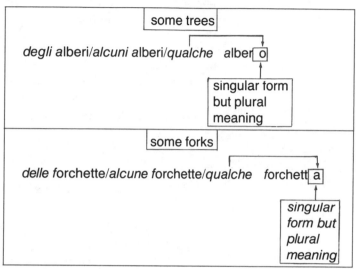

- *Qualche* or *alcuni/alcune* are often used at the start of sentences, rather than the more awkward *degli/dei/delle* forms. Once again, be careful with *qualche:* it requires a *singular* verb!

- In current Italian, it is not unusual to find that the partitive is omitted (when the noun is not the first word in a sentence).

EXAMPLES

Voglio *della* carne. OR Voglio carne. (I want [some] meat.)
Mangio *degli* spaghetti. OR Mangio spaghetti. (I'm eating [some] spaghetti.)

- In negative sentences, the partitive (translated as "any") is omitted.

EXAMPLES

Affirmative Sentence	Negative Sentence
Ho dei biglietti. / I have some tickets.	*Non ho biglietti.* / I don't have any tickets.
Voglio delle paste. / I want some pastries.	*Non voglio paste.* / I don't want any pastries.

• The partitive can also be rendered by *non . . . nessuno*. Think of *nessuno* as being made up of "ness" + *indefinite article*.

---

nessuno corresponds to *uno: uno studente/nessuno studente*

nessun corresponds to *un: un biglietto/nessun biglietto*

nessuna corresponds to *una: una signora/nessuna signora*

nessun' corresponds to *un': un'automobile/nessun' automobile*

• This means that after the forms of *nessuno* the noun is always in the singular, even though the meaning is plural.

EXAMPLES

Affirmative Sentence	Negative Sentence
Carlo compra degli specchi. / Charles buys some mirrors.	*Carlo non compra nessuno specchio.* / Charles does not buy any mirrors.
Carla compra delle caramelle. / Carla buys some candies.	*Carla non compra nessuna caramella.* / Carla does not buy any candies.

§6.3 WITH NON-COUNT NOUNS

With noncount nouns (see §4.1), the partitive is rendered by *di* + the singular forms of the definite article (according to the noun), or by the expression *un po' di* ("a bit of").

EXAMPLES

Voglio del pane. OR *Voglio un po' di pane.*/I want some bread.

$$\boxed{di + il}$$

Lui vuole dello zucchero. OR *Lui vuole un po' di zucchero.*/
He wants some sugar.

$$\boxed{di + lo}$$

*Maria mangia dell'insalata.*OR *Maria mangia un po' di insalata.*/
Mary eats some salad.

$$\boxed{di + l'}$$

Preferisco mangiare della carne. OR *Preferisco mangiare un po' di carne.*/I prefer to eat some meat.

$$\boxed{di + la}$$

§6.4
SUMMARY

The following chart summarizes the various partitive forms:

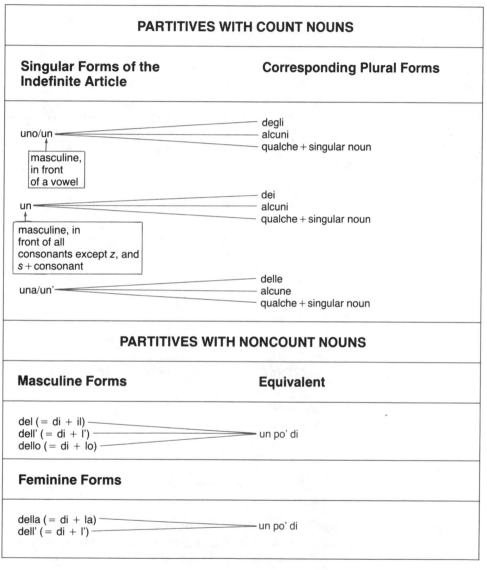

PARTITIVES WITH COUNT NOUNS	
Singular Forms of the Indefinite Article	**Corresponding Plural Forms**
uno/un — *masculine, in front of a vowel*	degli alcuni qualche + singular noun
un — *masculine, in front of all consonants except z, and s + consonant*	dei alcuni qualche + singular noun
una/un'	delle alcune qualche + singular noun

PARTITIVES WITH NONCOUNT NOUNS	
Masculine Forms	**Equivalent**
del (= di + il) dell' (= di + l') dello (= di + lo)	un po' di
Feminine Forms	
della (= di + la) dell' (= di + l')	un po' di

● Remember! As in the case of articles and demonstratives (see chapter 5), you might have to change the partitive forms when an adjective precedes the noun.

degli zii BUT *dei simpatici zii*

§7.

Adjectives

§7.1
WHAT ARE ADJECTIVES?

Adjectives are words that modify, or describe, nouns. They are placed before or after the noun they modify.

È una casa nuova. / It's a new house.
È il mio libro. / It's my book.

§7.2
AGREEMENT

Adjectives must agree with the nouns they modify. This means that an adjective must correspond in gender and number with the noun. Thus, the ending of an adjective depends on whether the noun is masculine or feminine, singular or plural.

There are two types of adjectives according to their endings.

- Adjectives that end in *-o* (masculine singular) have the following set of endings that agree with the noun:

	Singular	Plural
Masculine	-o	-i
Feminine	-a	-e

EXAMPLES

Singular

l'uomo alt $\boxed{o}$ /
the tall man

il figlio alt $\boxed{o}$ /
the tall son

la donna alt $\boxed{a}$ /
the tall woman

la madre alt $\boxed{a}$ /
the tall mother

Plural

gli uomini alt $\boxed{i}$ /the tall men

i figli alt $\boxed{i}$ /the tall sons

le donne alt $\boxed{e}$ /the tall women

le madri alt $\boxed{e}$ /the tall mothers

- Adjectives that end in *-e* in the singular have two endings, according to whether they modify a singular noun (masculine or feminine) or plural noun (masculine or feminine):

	Singular	Plural
Masculine or Feminine	-e	-i

EXAMPLES

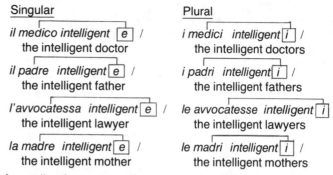

Singular	Plural
il medico intelligent $\boxed{e}$ / the intelligent doctor	*i medici intelligent* $\boxed{i}$ / the intelligent doctors
il padre intelligent $\boxed{e}$ / the intelligent father	*i padri intelligent* $\boxed{i}$ / the intelligent fathers
l'avvocatessa intelligent $\boxed{e}$ / the intelligent lawyer	*le avvocatesse intelligent* $\boxed{i}$ / the intelligent lawyers
la madre intelligent $\boxed{e}$ / the intelligent mother	*le madri intelligent* $\boxed{i}$ / the intelligent mothers

- A few adjectives are invariable, that is, their ending never changes. The most common are the adjectives of color: *marrone* (brown), *arancione* (orange), *viola* (violet, purple), *rosa* (pink), and *blu* (dark blue).

EXAMPLES

Singular	Plural
il vestito marrone / the brown suit	*i vestiti marrone* / the brown suits
la giacca marrone / the brown jacket	*le giacche marrone* / the brown jackets

- When two nouns are modified, the adjective is always in the plural. If the two nouns are feminine, then use a feminine plural ending. If the two nouns are both masculine, or of mixed gender, then use the masculine plural ending.

EXAMPLES

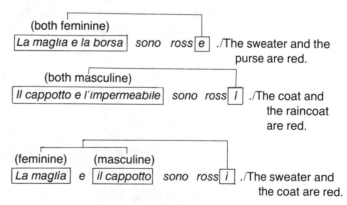

(both feminine)
$\boxed{\text{La maglia e la borsa}}$ *sono ross* $\boxed{e}$ ./The sweater and the purse are red.

(both masculine)
$\boxed{\text{Il cappotto e l'impermeabile}}$ *sono ross* $\boxed{i}$ ./The coat and the raincoat are red.

(feminine)   (masculine)
$\boxed{\text{La maglia}}$ *e* $\boxed{\text{il cappotto}}$ *sono ross* $\boxed{i}$ ./The sweater and the coat are red.

**§7.3
POSITION**

Interrogative (see §7.4–2) and possessive (see §7.4–3) adjectives *precede* the noun they modify, whereas descriptive adjectives (see §7.4–1) generally *follow* the noun.

Quante scarpe hai comprato?/How many shoes did you buy?

$\boxed{\text{interrogative adjective}}$

I tuoi pantaloni sono lunghi./Your pants are long.

possessive
adjective

Ieri ho comprato una camicia bianca./Yesterday I bought a
white shirt.

descriptive
adjective

Some descriptive adjectives, however, can be used before
or after.

EXAMPLES

È una bella camicia.   OR   *È una camicia bella.*/It's a
beautiful shirt.

Maria è una ragazza simpatica. OR *Maria è una simpatica ragazza./*
Mary is a nice girl.

- You will eventually learn which descriptive adjectives can
  come before through practice and use.

- Be careful! As discussed in Chapter 5, you might have to
  change the form of the article when you put the adjective
  before.

lo zio simpatico BUT *il simpatico zio*

before *z*   before *s*

- Some common descriptive adjectives that can come before
  or after a noun are:

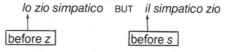

bello/	*cattivo*/bad	*piccolo*/small, little
beautiful	*giovane*/young	*povero*/poor
brutto/ugly	*grande*/big, large	*simpatico*/nice,
buono/good	*nuovo*/new	charming
caro/dear		*vecchio*/old

- But be careful! A few of these adjectives change meaning
  according to their position.

EXAMPLES
È un ragazzo povero. = He is a poor (not wealthy) boy.
È un povero ragazzo. = He is a poor (deserving of pity) boy.

È un amico vecchio. = He is an old (in age) friend.
È un vecchio amico. = He is an old (for many years) friend.

- As always, when you are unsure of the meaning and use of
  an adjective, check a dictionary.

Descriptive adjectives can also be separated from the noun they modify by what is called a *linking* verb. The most common linking verbs are *essere* (to be), *sembrare* (to seem), and *diventare* (to become).

EXAMPLES

Quella casa è nuov[a] *.*/That house is new.

Quell'uomo sembra giovan[e] *.*/That man seems young.

- Adjectives used in this way are known as *predicate adjectives* because they occur in the predicate slot, *after* the verb that links them to the noun they modify.

One final word about the position of descriptive adjectives! When these adjectives are accompanied by an adverb, another adjective, or some other part of speech, they must *follow* the noun.

EXAMPLES

È un [simpatico] *ragazzo.*/He is a pleasant boy.

BUT

È un ragazzo [molto simpatico.] /He is a very pleasant boy.

È un ragazzo [simpatico e buono.] /He is a pleasant and good boy.

§7.4
TYPES

The four most common types of adjectives are *demonstrative, descriptive, interrogative,* and *possessive.* Demonstrative adjectives have already been discussed in §5.2–3.

§7.4 – 1
Descriptive

Descriptive adjectives specify a quality of the noun they modify. They make up the largest group of adjectives. As already discussed (see §6.2), descriptive adjectives generally follow the noun.

È un esame difficile./It's a difficult exam.

Of the adjectives that can come *before* the noun, *buono* (good), *bello* (beautiful), *santo* (saint[ly]), and *grande* (big, large), change in form when they are placed before.

- *Buono* changes exactly like the indefinite article (see §5.2–2).

BEFORE MASCULINE NOUNS		
	Singular	**Plural**
Beginning with *z, s* + consonant, *ps, gn*	*buono*	*buoni*
Beginning with any other sound (vowel or consonant)	*buon*	
BEFORE FEMININE NOUNS		
Beginning with any consonant	*buona*	*buone*
Beginning with any vowel	*buon*	

- When it is placed after the noun, *buono* is a normal adjective ending in *-o* (see §7.2).

  EXAMPLES
  Singular:

  un buono zio OR *uno zio buon[o]* (a good uncle)

  un buon libro OR *un libro buon[o]* (a good book)

  un buon amico OR *un amico buon[o]* (a good friend)

  una buona macchina OR *una macchina buon[a]* (a good car)

  una buon'amica OR *un'amica buon[a]* (a good friend)

  Plural:

  dei buoni zii OR *degli zii buon[i]* ([some] good uncles)

  dei buoni amici OR *degli amici buon[i]* ([some] good friends)

  delle buone macchine OR *delle macchine buon[e]* ([some] good cars)

  delle buone amiche OR *delle amiche buon[e]* ([some] good friends)

- Notice that the apostrophe is used only with the feminine form (*buon'*), as is the case for the indefinite article (see §5.2–2).

- When referring to people, *buono* means "good," in the sense of "good in nature." If "good at doing something" is intended, then you must use the adjective *bravo*.

  È un buon ragazzo. = He is a good (natured) boy
  È un bravo studente. = He is a good student. (i.e., He is good at being a student.)

- *Bello* changes exactly like the definite article (see §5.2–1) and the demonstrative quello (see §5.2–3).

BEFORE MASCULINE NOUNS		
	Singular	**Plural**
Beginning with *z, s* + consonant, *ps, gn*	bello	begli
Beginning with any vowel	bell'—	begli
Beginning with any other consonant	bel——— bei	
BEFORE FEMININE NOUNS		
Beginning with any consonant	bella	belle
Beginning with any vowel	bell'—	belle

- If placed after the noun, *bello* is a normal adjective ending in *-o* (see §7.2).

  EXAMPLES

  Singular:

  un bello sport OR *uno sport bell* o   (a beautiful sport)
  un bell'orologio OR *un orologio bell* o   (a beautiful watch)
  un bel fiore OR *un fiore bell* o   (a beautiful flower)
  una bella donna OR *una donna bell* a   (a beautiful woman)
  una bell'automobile OR *un'automobile bell* a   (a beautiful automobile)

  Plural:

  dei begli sport OR *degli sport bell* i   ([some] beautiful sports)
  dei begli orologi OR *degli orologi bell* i   ([some] beautiful watches)
  dei bei fiori OR *dei fiori bell* i   ([some] beautiful flowers)
  delle belle automobili OR *delle automobili bell* e   ([some] beautiful automobiles)

- *Santo* has the following forms when placed before the noun.

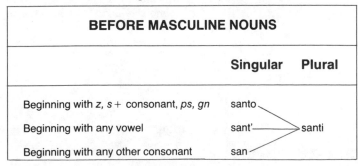

BEFORE MASCULINE NOUNS		
	Singular	**Plural**
Beginning with *z, s* + consonant, *ps, gn*	santo	santi
Beginning with any vowel	sant'—	santi
Beginning with any other consonant	san	

BEFORE FEMININE NOUNS		
	Singular	**Plural**
Beginning with any consonant	santa	sante
Beginning with any vowel	sant'	sante

EXAMPLES

Singular	*Plural*
Santo Stefano	*i santi Stefano, Antonio, e Pietro* (Saints Stephen, Anthony, and Peter)
Sant'Antonio	
San Pietro	
Santa Caterina	*le sante Caterina e Anna* (Saints Catherine and Anne)
Sant'Anna	

- *Grande* has the optional forms *gran* (before a masculine singular noun beginning with any consonant except *z, s* + consonant, *ps*, and *gn*), and *grand'* before any singular noun beginning with a vowel. Otherwise, it is a normal adjective ending in *-e* (see §7.2).

EXAMPLES

  un gran film (a great film) OR *un grande film*
  un grand'amico (a great friend) OR *un grande amico*

- Note that in the preceding examples, the articles and partitives are changed according to the initial sound of the word they precede—noun or adjective (see §5.2–1, §5.2–2, §5.2–3).

Those adjectives ending in *-co, -go, -cio*, and *-gio* have the same spelling patterns when pluralized as the nouns ending in these sounds (see §4.3–4).

EXAMPLES

Singular	*Plural*
un uomo simpatico / a pleasant man	*degli uomini simpatici* / (some) nice men
una strada lunga / a long street	*delle strade lunghe* / (some) long streets
un vestito grigio / a gray suit	*dei vestiti grigi* / (some) gray suits

§7.4 – 2
Interrogative

Interrogative adjectives allow us to ask questions about nouns.

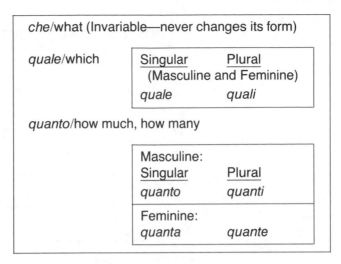

che/what (Invariable—never changes its form)

quale/which

Singular	Plural
(Masculine and Feminine)	
quale	*quali*

quanto/how much, how many

Masculine:	
Singular	Plural
quanto	*quanti*
Feminine:	
quanta	*quante*

These adjectives always come before the noun.

EXAMPLES

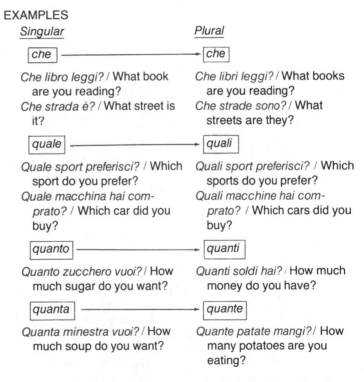

Singular	*Plural*
che	che

Che libro leggi? / What book are you reading?

Che strada è? / What street is it?

Che libri leggi? / What books are you reading?

Che strade sono? / What streets are they?

| quale | quali |

Quale sport preferisci? / Which sport do you prefer?

Quale macchina hai comprato? / Which car did you buy?

Quali sport preferisci? / Which sports do you prefer?

Quali macchine hai comprato? / Which cars did you buy?

| quanto | quanti |

Quanto zucchero vuoi? / How much sugar do you want?

Quanti soldi hai? / How much money do you have?

| quanta | quante |

Quanta minestra vuoi? / How much soup do you want?

Quante patate mangi? / How many potatoes are you eating?

§7.4 – 3
Possessive

Possessive adjectives allow us to indicate ownership of, or relationship to, a noun.

il mio libro / my book (ownership of)
le nostre amiche / our (female) friends (relationship to)

Like all adjectives, possessive adjectives agree in number and gender with the noun they modify.

	POSSESSIVE ADJECTIVE FORMS			
	Before Masculine Nouns		**Before Feminine Nouns**	
	Singular	**Plural**	**Singular**	**Plural**
my	il mio	i miei	la mia	le mie
your (familiar singular)	il tuo	i tuoi	la tua	le tue
his, her, its	il suo	i suoi	la sua	le sue
your (polite singular)	il Suo	i Suoi	la Sua	le Sue
our	il nostro	i nostri	la nostra	le nostre
your (familiar plural)	il vostro	i vostri	la vostra	le vostre
their	il loro	i loro	la loro	le loro
your (polite plural)	il Loro	i Loro	la Loro	le Loro

EXAMPLES

With Singular Nouns

il mio cappotto / my coat
la tua bicicletta / your (familiar, singular) bicycles
il suo biglietto / his, her ticket
la nostra camera / our bedroom

il vostro passaporto / your (familiar, plural) passport
la loro casa / their house
il Suo indirizzo / your (polite, singular) address
il Loro lavoro / your (polite, plural) job

With Plural Nouns

i miei cappotti / my coats
le tue biciclette / your bicycles

il suoi biglietti / his, her tickets
le nostre camere / our bedrooms

i vostri passaporti / your passports
le loro case / their houses
i Suoi indirizzi / your addresses

i Loro lavori / your jobs

- As you can see, possessives are adjectives that come before the noun and agree with it in gender and number.

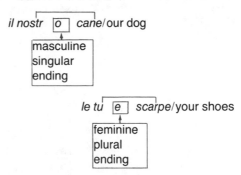

il nostr $\boxed{o}$ *cane*/our dog
↑
masculine
singular
ending

le tu $\boxed{e}$ *scarpe*/your shoes
↑
feminine
plural
ending

- The only invariable form is *loro*: it *never* changes.

- Notice that the definite article (in its appropriate form) is part of the possessive adjective. It is, however, dropped for all forms except *loro* when the noun modified has the following characteristics.

| It is a kinship noun (i.e, it refers to family members or relatives). |
| It is singular. |
| It is unmodified (i.e., it is not accompanied by another adjective, or altered by a suffix — §4.5). |

used when kinship
noun is plural

tuo cugino / your cousin		*i tuoi cugini* / your cousins
mia sorella / my sister	BUT	*le mie sorelle* / my sisters
nostro fratello / our brother		*i nostri fratelli* / our brothers

used when kinship
noun is modified

il tuo nonno americano/ your American grandfather
la mia sorellina/ my little sister (see §4.5)
la nostra nonna italiana/ our Italian grandmother

- As already mentioned, the article is always retained with *loro*.

il loro figlio/ their son
la loro figlia / their daughter
il loro fratello / their brother

- The only kinship nouns to which the above rules do not apply are *mamma* (mom) and *papà (babbo)* (dad).

mia madre / my mother	BUT	*la mia mamma* / my mom
tuo padre / your father		*il tuo papà* / your dad

- Notice that both "his" and "her" are expressed by the same possessive (which takes on the appropriate form before the noun).

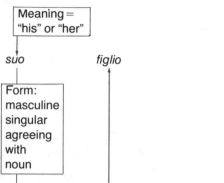 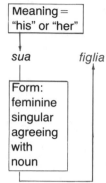

- As a handy guideline, make the possessive adjective agree with the noun first. Then worry about what it means in English. Otherwise, you will confuse its form with its meaning!

- Notice that "your" has both *familiar* and *polite* forms. More will be said about this distinction in the next chapter (see §8.3–1). As these terms imply, you use familiar forms with the people you know well and with whom you are on familiar terms; otherwise you use the polite forms.

- Note also that the polite forms are identical to the "his, her" forms in the singular, and the "their" forms in the plural. To keep the two types distinct in writing, the polite forms are often capitalized, as has been done here. But this is *not* an obligatory rule.

- Thus, when you see or hear these forms, you will have to figure out what they mean from the context.

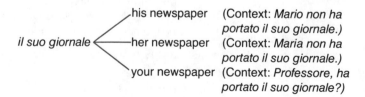

> First context: Mario didn't bring his newspaper.
> Second context: Mary didn't bring her newspaper.
> Third context: Professor, did you bring your newspaper?

- In current Italian, it is not unusual to find only the *vostro* forms used as the plural of both the familiar and polite singular forms.

	"Your book"	
Singular		Plural
il tuo libro (familiar)		il vostro libro (familiar and
il Suo libro (polite)		polite)

- The use of Loro as the polite plural possessive is restricted to very formal situations (see §8.3–1).

- The possessive adjective can be put after the noun for emphasis.

    È il mio cane./It's my dog.   *È il cane mio!*/It's my dog!

- If the possessive adjective is preceded by the indefinite article, it expresses the idea "of mine," "of yours," etc.

EXAMPLES
    un mio zio / an uncle of mine
    una sua amica / a friend of his, hers

- To express "own," use the adjective *proprio*.

    il mio proprio cane / my own dog
    la (sua) propria chiave / his, her own key

- Notice, finally, that the article is dropped when speaking directly to someor.

    Figlio mio, che fai? / My son, what are you doing?

§7.4 – 4 Other Common Adjectives

There are a few other adjectives you should know. Some of these are known formally as *indefinite* adjectives. The most common are:

Invariable	Like regular adjectives ending in -o
abbastanza/enough	*altro*/other
assai/quite, enough	*certo*/certain
ogni/each, every	*molto*/much, many, a lot
qualsiasi/whichever, any	*poco*/little, few
qualunque/ whichever, any	*parecchio*/several, a lot
	tanto/much, many, a lot
	troppo/too much
	stesso/the same
	ultimo/last
	tutto/all

EXAMPLES

<u>Invariable</u>

Non ho abbastanza soldi. / I do not have enough money.
Lui mangia assai carne. / He eats quite a lot of meat.
Ogni mattina leggiamo il giornale. / Every morning we read the
  newspaper.
In Italia puoi andare a qualsiasi (qualunque) ristorante /
  In Italy you can go to any restaurant.

<u>Variable</u>

Chi è l'altra ragazza? / Who is the other girl?
Conosco un certo signore che si chiama Roberto. / I know a certain gentle-
  man (who
  is) named
  Robert.

Ieri ho mangiato molti (tanti) dolci. /
  Yesterday I ate a lot of sweets.
Ci sono poche studentesse in questa classe. / There are few
  female stu-
  dents in this
  class.
Parecchi turisti visitano Venezia. / Several (a lot of) tourists visit
  Venice.
Abbiamo mangiato troppo gelato. / We ate too much ice cream.
Questi sono gli stessi libri.   These are the same books.
Questa è l'ultima volta che ti telefonerò. / This is the last time I'm
  going to call you.

- The adjectives *ogni, qualsiasi*, and *qualunque* are always followed by a *singular* noun.

- *Alcuni, alcune* (some), *qualche* (some), and *nessuno* (any) are technically indefinite adjectives. However, they are used primarily with a partitive function (see §6.2).

- Notice that *tutto* is separated from the noun by the definite article.

EXAMPLES

Lei ha mangiato tutto il riso. / She ate all the rice.
Mario ha mangiato tutta la minestra. / Mario ate all the soup.

- *Molto, tanto, poco*, and *troppo* are also used as adverbs, in which case there is no agreement. More will be said about this in Chapter 10 (see §10.3).

§7.5 COMPARISON OF ADJECTIVES

We make a comparison of descriptive adjectives (see §7.4–1) when we want to indicate that some quality has a relatively equal, greater, or lesser degree of the quality.
The three degrees of comparison are: *positive, comparative*, and *superlative*.

> For the positive degree use either *così . . . come* or *tanto . . . quanto.*

EXAMPLES

Paola è così felice come sua sorella. / Paula is as happy as her sister.

Quei ragazzi sono tanto noiosi quanto gli altri. / Those boys are as boring as the others.

● The first words (*così* or *tanto*) are optional.
Paola è felice come sua sorella.
Quei ragazzi sono noiosi quanto gli altri.

> For the comparative degree simply use *più* (more) or *meno* (less), as the case may be.

EXAMPLES

Maria è più studiosa di sua sorella. / Mary is more studious than her sister.

Maria è meno alta di suo fratello. / Mary is shorter than her brother.

Quei ragazzi sono più generosi degli altri. /
Those boys are more generous than the others.

Quei ragazzi sono meno intelligenti di quelle ragazze. / Those boys are less intelligent than those girls.

> For the *superlative degree* use the definite article (in its proper form, of course!) followed by *più* or *meno*, as the case may be.

EXAMPLES

Maria è la più studiosa della sua classe. / Mary is the most studious in her class.

Quel ragazzo è il più simpatico della famiglia. / That boy is the nicest in his family.

Le patate sono le meno costose. / Potatoes are the least expensive.

● In superlative constructions, the definite article is not repeated if it is already in front of a noun.

Maria è la ragazza più studiosa della classe. / Mary is the most studious girl in the class.

Lui è il ragazzo meno intelligente della classe. / He is the least intelligent boy in the class.

- Notice that "in the" is rendered by *di* + definite article (if needed).

  Gina è la più elegante della scuola./Gina is the most elegant in the school.

  di + la

  Lui è il meno generoso dei miei amici./He is the least generous of my friends.

  di + i

  È il ristorante più caro di Roma./It's the most expensive restaurant in Rome.

- In comparative constructions, the word "than" is rendered in one of two ways according to the following patterns:

If two nouns are compared by one adjective, use *di*.

EXAMPLES

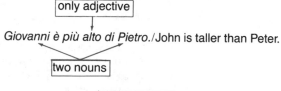

only adjective

Giovanni è più alto di Pietro./John is taller than Peter.

two nouns

only adjective

Questo signore è meno elegante dell'altro signore./

two nouns

This gentleman is less elegant than the other gentleman.

If one noun and two adjectives modifying the same noun are involved, then use *che*.

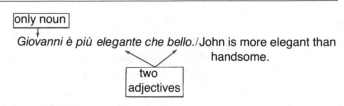

only noun

Giovanni è più elegante che bello./John is more elegant than handsome.

two adjectives

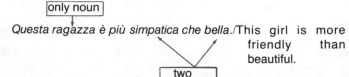

only noun

Questa ragazza è più simpatica che bella./This girl is more friendly than beautiful.

two adjectives

● If "than what" (= "than that which") is needed, then use *di quello che*/*di quel che*/*di ciò che*.

$$\textit{È più intelligente di} \begin{cases} \textit{quello} \\ \textit{quel che crediamo.} \\ \textit{ciò} \end{cases} \text{/ He is more intelligent than we believe.}$$

Some adjectives have both regular and irregular comparative and superlative forms. The most commonly used ones are:

Adjective	Comparative	Superlative
buono / good	*più buono* OR *migliore**	*il più buono* OR *il migliore*
cattivo / bad	*più cattivo* OR *peggiore**	*il più cattivo* OR *il peggiore*
grande / big, large	*più grande* OR *maggiore*	*il più grande* OR *il maggiore*
piccolo / small	*più piccolo* OR *minore*	*il più piccolo* OR *il minore*

*Before nouns, the *e* of these forms is normally dropped (e.g., *il miglior vino; il peggior vino*).

EXAMPLES

Questo vino è più buono. / This wine is better.

OR

Questo vino è migliore.

Quel vino è il più cattivo. / That wine is the worst.

OR

Quel vino è il peggiore.

To express "very" as part of the adjective, just drop the final vowel and add *-issimo*. Don't forget to make this newly-formed adjective agree with the noun!

EXAMPLES

Giovanni è intelligentissimo. / John is very intelligent.
Anche Maria è intelligentissima. / Mary is also very intelligent.

§8.

Pronouns

§8.1
WHAT ARE PRONOUNS?

Pronouns are words used in place of a noun or noun phrase, that is, a noun accompanied by an article or demonstrative (with or without an adjective).

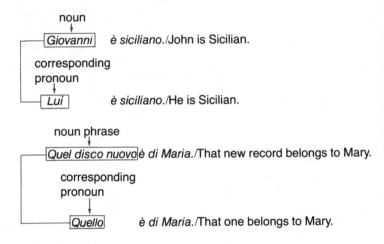

§8.2
DEMONSTRA-TIVE, POS-SESSIVE, AND INTERROGA-TIVE PRONOUNS

Demonstrative pronouns replace a noun phrase containing a demonstrative adjective (see §5.2–3).

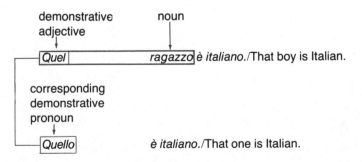

These pronouns correspond to the English "this one," "these," "that one," "those."

● Demonstrative pronouns agree in gender and number with the noun they replace.

Demonstrative Adjectives	Corresponding Demonstrative Pronouns
"this/these"	"this one/these"
With Masculine Nouns Singular	
questo— quest'——————————————— questo	
Plural	
questi ————————————— questi	
With Feminine Nouns Singular	
questa— quest'——————————————— questa	
Plural	
queste ————————————— queste	

Demonstrative Adjectives	Corresponding Demonstrative Pronouns
"that/those"	"that one/those"
With Masculine Nouns Singular	
quello— quell'——— quel——————————————— quello	
Plural	
quegli— quei——————————— quelli	
With Feminine Nouns Singular	
quella——— quell'——————————————— quella	
Plural	
quelle ————————————— quelle	

EXAMPLES

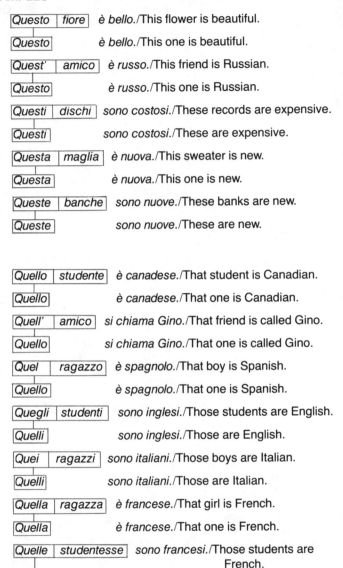

Questo | fiore | è bello./This flower is beautiful.

Questo | è bello./This one is beautiful.

Quest' | amico | è russo./This friend is Russian.

Questo | è russo./This one is Russian.

Questi | dischi | sono costosi./These records are expensive.

Questi | sono costosi./These are expensive.

Questa | maglia | è nuova./This sweater is new.

Questa | è nuova./This one is new.

Queste | banche | sono nuove./These banks are new.

Queste | sono nuove./These are new.

Quello | studente | è canadese./That student is Canadian.

Quello | è canadese./That one is Canadian.

Quell' | amico | si chiama Gino./That friend is called Gino.

Quello | si chiama Gino./That one is called Gino.

Quel | ragazzo | è spagnolo./That boy is Spanish.

Quello | è spagnolo./That one is Spanish.

Quegli | studenti | sono inglesi./Those students are English.

Quelli | sono inglesi./Those are English.

Quei | ragazzi | sono italiani./Those boys are Italian.

Quelli | sono italiani./Those are Italian.

Quella | ragazza | è francese./That girl is French.

Quella | è francese./That one is French.

Quelle | studentesse | sono francesi./Those students are French.

Quelle | sono francesi./Those are French.

- Be careful! Some of the forms match exactly; others do not.

  A possessive pronoun replaces a noun phrase containing a possessive adjective (see §7.4–3) and a noun. The Italian possessive pronouns correspond to English "mine," "yours," "his," "hers," "ours," "theirs."

- In this case there is a perfect match between the adjective and pronoun forms of the possessive. So, just go over the chart in §7.4–3, and it will give you the pronoun forms as well.

EXAMPLES

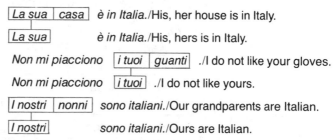

- The article is always used with the pronoun forms, even in the case of singular, unmodified, kinship nouns (review §7.4–3).

EXAMPLES

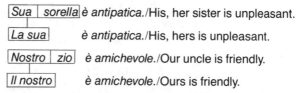

- The article can be dropped if the pronoun occurs as a predicate; i.e., if it occurs after the verb *essere* (to be), or some other linking verb (see §7.3).

EXAMPLES

Questo denaro è mio. / This money is mine.
È tua questa borsa? / Is this purse yours?
Quei biglietti sono suoi. / Those tickets are his, hers.

An interrogative pronoun replaces a noun or noun phrase introducing a question. The interrogative adjectives discussed in §7.4–2 of the previous chapter have identical pronoun forms.

EXAMPLES

| Che | libro | *leggi?*/What book are you reading?

| Che | *leggi?*/What are you reading?

> The forms *che*, *che cosa*, and *cosa* are synonyms for "what?" *Che leggi?/Che cosa leggi?/Cosa leggi?*

| Quali | riviste | *hai comprato?*/Which magazines did you buy?

| Quali | *hai comprato?*/Which did you buy?

| Quanti | studenti | *erano presenti?*/How many students were present?

| Quanti | *erano presenti?*/How many were present?

- Here are a few other useful interrogative pronouns:

> *chi* = who, whom
> *Chi abita a Roma?*/Who lives in Rome?
> *Chi conosci qui?*/Whom do you know here?

> *di chi* = whose
> *Di chi è questo portafoglio?*/Whose wallet is this?

> *a chi* = to whom
> *A chi hai parlato?*/To whom did you speak?

> *da chi* = from whom
> *Da chi hai comprato la macchina?*/From whom did you buy the car?

The following words are not, strictly speaking, pronouns. But since they allow you to ask questions in exactly the same way, they are listed here for you:

> *come* = how
> *Come si scrive quella parola?*/How does one write that word?

> *dove* = where
> *Dove abiti?*/Where do you live?

> *perché* = why
> *Perché dici così?*/Why do you say that?

> *quando* = when
> *Quando andrai in Italia?*/When are you going to Italy?

- In writing, it is normal to drop the *e* in *come, dove,* and *quale* before the verb form *è* (is). For both *come* and *dove* an apostrophe is used. But this is not the case for *quale*!

> *Com'è?*/How is it?
> *Dov'è?*/Where is it?
> BUT
> *Qual è?*/Which is it?

§8.3 PERSONAL PRONOUNS

Personal pronouns refer to a person ("I," "you," "we," etc.). They can be classified as a subject, an object, or a reflexive pronoun. Personal pronouns are also classified according to the person speaking (= first person), the person spoken to (= second person), or the person spoken about (= third person). The pronoun can, of course, be in the singular (= referring to one person) or in the plural (= referring to more than one person).

§8.3 – 1 Subject

Subject pronouns are used as the subject of a verb (review the definition of "subject" in §2.1).

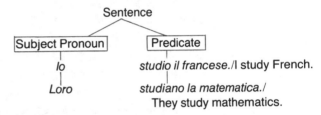

The Italian subject pronouns are:

	Person	Italian Forms	English Equivalents	Examples
Singular	1st	*io*	I	*Io non capisco.*/I do not understand.
	2nd	*tu*	you (familiar)	*Tu sei simpatico.*/You are nice
	3rd	*lui*	he	*Lui è americano.*/He is American.
		lei	she	*Lei è americana.*/She is American.
		Lei	you (polite)	*Come si chiama, Lei?*/What is your name?
Plural	1st	*noi*	we	*Noi non lo conosciamo.*/We do not know him.
	2nd	*voi*	you	*Voi arrivate sempre in ritardo.*/You always arrive late.
	3rd	*loro*	they	*Loro vanno in Italia.*/They are going to Italy.
		Loro	you (formal)	*Come si chiamano, Loro?*/What is your name?

- Notice that *io* (I) is not capitalized (unless it is the first word of a sentence).

- Subject pronouns are optional in normal affirmative sentences (see §2.2–1) because it is easy to tell from the verb ending which person is referred to.

  Io non capisco./I do not understand. OR *Non capisco.*

  > tells us
  > that *io* is
  > the subject

  Loro vanno in Italia./They are going to Italy. OR *Vanno in Italia.*

  > tells us
  > that *loro* is
  > the subject

- Sometimes, however, the way a sentence is constructed makes it impossible to avoid using pronouns. This is particularly true when you want to emphasize the subject.

  EXAMPLES
  Devi parlare tu, non io! / You have to speak, not I!
  Non è possibile che l'abbiano fatto loro. / It's not possible that they did it.

- These pronouns must also be used to avoid confusion when more than one person is being referred to.

  EXAMPLES
  Mentre lui guarda la TV, lei ascolta la radio. / While he watches TV, she listens to the radio.
  Lui e io vogliamo che tu dica la verità. / He and I want you to tell the truth.

- They are used after the words *anche* (also, too) and *neanche* (neither, not even) (whose synonyms are *neppure* and *nemmeno*), and *proprio* (really).

  EXAMPLES
  Anche tu devi venire alla festa. / You too must come to the party.
  Non è venuto neanche lui. / He didn't come either.
  Signor Bianchi, è proprio Lei? / Mr. Bianchi, is it really you?

- The subject pronoun "it" usually is not stated in Italian.

  EXAMPLES
  È vero. / It is true.
  Pare che sia corretto. / It appears to be correct.

- However, if you should ever need to express this subject, use *esso* (m.)/*essa* (f.); plural forms: *essi* (m.), *esse* (f.).

È una buona scusa *, ma neanche* essa *potrà aiutarti adesso./*
It's a good excuse, but not even it can help you now.

- Notice that "you" has both familiar and polite forms. These are not optional! If you address someone incorrectly, it might be taken as rudeness! So, be careful.

- The familiar forms (and their corresponding verb forms) are used, as the name suggests, with people with whom you are on familiar terms: that is, members of the family, friends, etc. If you call someone by a first name, then you are obviously on familiar terms.

  Maria, anche tu studi l'italiano? / Mary, are you studying Italian too?

- The polite forms are used with all other persons.

  Signora Bianchi, anche Lei studia l'italiano? / Mrs. Bianchi, are you studying Italian too?

- In writing, the polite forms (*Lei, Loro*) are often capitalized in order to distinguish them from *lei* (she) and *loro* (they), but this is not obligatory.

- In the plural, there is a strong tendency in current Italian to use *voi* as the plural of both *tu* and *Lei*. *Loro* is restricted to very formal situations (when addressing an audience, when a waiter takes an order, etc.)

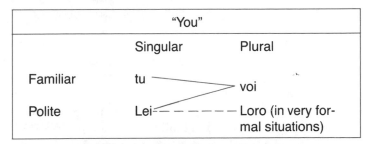

	"You"	
	Singular	Plural
Familiar	tu	voi
Polite	Lei	Loro (in very formal situations)

- The forms *lui* (he) and *lei* (she) are used in ordinary conversation. However, there are two more formal pronouns that are limited to such things as writing essays: *egli* (he) and *ella* (she).

  Normal Conversational Italian
  Giovanni è italiano, ma neanche lui capisce i pronomi!/
  John is Italian, but he doesn't understand pronouns either!

  Formal (Usually Written) Italian
  Dante scrisse la Divina Commedia. Egli era fiorentino./
  Dante wrote the *Divine Comedy*. He was Florentine.

§8.3 – 2
Object

Object pronouns are used as the object of a verb. As discussed in Chapter 2 (review section §2.2–1), the object can be direct or indirect.

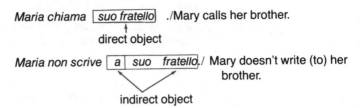

Maria chiama | suo fratello | ./Mary calls her brother.
           direct object

Maria non scrive | a | suo | fratello |./ Mary doesn't write (to) her brother.
           indirect object

The corresponding pronouns are also known as direct and indirect. Italian object pronouns generally come right *before* the verb.

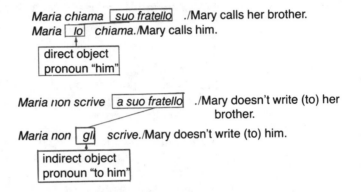

Maria chiama | suo fratello | ./Mary calls her brother.
Maria | lo | *chiama.*/Mary calls him.
direct object
pronoun "him"

Maria non scrive | a suo fratello | ./Mary doesn't write (to) her brother.

Maria non | gli | *scrive.*/Mary doesn't write (to) him.
indirect object
pronoun "to him"

The Italian object pronouns are detailed in the following charts.

● Notice that the first and second person pronouns are identical. Differences occur only in the third person.

● As mentioned in the previous section (see §8.3–1), there are both familiar and polite forms in the singular, but in the plural there is a tendency to use only the second person forms.

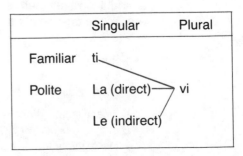

	Singular	Plural
Familiar	ti	
Polite	La (direct)	vi
	Le (indirect)	

	Person	Object Pronouns		English Equivalents		Examples
		Direct	**Indirect**			
S i n g u l a r	1st	*mi*	*mi*	me	to me	*Maria mi chiama.*/Mary calls me. *Maria mi scrive.*/Mary writes (to) me.
	2nd familiar	*ti*	*ti*	you	to you	*Ti chiamo fra mezz'ora.*/I'll call you in a half hour. *Ti scrivo fra un mese.*/I'll write (to) you in a month.
	3rd	*lo (m.)*	*gli (m.)*	him	to him	*Maria lo chiama.*/Mary calls him. *Maria gli scrive spesso.*/ Mary writes (to) him often.
		la (f.)	*le (f.)*	her	to her	*Maria la chiama.*/Mary calls her. *Maria le scrive spesso.*/ Mary writes (to) her often.
	polite	*La*	*Le*	you	to you	*Signore, La chiamo domani.*/Sir, I'll call you tomorrow. *Signore, Le scrivo fra un mese.*/Sir, I'll write (to) you in a month.
P l u r a l	1st	*ci*	*ci*	us	to us	*Perché non ci chiami?*/Why don't you call us? *Perché non ci scrivi?*/Why don't you write to us?
	2nd	*vi*	*vi*	you	to you	*Domani vi chiamo.*/Tomorrow I'll call you. *Vi scrivo dall'Italia.*/I'll write (to) you from Italy.
	3rd	*li (m.)*	*gli (m.)*	them	to them	*Li chiamo dopo.*/I'll call them after.
		le (f.)	*gli (f.)*	them	to them	*Maria e Claudia? Le chiamo domani, ma non gli scrivo.*/Mary and Claudia? I'll call them tomorrow, but I won't write to them.

- Notice that the plural of the indirect object pronouns *gli* (to him) and *le* (to her) is *gli* (to them). This is very common in current ordinary Italian. However, in more formal situations, some Italians prefer to use *loro* (to them), which goes *after* the verb.

Normal Usage	Very Formal Usage
I ragazzi? Gli parlo domani. / The boys? I'll speak to them tomorrow.	*I signori? Parlo loro domani.* / The gentlemen? I'll speak to them tomorrow.
Le ragazze? Gli parlo domani. / The girls? I'll speak to them tomorrow.	*Le signore? Parlo loro domani.* / The ladies? I'll speak to them tomorrow.

- The English direct object pronoun "it" (plural, "them") is expressed by the third person direct object pronoun. Be careful! Choose the pronoun according to the gender and number of the noun it replaces.

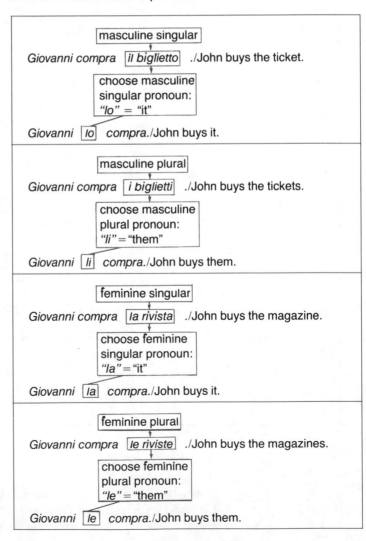

- The past participle of the verb agrees in gender and number with these four pronouns (*lo, la, li, le*) (see Chapter 8 for verb forms using the past participle).

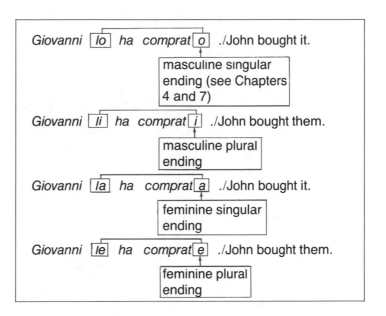

- Note that only the singular forms *lo* and *la* can be elided with the auxiliary forms of *avere: ho, hai, ha, hanno* (see §9.2–2).

  Giovanni lo ha comprato. OR *Giovanni l'ha comprato.*
  Giovanni la ha comprata. OR *Giovanni l'ha comprata.*

- **Agreement with the other direct object pronouns *mi, ti, ci, vi* is optional.**

  Giovanni ci ha chiamato / John called us. (= no agreement)

  OR

  Giovanni ci ha chiamati / John called us. (= agreement)

- **Recall that the ending *-i* is used when referring to both male and female persons (review §3.3–1).**

- There is *no* agreement with indirect object pronouns.

  Giovanni gli ha scritto. / John wrote (to) him, (to) them.
  Giovanni le ha scritto. / John wrote (to) her.

- But be very careful! The pronoun form *le* has two meanings.

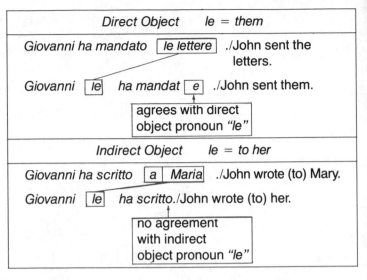

- Direct object pronouns normally follow an infinitive or gerund and are attached to it (see §9.6–1 and §9.6–2). In the case of the infinitive, you must drop the final -*e:* parlare:⟶ parlar⟶ parlar*mi*, parlar*ti*, etc.

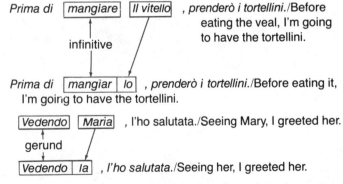

- They are also attached to the form *ecco* (here is, here are, there is, there are) (see §12.3).

  Ecco | la ricetta | ./Here is the recipe.

  Ecco| la | ./Here it is.

  Ecco | i nostri genitori | ./Here are our parents.

  Ecco| li | ./Here they are.

- With *modal* verbs such as *potere* (to be able to), *dovere* (to have to) and *volere* (to want) (see §9.9), you can either attach the direct object pronoun to the infinitive, or put it before the modal.

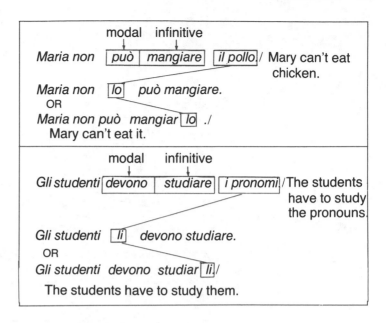

- These pronouns are also attached to the nonpolite forms of the imperative (see §9.3).

Giovanni, paga [*il conto*] *!*/John, pay the bill!

Giovanni, paga [lo] *!*/John, pay it!

BUT

Signor Verdi, paghi [*il conto*] *!*/Mr. Verdi, pay the bill!

Signor Verdi, [lo] *paghi!*/Mr. Verdi, pay it!

- More will be said about the use of direct object pronouns with imperatives and modal verbs in Chapter 10.

  Now comes the complicated task of sequencing indirect and direct objects! Just remember the following, and you won't have too much difficulty:

The indirect object always precedes the direct object *lo, la, li,* or *le.*

Giovanni me lo dà./John gives it to me.

indirect object pronoun | direct object pronoun

> Change the indirect forms *mi, ti, ci, vi* to *me, te, ce,* and *ve,* respectively.

Giovanni mi dà l'indirizzo ./John gives me the address.
Giovanni me lo dà./John gives it to me.

Giovanni ti manda i francobolli ./John sends you the stamps.
Giovanni te li manda./John sends them to you.

Giovanni ci scrive una cartolina./John writes us a card.
Giovanni ce la scrive./John writes it to us.

Giovanni vi scrive una cartolina ./John writes you a card.
Giovanni ve la scrive./John writes it to you.

> Change both the indirect forms *gli* and *le* to *glie,* and combine it with *lo, la, li,* or *le* to form one word: *glielo, glieli, gliela, gliele.*

Lo studente gli porta gli esercizi ./The student brings the exercises to him, them.
Lo studente glieli porta./The student brings them to him, them.

Lo studente le porta le dispense ./The student brings the course notes to her.
Lo studente gliele porta./The student brings them to her.

- When the pronouns are attached to a verb (in the cases discussed above), you always write them as one word.

  Prima di mandarti la lettera *, ti telefono.*/Before sending you the letter, I'll phone you.
  Prima di mandartela, ti telefono./Before sending it to you, I'll phone you.

  Giovanni, paga il conto al cameriere !/John, pay the bill to the waiter!

  lo   gli

  Giovanni, pagaglielo!/John, pay it to him!

  Maria deve comprarmi una borsa ./Mary has to buy me a purse.
  Maria deve comprarmela./Mary has to buy it for me.

- And do not forget that when *lo, la, li, le* are put before a past participle, there must be agreement.

  Lo studente gliele ha portate./The student brought them to her.

- The forms *glielo* and *gliela* can be elided with the auxiliary forms *ho, hai, ha, hanno.*

  Gliel'hanno portato. / They brought it to him, her, them.

There is a second type of object pronoun that goes after the verb. It is known as a *stressed* pronoun.

Before Verb	After Verb	Translation
mi ———————————— me		me
ti ———————————— te		you
lo ——————⟍		
gli ——————⟋ lui		him
la ——————⟍		
le ——————⟋ lei		her/you (pol.)
ci ———————————— noi		us
vi ———————————— voi		you
gli (pl.) ——————————— loro		they

- These allow you to put greater emphasis on the object.

  Normal Speech
  Maria mi chiama. / Mary calls me.
  Giovanni gli dice la verità. / John tells him the truth.

  Emphasis
  Maria chiama me, non te! / Mary calls me, not you!
  Giovanni dice la verità a lui, non a loro! / John tells him, not them, the truth!

- They also allow you to be precise and clear about the person you are referring to.

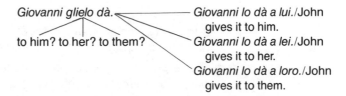

  Giovanni glielo dà.
  to him? to her? to them?
  Giovanni lo dà a lui./John gives it to him.
  Giovanni lo dà a lei./John gives it to her.
  Giovanni lo dà a loro./John gives it to them.

- These are the *only* object pronouns you can use after a preposition.

  EXAMPLES

  Maria viene con noi./Mary is coming with us.

  Il professore parla di te./The professor is speaking of you.

  L'ha fatto per me./He did it for me.

§8.3 – 3 Reflexive

Reflexive pronouns, "reflect" the subject of a verb. Like object pronouns, reflexives generally come before the verb.

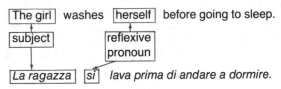

The Italian reflexive pronouns are:

	Person	Italian Forms	English Equivalents	Examples
S i n g u l a r	1st	*mi*	myself	*Io mi lavo.*/I wash (myself).
	2nd familiar	*ti*	yourself	*Tu ti diverti.*/You enjoy yourself.
	3rd	*si*	himself, herself, oneself, itself	*Lui si diverte.*/He enjoys himself. *Anche lei si diverte.*/She enjoys herself too.
	3rd polite	*Si*	yourself	*Si diverte, Lei?*/Are you enjoying yourself?
P l u r a l	1st	*ci*	ourselves	*Anche noi ci divertiamo.*/We too are enjoying ourselves.
	2nd	*vi*	yourselves	*Vi divertite, voi?*/Are you enjoying yourselves?
	3rd	*si*	themselves	*Loro si divertono sempre.*/They always enjoy themselves.
	3rd polite	*Si*	yourselves	*Si divertono, Loro?*/Are you enjoying yourselves?

- Notice that the third person also gives you the polite form of address (which is often capitalized to distinguish it from the other third person forms in writing) (see also §8.3–1).

- These pronouns also express the *reciprocal* forms "to each other," "to themselves," etc.

    Si telefonano ogni sera. / They phone each other every night.
    Noi ci scriviamo ogni mese. / We write each other every month.

- After prepositions (especially *da*), use the forms *me, te, sé, noi, voi.*

    Ci vado da me. / I'm going there by myself.
    Lo farà da sé. / He'll do it by himself.

- Notice that *sé* is written with an accent. However, in the expression *se stesso* ([by] himself), *se stessa* ([by] herself), *se stessi* ([by] themselves) and *se stesse,* the accent is omitted.

Ci andrà se stesso. / He'll go by himself.
Maria gli scriverà se stessa. / Mary will write to him herself.

● For more information on these pronouns, see §9.7.

§8.4 RELATIVE PRONOUNS

As discussed in Chapter 2 (review §2.3–1), a relative clause is introduced into a sentence by means of a *relative* pronoun, which serves as a subject or an object in the clause. The relative pronouns in Italian are:

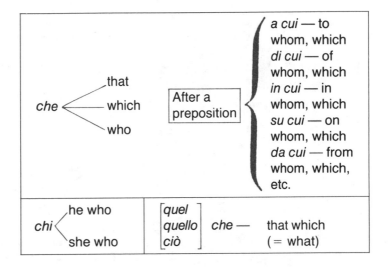

EXAMPLES

$\boxed{che}$

Quella donna che legge il giornale è mia sorella. / That woman who is reading the newspaper is my sister.

Il vestito che ho comprato ieri è molto bello. / The dress I bought yesterday is very beautiful.

Mi piace la poesia che stai leggendo. / I like the poem (that) you are reading.

$\boxed{cui}$

Il ragazzo a cui ho dato il regalo è mio cugino./The boy to whom I gave the gift is my cousin.

Non trovo il cassetto in cui ho messo il mio anello./I can't find the drawer in which I put my ring.

Ecco la rivista di cui ho parlato./Here is the magazine of which I spoke.

chi

Chi va in Italia si divertirà. / He, she who goes to Italy will enjoy himself, herself.

C'è chi dorme e c'è chi lavora! / Some sleep, some work! (*lit.*, There is he who sleeps and there is he who works!)

quel/quello/ciò che

Quello che dici è vero. / What (that which) you are saying is true.

Non sai quel che dici. / You don't know what you are saying.

- Both *che* and *cui* can be replaced by *il quale*, if there is an antecedent. It changes in form according to the noun it refers to and is always preceded by the definite article.

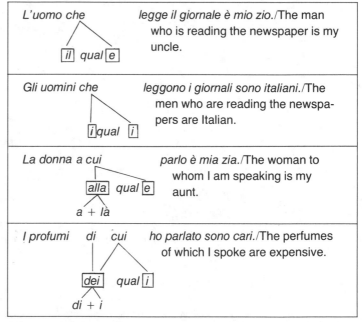

L'uomo che	legge il giornale è mio zio./The man who is reading the newspaper is my uncle.
il qual e	
Gli uomini che	leggono i giornali sono italiani./The men who are reading the newspapers are Italian.
i qual i	
La donna a cui	parlo è mia zia./The woman to whom I am speaking is my aunt.
alla qual e a + là	
I profumi di cui	ho parlato sono cari./The perfumes of which I spoke are expensive.
dei qual i di + i	

- When there is no antecedent, only *che* is used.

- *Il quale, la quale,* etc., are used when you want to be clear about which noun is being referred to.

- To express "whose," use *il cui,* changing the article according to the gender and number of the noun modified.

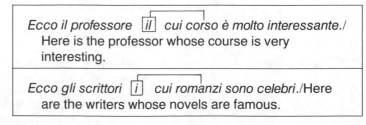

Ecco il professore il *cui corso è molto interessante./* Here is the professor whose course is very interesting.

Ecco gli scrittori i *cui romanzi sono celebri./*Here are the writers whose novels are famous.

> *Ecco la ragazza* ⌐la⌐ *cui intelligenza è straordinaria./*
> Here is the girl whose intelligence is extraordinary.

> *Ecco la ragazza* ⌐le⌐ *cui amiche sono italiane./*Here
> is the girl whose friends are Italian.

§8.5 OTHER PRONOUNS

The indefinite adjectives discussed in Chapter 7 have corresponding indefinite pronouns. The pronouns have only one form (review the chart in §7.4–4).

EXAMPLES

Lui mangia assai.   He eats quite a lot.
Tuo fratello dorme molto, no? / Your brother sleeps a lot, doesn't he?
Ieri ho mangiato troppo. / Yesterday I ate too much.

- When referring to people in general, use the plural forms *molti, alcuni, tanti, pochi, parecchi, tutti,* etc.

EXAMPLES

Molti vanno in Italia quest'anno. / Many are going to Italy this year.
Alcuni dormono alla mattina, ma parecchi lavorano già. / Some sleep in the morning, but quite a few are working already.
Tutti sanno quello. / Everyone knows that.

- Use the corresponding feminine forms (*molte, alcune,* etc.) when referring only to females.

EXAMPLES

Di quelle ragazze, molte sono italiane. / Of those girls, many are Italian.
Di tutte quelle donne, alcune sono americane. / Of all those women, some are American.

- Notice the expression *alcuni . . . altri* (some . . . others).

Alcuni andranno in Italia; altri, invece, andranno in Francia. / Some will go to Italy; others, instead, will go to France.

The pronoun *ne* has four main functions. It is used to replace:

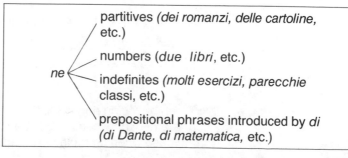

ne 〈
- partitives (*dei romanzi, delle cartoline,* etc.)
- numbers (*due libri,* etc.)
- indefinites (*molti esercizi, parecchie classi,* etc.)
- prepositional phrases introduced by *di* (*di Dante, di matematica,* etc.)

Like most object pronouns, it is usually placed before the verb (except in those cases discussed in §8.3–2).

EXAMPLES

Partitive: *ne* = "some"

Domani scriverò delle cartoline ./Tomorrow I'm going to write some postcards.

Domani ne *scriverò.*/Tomorrow I'm going to write some.

Anch'io devo comprare della carne ./I too have to buy some meat.

Anch'io ne *devo comprare.*/I too have to buy some.

Numbers: *ne* = "of them" (retain the number)

Domani comprerò tre matite ./Tomorrow I will buy three pencils.

Domani ne *comprerò* tre ./Tomorrow I will buy three (of them).

Voglio comprare quattro dischi ./I want to buy four records.

Ne *voglio comprare* quattro ./I want to buy four (of them).

Indefinites: *ne* = "of them" (retain the indefinite)

Domani vedrò molte amiche ./Tomorrow I'm going to see many (female) friends.

Domani ne *vedrò* molte./Tomorrow I'm going to see many of them.

Devo comprare parecchi regali ./I have to buy quite a few presents.

Ne *devo comprare* parecchi ./I have to buy quite a few of them.

Phrases introduced by *di*: *ne* = "of him, her, it, them"/"about him, her," etc.

Il professore parlerà di matematica ./The professor will speak about mathematics.

Il professore ne *parlerà.*/The professor will speak about it.

Lei parlerà del suo amico ./She will speak about her friend.

Lei ne *parlerà.*/She will speak about him.

- When replacing partitives, numbers, and definites, there is agreement between *ne* and the past participle. This is not the case when *ne* replaces a phrase introduced by *di*.

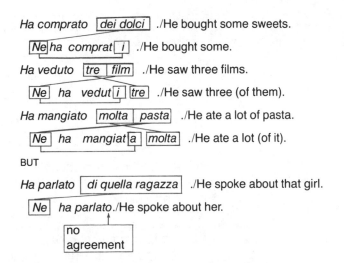

Ha comprato dei dolci ./He bought some sweets.

Ne ha comprat i ./He bought some.

Ha veduto tre | film ./He saw three films.

Ne ha vedut i tre ./He saw three (of them).

Ha mangiato molta | pasta ./He ate a lot of pasta.

Ne ha mangiat a molta ./He ate a lot (of it).

BUT

Ha parlato di quella ragazza ./He spoke about that girl.

Ne ha parlato./He spoke about her.

no
agreement

The pronoun *ci* (identical to the object and reflexive *ci* discussed above) can also mean "there." As always, it goes before the verb (except in the cases mentioned in §8.3–2).

ci = "there"

Andremo in Inghilterra *domani.*/We are going to England
tomorrow.

Ci andremo domani./We are going there tomorrow.

Chi abita in quella città ?/Who lives in that city?

Chi ci abita?/Who lives there?

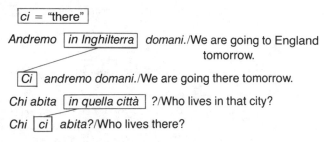

- However, to express "from there," you have to use *ne* (again!).

Tu vai in Italia *, e io vengo* dall'Italia./You are going to Italy,
and I'm coming
from Italy.

Tu ci *vai, e io* ne *vengo.*/You are going there, and I'm
coming from there.

In these cases, there is no agreement between *ci* and *ne* and the past participle.

Both *ci* and *ne* can occur in sequence with object pronouns.

Ci is changed to *ce* when it precedes other pronouns.

Io metto il portafoglio nel cassetto ./I put my wallet in the
drawer.

Io ce lo *metto.*/I put it there.

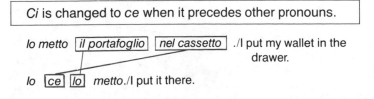

> *Ne* is placed after the indirect object pronouns in the normal fashion.

Giovanni mi dà delle rose ./John gives me some roses.

Giovanni me ne dà./John gives some to me.

Il medico gli dà delle pillole ./The doctor gives him some pills.

Il medico gliene dà./The doctor gives some to him.

And now for the last pronoun to be discussed! The impersonal *si* (one, in general) has the following peculiar characteristics:

> Unlike its synonym *uno*, with *si* the verb agrees with what appears to be the predicate!

Uno compra quel libro solo in Italia./One buys that book only in Italy.

Si compra quel libro solo in Italia.

Uno compra quei libri solo in Italia./One buys those books only in Italy.

Si comprano quei libri solo in Italia.

> All compound tenses using *si* (see §9.2–2), are conjugated with *essere* (to be), with the past participle agreeing, apparently, with the predicate!

Uno ha veduto quei film solo in Italia./One has seen those films only in Italy.

Si sono vedut i *quei film solo in Italia.*

> When followed by a predicate adjective (see §7.3), the adjective is always in the plural (usually in *-i*!).

Uno è contento in Italia./One is happy in Italy.

Si è content i *in Italia.*

> Direct object pronouns are placed before it!

Uno deve dire la verità ./One has to tell the truth.

Uno la *deve dire.*/One has to tell it.

La *si deve dire.*

> In front of the reflexive *si* (see §8.3–3)/"oneself", *si* changes to *ci*!

*Uno si diverte in Italia./*One enjoys oneself in Italy.

Si

Ci si diverte in Italia.

§9.

Verbs

Verbs are words that indicate the action performed by the subject. For this reason, the verb agrees with the subject's *person* (first, second, third — see §9.3) and *number* (singular or plural).

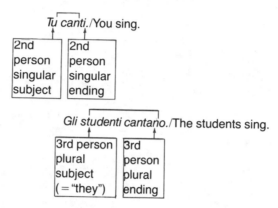

- For the kinds of objects that verbs can take, go over §2.2–1.

- In Italian a verb is listed in a dictionary in its definitive form (see also §9.6–1). Italian verbs are divided into three conjugations according to their infinitive endings.

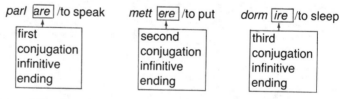

- These infinitive endings allow you to determine which person and number endings a verb must take when you conjugate it (that is, when you attach the endings to the verb according to some pattern).

- A verb tense indicates the time the action occurred: *now* (present tense), *before* (past tense), or *after* (future tense).

  > *La mangio adesso.* / I'm eating it now. (present tense)
  > *L'ho mangiata ieri.* / I ate it yesterday. (past tense)
  > *La mangerò domani.* / I will eat it tomorrow. (future tense)

- Not only do verbs allow you to express a time relationship but they also allow you to convey your manner of thinking, point of view, etc. This aspect of a verb is known as its *mood*.

Maria scrive la lettera. (indicative mood—states something)
Maria, scrivi la lettera! / Mary, write the letter! (imperative
                                  mood—allows you to make
                                  commands)

È probabile che Maria scriva la lettera./ It's probable that Mary is
                                  writing the letter (sub-
                                  junctive mood—allows
                                  you to express proba-
                                  bility, doubt, etc.)

We will study the tenses of the different moods of *regular*
verbs in this chapter. A regular verb is one whose conjugations follow a general pattern. Verbs that do not are known
as *irregular.* You will find some common irregular verbs in
the "Verb Charts" section at the end of this book.

§9.2 THE INDICATIVE TENSES

The *indicative* mood allows you to express or indicate facts.
It is used for ordinary statements and questions, and is the
most commonly used mood in everyday conversation.

§9.2 – 1 Present

The present tense is formed as follows:

- Drop the infinitive ending of the verb and add the following
  endings to the stem according to the conjugation.

	Person	Endings		
		1st Conjugation = are	**2nd Conjugation = ere**	**3rd Conjugation = ire**
Singular 1st	1st	-o	-o	-o
	2nd	-i	-i	-i
	3rd	-a	-e	-e
Plural	1st	-iamo	-iamo	-iamo
	2nd	-ate	-ete	-ite
	3rd	-ano	-ono	-ono

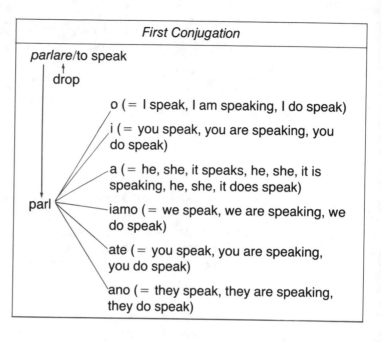

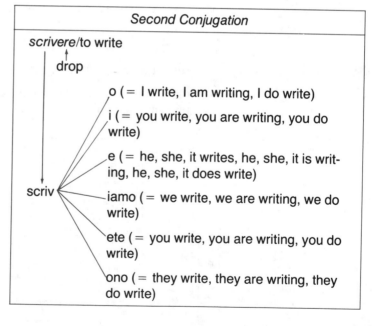

EXAMPLES

Lui parla molto bene. / He speaks very well.
Quando scrivi quella lettera? / When are you writing that letter?
Non apriamo mai le finestre d'inverno. / We never open the windows in the winter.
È vero; lei scrive molto bene. / It's true; she does write very well.

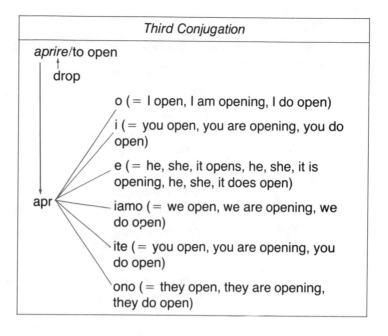

- There is a second type of third conjugation verb that has an additional *-isc-* in front of the endings *-o, -i, -e,* and *-ono.*

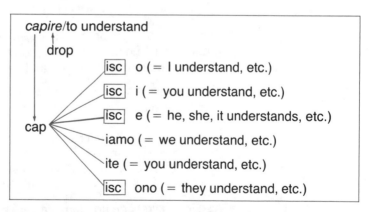

- Two other common verbs conjugated in this fashion are *finire* (to finish) and *preferire* (to prefer).

EXAMPLES

Gli studenti non capiscono la lezione. / The students do not understand the lesson.
Finisco di lavorare alle sei. / I finish working at six.
Quale preferisce, Lei? / Which one do you (*pol.*) prefer?

- You will have to learn whether a given third conjugation verb follows this pattern or the other one (*aprire*). A good dictionary will provide this kind of information.

- Be careful when you pronounce the third person plural forms! The accent is *not* placed on the ending.

  parlano/they speak   *scrivono*/they write
    ↑   ↑
  stress   stress

- Recall from the previous chapter (see §8.3–1) that subject pronouns are optional with the indicative tenses. The reason is obvious: the endings make it clear which person is being referred to.

- The third person forms are used, of course, with subjects that are not pronouns.

  La ragazza studi a ./The girl studies.

  Quegli studenti non studi ano ./Those students do not study.

- Remember as well (§8.3–1) that for the singular polite "you," the third person singular form is used.

  Cosa preferisci, tu? / What do you (*fam.*) prefer?
  Cosa preferisce, Lei? / What do you (*pol.*) prefer?

- And do not forget that the subject pronoun "it" (plural "they") is not normally expressed (§8.3–1).

  Apre a mezzogiorno. / It opens at noon.

- In the first conjugation only, if a verb ends in hard *c* or hard *g* before the ending *-are*, you retain the hard sound by adding an *h* before the endings *-i* and *-iamo*.

cercare/ to search for	*pagare* / to pay (for)
cerco/ I search	*pago*./ I pay
cerchi/ you search	*paghi*/ you pay
cerca/ he, she, it searches	*paga*/ he, she, it pays
cerchiamo/ we search	*paghiamo* / we pay
cercate/ you search	*pagate* / you pay
cercano/ they search	*pagano* / they pay

- Also in the first conjugation, if a verb ends in soft *c* or soft *g*, written as *-ciare* and *-giare*, then you do not keep the *i* before *-i* or *-iamo*.

cominciare / to start, begin	*mangiare*/ to eat
comincio / I start	*mangio*/ I eat
cominci / you start	*mangi*/ you eat
comincia / he, she, it starts	*mangia*/ he, she, it eats
cominciamo / we start	*mangiam* / we eat
cominciate / you start	*mangiate*/ you eat
cominciano / they start	*mangiano*/ they eat

- Note that the Italian present indicative is equivalent to **three** English verb tenses.

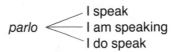

- In addition, it can be used with the preposition *da* (which, in this case, means both "since" and "for") to express the present perfect progressive tense in English.

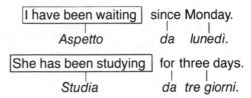

- Finally, you can use this versatile tense to express a future action that is not too far off in the future.

> *Domani andiamo al teatro.* / Tomorrow we are going to the theater.
> *Domani parlo al professore.* / Tomorrow I will speak to the professor.

§9.2 – 2 Present Perfect

The present perfect tense expresses simple past actions in the indicative mood (see also §8.2–3). It is a compound tense, that is, it is formed by the appropriate form of the auxiliary verb plus the past participle of the verb, in that order.

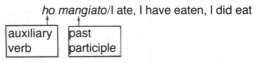

- To form the past participle of regular verbs in Italian, drop the infinitive ending and add the following endings:

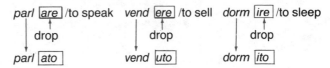

- In Italian there are two auxiliary verbs: *avere* (to have) and *essere* (to be). In the present perfect, these verbs are conjugated, logically enough, in the present indicative. Both are irregular, and you will find their conjugations in the "Verb Charts" section. The three verbs listed above are conjugated with *avere*.

ho	*parlato* (= I spoke, I have spoken, I did speak) *venduto* (= I sold, etc.) *dormito* (= I slept, etc.)
hai	*parlato* (= you spoke, etc.) *venduto* (= you sold, etc.) *dormito* (= you slept, etc.)
ha	*parlato* (= he, she, it spoke, etc.) *venduto* (= he, she, it sold, etc.) *dormito* (= he, she, it slept, etc.)
abbiamo	*parlato* (= we spoke, etc.) *venduto* (= we sold, etc.) *dormito* (= we slept, etc.)
avete	*parlato* (= you spoke, etc.) *venduto* (= you sold, etc.) *dormito* (= you slept, etc.)
hanno	*parlato* (= they spoke, etc.) *venduto* (= they sold, etc.) *dormito* (= they slept, etc.)

EXAMPLES

Maria ha venduto la sua macchina. / Mary sold her car.
Ieri ho parlato al signor Verdi. / Yesterday, I spoke to Mr. Verdi.
Loro hanno dormito troppo ieri. / They slept too much yesterday.
Ho già mangiato. / I have already eaten.

- The verbs *arrivare* (to arrive), *cadere* (to fall), and *partire* (to leave, depart) are conjugated with *essere*. In this case, the final vowel of the past participle agrees with the subject in the same way that an adjective does (see §7.2).

Singular		
(io) sono	*arrivato* *(-a)* *caduto* *(-a)* *partito* *(-a)*	(= I arrived) (= I fell) (= I left)
(tu) sei	*arrivato* *(-a)* *caduto* *(-a)* *partito* *(-a)*	(= you arrived) (= you fell) (= you left)
(lui) è	*arrivato* *caduto* *partito*	(= he arrived) (= he fell) (= he left)

Singular		
(lei) è	*arrivata* *caduta* *partita*	(=she arrived) (=she fell) (=she left)

- Remember that *Lei* is the polite form of address. In this case, choose the ending according to the sex of the person you are addressing.

   Signor Verdi, è caduto, Lei? / Mr. Verdi, did you fall?
   Signora Verdi, è caduta, Lei? / Mrs. Verdi, did you fall?

- In the plural, do not forget that the masculine ending *-i* refers to people of both genders (review §7.2).

Plural		
(noi) siamo	*arrivati (-e)* *caduti (-e)* *partiti (-e)*	(= we arrived) (= we fell) (= we left)
(voi) siete	*arrivati (-e)* *caduti (-e)* *partiti (-e)*	(=you arrived) (=you fell) (=you left)
(loro) sono	*arrivati (-e)* *caduti (-e)* *partiti (-e)*	(=they arrived) (=they fell) (=they left)

- Do not forget all the things you know about the use of subject pronouns with the indicative (see §8.3–1)

- When do you use *avere* or *essere*? The answer to this question is quite complicated. The best learning strategy is to assume that most verbs are conjugated with *avere* (which is true!), and then memorize those few verbs conjugated with *essere*. Here are some of them. Notice that these verbs are all intransitive.

andare/to go	*nascere*/to be born
arrivare/to arrive	*partire*/to leave, depart
cadere/to fall	*stare*/to stay, remain
entrare/to enter	*sembrare*/to seem
essere/to be	*tornare*/to return
diventare/to become	*uscire*/to go out
morire/to die	*venire*/to come

- There are a few verbs that are never conjugated in the normal fashion with a subject pronoun. These *impersonal* verbs occur only in the third person form, and are conjugated with *essere*.

   Lo spettacolo è durato tre ore. / The show lasted three hours.

- Remember! To be sure about which auxiliary to use, look up the main verb in a good dictionary.

- Notice that this tense is also equivalent to three English tenses.

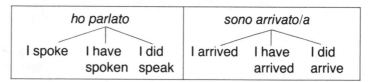

- Recall that the past participle must agree with the direct object pronouns *lo, la, li, le* (§8.3–2) and the pronoun *ne* (§8.5).

  Le ho mangiate./I ate them.

  Ne ho mangiati tre./I ate three of them.

- Only verbs conjugated with *avere* can have *direct object* pronouns.

§9.2 – 3 Imperfect

As you know, the present perfect allows you to express a finished past action, that is, an action you visualize as having started and ended.

Ieri ho dormito due ore./Yesterday I slept (for) two hours.

If, however, you wish to indicate that an action continued for an indefinite period of time, then the imperfect tense is called for.

Ieri, mentre io dormivo, tu guardavi la TV./Yesterday, while I was sleeping, you watched TV.

The imperfect is used to indicate that an action was habitual or repeated in the past.

Quando ero giovane, suonavo il pianoforte./When I was young, I used to play the piano.

It is also used to describe the physical characteristics of people and things as they used to be in the past.

> *Da giovane, Maria aveva i capelli biondi.*/As a youth, Mary had (= used to have) blonde hair.

- To form the imperfect, drop the infinitive ending and add the following endings (see §9.2–1):

	Person	Endings		
		1st Conj. **= are**	**2nd Conj.** **= ere**	**3rd Conj.** **= ire**
S i n g u l a r	1st	-avo	-evo	-ivo
	2nd	-avi	-evi	-ivi
	3rd	-ava	-eva	-iva
P l u r a l	1st	-avamo	-evamo	-ivamo
	2nd	-avate	-evate	-ivate
	3rd	-avano	-evano	-ivano

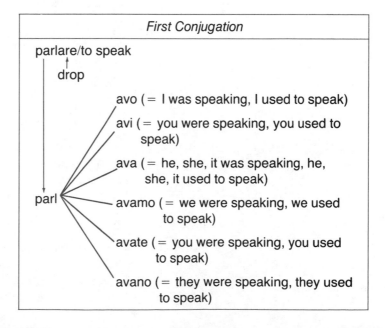

First Conjugation

parlare/to speak

↑ drop

parl

- avo (= I was speaking, I used to speak)
- avi (= you were speaking, you used to speak)
- ava (= he, she, it was speaking, he, she, it used to speak)
- avamo (= we were speaking, we used to speak)
- avate (= you were speaking, you used to speak)
- avano (= they were speaking, they used to speak)

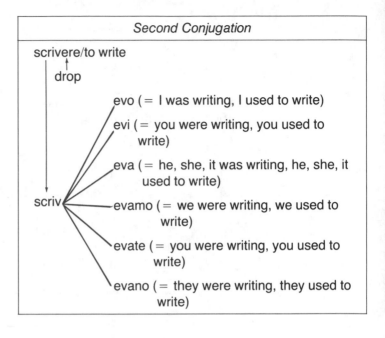

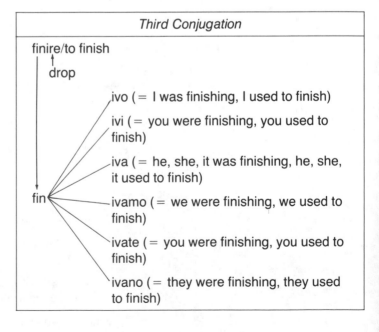

EXAMPLES

Mentre tu studiavi, tuo fratello suonava il violino. / While you were studying, your brother was playing the violin.

L'anno scorso mio cugino scriveva ogni mese. / Last year my cousin wrote (used to write) every month.

Quando andava a scuola, Maria studiava molto. / When she was going to school, Mary studied (used to study) a lot.

- Note that the third person plural forms are *not* stressed on the last syllable.

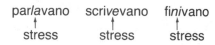

par*la*vano   scri*ve*vano   fi*ni*vano
stress   stress   stress

- The Italian imperfect is equivalent to two English tenses:

parlavo ⟨ I was speaking
          I used to speak

- Sometimes English uses a perfect form that is normally covered by the Italian present perfect (§9.2–1). In all cases, this is merely another way of expressing an imperfect action.

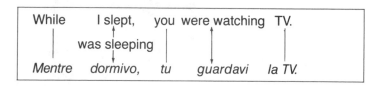

While	I slept,	you	were watching	TV.
	was sleeping			
Mentre	*dormivo,*	*tu*	*guardavi*	*la TV.*

- Compare this with the following.

Yesterday	I slept	for only two hours.
Ieri	*ho dormito*	*solo due ore.*

- You must therefore always look for clues among the other words in a sentence to determine whether the imperfect should be used. Words such as *mentre* (while) and *sempre* (always) often indicate that a past action is imperfect in the dependent clause.

§9.2 – 4 Past Absolute

As we shall soon see, the uses of the past absolute are similar, in many ways, to the present perfect (§9.2–2). It is formed by dropping the infinitive ending and then adding the following endings to the stem:

Person		Endings		
		1st Conjugation = are	**2nd Conjugation = ere**	**3rd Conjugation = ire**
Singular	1st	-ai	-ei (-etti)	-ii
	2nd	-asti	-esti	-isti
	3rd	-ò	-è (-ette)	-ì
Plural	1st	-ammo	-emmo	-immo
	2nd	-aste	-este	-iste
	3rd	-arono	-erono (-ettero)	-irono

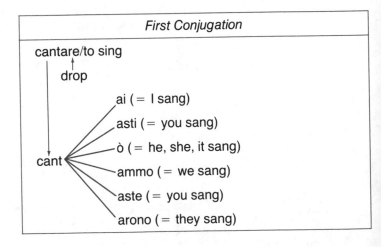

First Conjugation

cantare/to sing
↑ drop

cant
- ai (= I sang)
- asti (= you sang)
- ò (= he, she, it sang)
- ammo (= we sang)
- aste (= you sang)
- arono (= they sang)

EXAMPLES

I miei genitori tornarono in Italia nel 1976. / My parents returned to Italy in 1976.

Marco Polo portò tante belle cose indietro dalla Cina. / Marco Polo brought back many beautiful things from China.

Dopo che vendè (vendette) la macchina, Gino comprò una motocicletta. / After he sold the car, Gino bought a motorcycle.

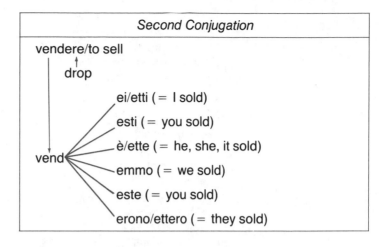

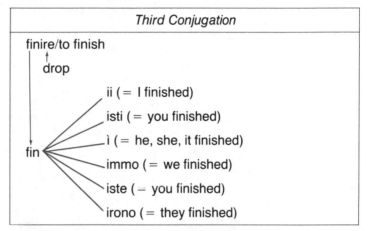

- Recall that the present perfect is equivalent to three English tenses (§9.2–2). One of these tenses is also covered by the past absolute.

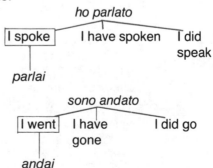

- However, the past absolute cannot be used with temporal adverbs such as *già* (already), *poco fa* (a little while ago), etc., which limit the action to the immediate past (occurring within less than twenty-four hours).

Only Present Perfect Used:

Maria è arrivata poco tempo fa. / Mary arrived a little while ago.

Ho già telefonato al signor Rossi. / I have already phoned Mr. Rossi.

- Outside this time restriction, the past absolute can be used as an alternative to the present perfect to cover the English perfect tense exemplified above (I spoke, I went, etc.).

Present Perfect		Past Absolute
Maria è arrivata in Italia nel 1980. / Mary arrived in Italy in 1980.	OR	*Maria arrivò in Italia nel 1980.*
Ieri ho telefonato al signor Rossi. / Yesterday I phoned Mr. Rossi.	OR	*Ieri telefonai al signor Rossi.*

- In Italy you will find that certain regions use one or the other tense in ordinary conversational situations. But the past absolute is preferred as a "literary" tense, particularly for the narration of historical events.

Colombo scoprì l'America nel 1492. / Columbus discovered America in 1492.

- Whatever tense you decide to use (following the above restrictions), you must use either tense consistently when several clauses are involved.

Quando sono arrivati, hanno telefonato a Maria. / When they arrived, they phoned Mary.

Quando arrivarano, telefonarono a Maria.

- If you have forgotten about clauses, review §2.3–1.

§9.2 – 5
Pluperfect

The pluperfect is a compound tense. As such, it has all the characteristics associated with this kind of verb form. (Review §9.2–2 of this chapter if you have forgotten about compound tenses.)

- The pluperfect is formed with the auxiliary in the imperfect tenses (§9.2–3).

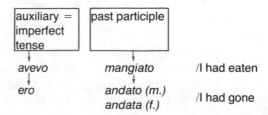

auxiliary = imperfect tense	past participle	
avevo	*mangiato*	/I had eaten
ero	*andato (m.)* *andata (f.)*	/I had gone

● Here are these two verbs fully conjugated:

avevo mangiato / I had eaten   *ero andato(-a)* / I had gone
avevi mangiato / you had eaten *eri andato(-a)* / you had gone
aveva mangiato / he, she, it   *era andato(-a)* / he, she, it had
   had eaten   gone
avevamo mangiato / we had   *eravamo andati(-e)* / we had
   eaten   gone
avevate mangiato / you had   *eravate andati(-e)* / you had
   eaten   gone
avevano mangiato / they had   *erano andati(-e)* / they had
   eaten   gone

● If you have forgotten the rule of thumb on using one auxiliary verb or the other, go over §9.2–2.

● The pluperfect tense (literally, "more than perfect" or "more than past") allows you to express an action that occurred *before* a simple past action (as expressed by the present perfect, the imperfect, or the past absolute).

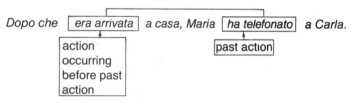

Dopo che era arrivata *a casa, Maria* ha telefonato *a Carla.*

action occurring before past action   past action

After she had arrived home, Mary phoned Carla.

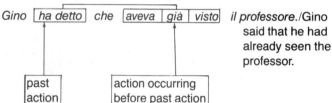

Gino ha detto *che* aveva già visto *il professore.*/Gino said that he had already seen the professor.

past action   action occurring before past action

● As you can see, this tense is rendered by the corresponding English pluperfect ("had" + past participle). But be careful! Sometimes this tense is only implied in English.

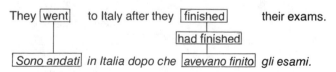

They went   to Italy after they finished   their exams.
                                              had finished

Sono andati *in Italia dopo che* avevano finito *gli esami.*

● Therefore, you will generally use this tense in dependent clauses, especially those introduced by a temporal conjunction (review §2.3–2).

● There exists another pluperfect tense that is limited to very formal literary usage. But it is used so seldom that you will probably never need it.

§9.2 – 6
Simple Future

The simple future, as its name implies, allows you to express an action that will occur in the future. It is formed in the following manner:

- Drop the final -e of the infinitives of all three conjugations. For verbs of the first conjugation (-are), change the a of the infinitive to e.

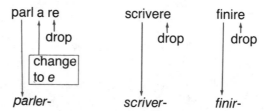

Then add the following endings to all three conjugations.

S i n g u l a r	Person	Endings for all Conjugations
	1st	-ò
	2nd	-ai
	3rd	-à
P l u r a l	1st	-emo
	2nd	-ete
	3rd	-anno

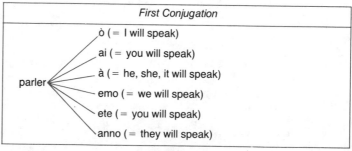

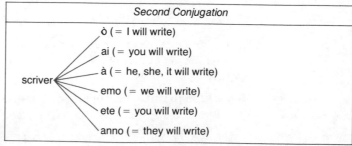

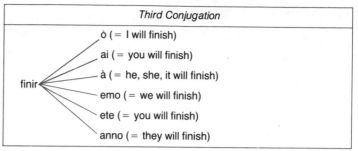

Third Conjugation
finir ò (= I will finish)
ai (= you will finish)
à (= he, she, it will finish)
emo (= we will finish)
ete (= you will finish)
anno (= they will finish)

- Recall that the hard *c* and hard *g* sounds are retained in the present indicative of first conjugation verbs by adding an *h* (see §9.2–1). This is the case for the future tense too. In writing, add the *h*.

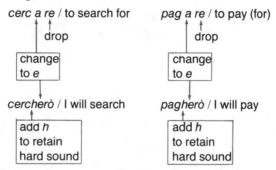

cerc a re / to search for

↓ drop

change to *e*

cercherò / I will search

add *h* to retain hard sound

pag a re / to pay (for)

↓ drop

change to *e*

pagherò / I will pay

add *h* to retain hard sound

- Similarly, remember that to write the corresponding soft sounds, you omit the *i* of the infinitive (see §9.2–1).

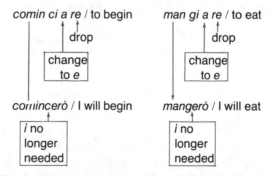

comin ci a re / to begin

↓ drop

change to *e*

comincerò / I will begin

i no longer needed

man gi a re / to eat

↓ drop

change to *e*

mangerò / I will eat

i no longer needed

- The future tense is normally rendered by the English future ("I will go," etc.). It can also be translated by using the expression "going to."

> *Scriverò.* / I will write OR I'm going to write.
> *Partiranno domani.* / They will leave tomorrow OR They are going to leave tomorrow.

- This tense is also used to express probability.

> *Quanto costa il tuo orologio?* / How much does your watch cost?
> *Costerà centomila lire.* / It must cost a hundred thousand lira.

- It can be used as well in temporal clauses introduced by *se* (if), *quando* (when), and *appena* (as soon as) (see §2.3–2) in order to agree with a future tense in the main clause.

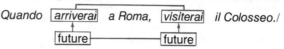

Quando [arriverai] *a Roma,* [visiterai] *il Colosseo./*

When you arrive in Rome, you will visit the Colosseum.

§9.2 – 7
Future Perfect

Like the present perfect (see §9.2–2) and the pluperfect (see §9.2–5), the future perfect is a compound tense.

- In this case, the auxiliary is in the future tense.

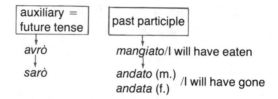

auxiliary = future tense | past participle

avrò | *mangiato*/I will have eaten

sarò | *andato* (m.) / I will have gone
andata (f.)

- Here are these two verbs fully conjugated:

avrò mangiato / I will have eaten
avrai mangiato / you will have eaten
avrà mangiato / he, she, it will have eaten
avremo mangiato / we will have eaten
avrete mangiato / you will have eaten
avranno mangiato / they will have eaten

sarò andato (-a) / I will have gone
sarai andato (-a) / you will have gone
sarà andato (-a) / he, she, it will have gone
saremo andati (-e) / we will have gone
sarete andati (-e) / you will have gone
saranno andati (-e) / they will have gone

- As you can see, this tense is rendered by the corresponding future perfect in English ("I will have eaten," etc.). It is used to express an action that occurred before a simple future action.

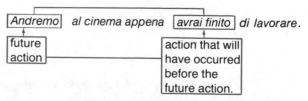

[Andremo] *al cinema appena* [avrai finito] *di lavorare.*

future action | action that will have occurred before the future action.

We will go to the movies as soon as you (will) have finished working.

- Thus, like the pluperfect, you will find it mainly in time clauses (see §9.2–5).

- In ordinary spoken Italian, there is a tendency to replace it with the simple future in temporal clauses.

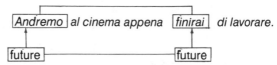

- It is also used to express probability (see §9.2–6) as in the following examples:

> *Quanto è costato il tuo orologio?* / How much did your watch cost?
> *Sarà costato centomila lire.* / It must have cost a hundred thousand lira.
> *A che ora ha telefonato?* / At what time did he phone?
> *Avrà telefonato alle sei.* / He must have phoned at six.

§9.3 THE IMPERATIVE

The imperative mood allows you to express commands and give advice. The only imperative tense is the present. You cannot command someone in the past!

- The imperative is formed by dropping the infinitive ending of the verb and adding the appropriate endings. There is, of course, no first person singular form. Note that the distinction between verbs conjugated with or without the *-isc-* (in the third conjugation) is once again applicable (see §9.2–1).

	Person	Endings		
		1st Conjugation = are	2nd Conjugation = ere	3rd Conjugation = ire
Singular	1st	—	—	—
	2nd	-a	-i	(-isc-)-i
	3rd	-i	-a	-(isc-)-a
Plural	1st	-iamo	-iamo	-iamo
	2nd	-ate	-ete	-ite
	3rd	-ino	-ano	(-isc-)-ano

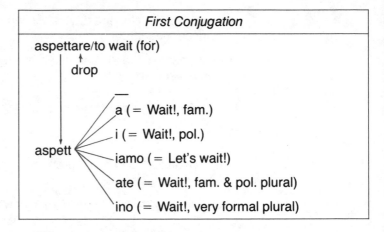

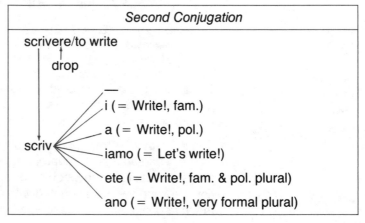

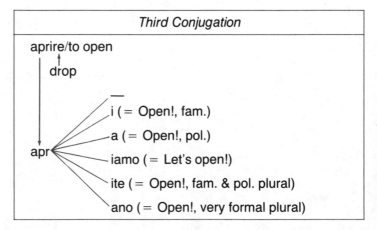

- As discussed in the previous chapter (see §8.3–1 and §8.3–2), the plural of both the familiar and polite forms tends to be the second person plural in this case as well. The third person plural is used rarely, being reserved for very formal situations.

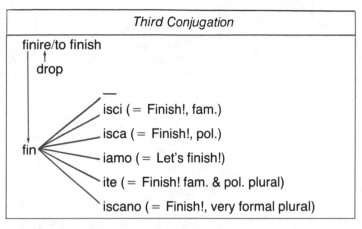

Third Conjugation
finire/to finish ↑ drop fin — isci (= Finish!, fam.) isca (= Finish!, pol.) iamo (= Let's finish!) ite (= Finish! fam. & pol. plural) iscano (= Finish!, very formal plural)

EXAMPLES

Giovanni, aspetta qui! / John, wait here!
Signora Binni, scriva il Suo nome qui. / Mrs. Binni, write your name here.
Gino, Maria, andiamo a un ristorante! / Gino, Mary, let's go to a restaurant!
Aprite i vostri libri a pagina 4. / Open your books at page 4.
Signora Binni e Signor Binni, aspettate qui! / Mrs. Binni and Mr. Binni, wait here!

- As in the case of the present indicative (see §9.2–1), the hard *c* and hard *g* sounds of first conjugation verbs are retained by adding an *h* in front of the *-i, -iamo,* and *-ino* endings. And the *i* of such verbs as *cominciare* (to begin) and *mangiare* (to eat) is not repeated in front of these endings.

EXAMPLES

Signor Dini, cerchi i Suoi occhiali, per favore. / Mr. Dini, look for your glasses, please!

Paghiamo il conto! / Let's pay the bill!
Signori, paghino il conto, per favore! / Gentlemen, pay the bill, please!
Signora, cominci per favore! / Madam, please begin!
E ora, mangiamo! / And now, let's eat!

- To form the negative imperative, add *non* in the usual way (see §2.2–2). But you must make one change: the second person singular becomes the infinitive of the verb.

EXAMPLES

Affirmative	Negative
2nd Person Singular	
Aspetta! / Wait!	*Non aspettare!* / Don't wait!
Scrivi! / Write!	*Non scrivere!* / Don't write!
Paga! / Pay!	*Non pagare!* / Don't pay!

Other Persons

Aspetti! / Wait! (pol.)	*Non aspetti!* / Don't wait!
Scriviamo! / Let's write!	*Non scriviamo!* / Let's not write!
Finite! / Finish!	*Non finite ora!* / Don't finish now!

- As pointed out in the previous chapter (see §9.3–2), the object pronouns are attached to the first and second person singular and plural forms. They are not attached to the polite forms.

EXAMPLES

Polite Forms

Signor Binni, mi parli! / Mr. Binni, speak to me!
Signora Dini, gliela scriva! / Mrs. Dini, write it to him!
Signori, ce li mandino! / Gentlemen, send them to us!

Other Forms

Giovanni, parlami! / John, speak to me!
Maria, Scrivigliela! / Mary, write it to him!
Ragazzi, mandateceli! / Boys, send them to us!

- The second person singular imperative forms of *dare* (to give), *dire* (to say), *fare* (to do, to make), *andare* (to go), and *stare* (to stay) are written with an apostrophe: *da', di', fa', va',* and *sta',* respectively (see the "Verb Charts" section). When you attach the object pronouns to these forms, then you must double the first letter.

EXAMPLES

Da' la penna $\boxed{a\ me}$! / Give me the pen!

Dammi la penna! / Give the pen to me!

Fa' $\boxed{quel\ favore\ |\ a\ noi}$! / Do us that favor!

Faccelo! / Do it for us!

Di' la verità $\boxed{a\ Maria}$! / Tell Mary the truth!

Dille la verità! / Tell her the truth!

- There is, of course, no double *gl*.

Digli la verità. / Tell him the truth.
Fagliela! / Do it for him!

- All the object pronoun patterns discussed so far apply as well to the reflexive pronouns (see §9.7).

- Recall that in the second person singular, the negative imperative form is the infinitive. With this form, the object pronouns can either be attached or put before.

EXAMPLES

Affirmative	Negative
Mangialo! / Eat it!	*Non mangiarlo!* OR *Non lo mangiare!* / Don't eat it!
Scrivimela! / Write it to me!	*Non scrivermela!* OR *Non me la scrivere!* / Don't write it to me!

§9.4 THE CONDI-TIONAL TENSES

The conditional mood allows you to express a condition: "I *would* go, if . . ."; "We *would* do it, but . . . ," etc. It corresponds to the English conditional and is used in exactly the same way.

§9.4 – 1 Present

The present conditional is formed in the same manner as the future (review §9.2–6).

● Drop the final -e of all three infinitives and add the appropriate set of endings to all three conjugations. Remember to change the *a* of the first conjugation (*are*) to *e* (parlar → parler).

	Person	Endings for all Three Conjugations
S i n g u l a r	1st	-ei
	2nd	-esti
	3rd	-ebbe
P l u r a l	1st	-emmo
	2nd	-este
	3rd	-ebbero

First Conjugation

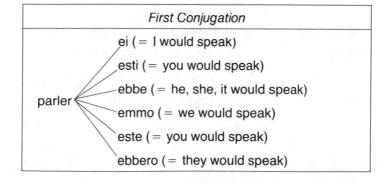

parler
— ei (= I would speak)
— esti (= you would speak)
— ebbe (= he, she, it would speak)
— emmo (= we would speak)
— este (= you would speak)
— ebbero (= they would speak)

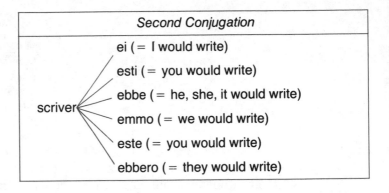

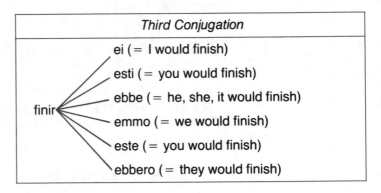

- The patterns used in the future for retaining the hard *c* and *g* sounds and writing the corresponding soft sounds in the first conjugation, apply in exactly the same way to the conditional. So go over §9.2–6 thoroughly.

EXAMPLES

Pagherei il conto, ma non ho soldi. / I would pay the bill, but I don't have any money.

Mangerebbe di più, ma non ha più tempo. / He would eat more, but he has no more time.

§9.4 – 2 Past

The past conditional is a compound tense (see §9.2–2).

- In this case, the auxiliary verb is in the present conditional.

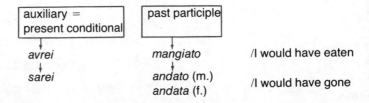

- Here are these two verbs fully conjugated:

  avrei mangiato / I would have eaten
  avresti mangiato / you would have eaten
  avrebbe mangiato / he, she, it would have eaten
  avremmo mangiato / we would have eaten
  avreste mangiato / you would have eaten
  avrebbero mangiato / they would have eaten

  sarei andato (-a) / I would have gone
  saresti andato (-a) / you would have gone
  sarebbe andato (-a) / he, she, it would have gone
  saremmo andati (-e) / we would have gone
  sareste andati (-e) / you would have gone
  sarebbero andati (-e) / they would have gone

- The past conditional corresponds to the English past conditional ("I would have . . ."; "You would have . . .," etc.) and is
  used in the same way. But notice that if the main verb is in
  a past tense, then English does not always use it, whereas
  Italian does.

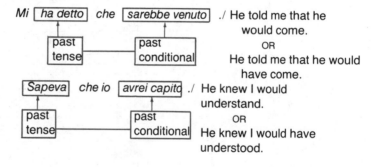

- In addition, both conditional tenses are used:

  —to express a polite request.
  Potrei parlare? / May I speak?
  —to quote someone else's opinion.
  Secondo loro, quella ragazza sarebbe spagnola. / According to
  them, that
  girl is
  Spanish.

§9.5
THE
SUBJUNCTIVE
TENSES

The subjunctive mood allows you to express a point of view,
fear, doubt, hope, possibility—anything that is not a fact. In
a way, the subjunctive is a counterpart to the indicative,
(the mood for stating facts and conveying information).

§9.5 – 1
Present

The present subjunctive is formed in the usual way by dropping the infinitive ending and attaching the following endings to the stem:

	Person	Endings		
		1st Conjugation = are	**2nd Conjugation = ere**	**3rd Conjugation = ire**
S i n g u l a r	1st	-i	-a	(-isc-)-a
	2nd	-i	-a	(-isc-)-a
	3rd	-i	-a	(-isc-)-a
P l u r a l	1st	-iamo	-iamo	-iamo
	2nd	-iate	-iate	-iate
	3rd	-ino	-ano	(-isc-)-ano

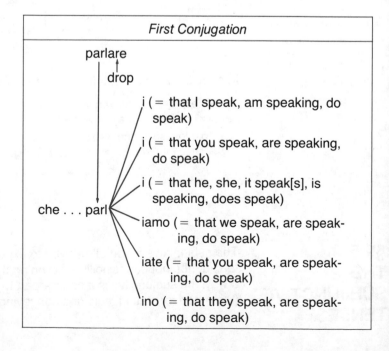

First Conjugation

parlare
↑
drop

che . . . parl

i (= that I speak, am speaking, do speak)

i (= that you speak, are speaking, do speak)

i (= that he, she, it speak[s], is speaking, does speak)

iamo (= that we speak, are speaking, do speak)

iate (= that you speak, are speaking, do speak)

ino (= that they speak, are speaking, do speak)

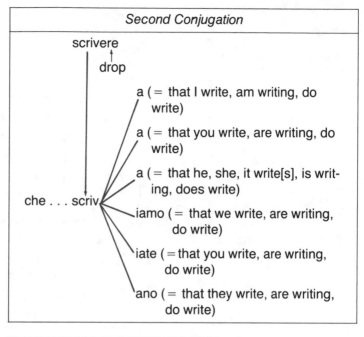

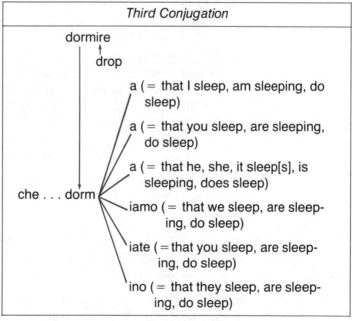

- Because the endings are often the same, you will need to use the subject pronouns with the subjunctive.

    Sembra che tu dica la verità. / It seems that you are telling the truth.

    Sembra che lei dica la verità. / It seems that she is telling the truth.

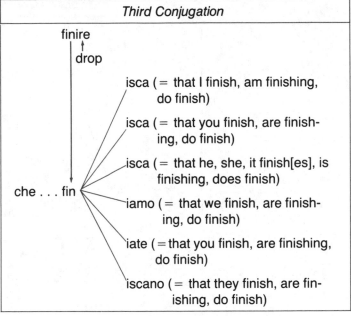

Third Conjugation

finire
↑
drop

che . . . fin

isca (= that I finish, am finishing, do finish)

isca (= that you finish, are finishing, do finish)

isca (= that he, she, it finish[es], is finishing, does finish)

iamo (= that we finish, are finishing, do finish)

iate (= that you finish, are finishing, do finish)

iscano (= that they finish, are finishing, do finish)

- Notice that in the third conjugation, we find once again the distinction between verbs conjugated with the *-isc-* and those without it (see §9.2–1).

- Also applicable to this tense is the pattern of retaining the hard *c* and hard *g* sounds, and of not repeating the *i* of verbs such as *cominciare* and *mangiare*, in the first conjugation (see §9.2–1). In this case, the *h* is used before all endings (since they begin with *i*).

  Vogliamo che lui paghi il conto./ We want him to pay the bill.
  Sembra che tu mangi troppo./ It seems that you eat too much.

The subjunctive is usually used in subordinate clauses, introduced by *che*. You will find it after a relative pronoun (see §2.3–1).

Spero che tu dica la verità./I hope you are telling the truth.

relative pronoun   subjunctive

- But not all verbs in relative clauses are necessarily in the subjunctive; only those connected to a main verb that expresses a nonfact (opinion, fear, supposition, anticipation, wish, hope, doubt etc.).

Sa   che   tu dici   *la verità.*/He knows that you are telling the truth.

expresses a fact ——— indicative

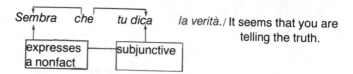

Sembra che tu dica la verità./ It seems that you are telling the truth.

- The best way to learn which of these verbs requires the subjunctive is to memorize the most commonly used ones. Here are eight of them:

credere/to believe	*pensare*/to think
desiderare/to desire	*sembrare*/to seem
dubitare/to doubt	*sperare*/to hope
immaginare/to imagine	*volere*/to want

EXAMPLES

Crede che loro arrivino stasera. / He thinks (that) they are arriving tonight.

Immagino che tu lo parli molto bene. / I imagine that you speak it very well.

Dubitano che voi finiate in tempo./ They doubt that you will finish in time.

- In current Italian, there is a tendency not to use the subjunctive in various situations. However, it is still used in writing and speaking when you want to emphasize the nonfactual nature of your thought. This is especially true when the main verb is in the negative.

Non credo che lui parli bene./ I do not think that he speaks well.

Impersonal verbs or expressions that precede the relative clause also require the subjunctive. An impersonal expression is a verb or expression that is used only in the third person.

EXAMPLES

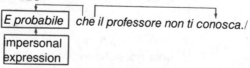

E probabile che il professore non ti conosca./

It's probable that the professor does not know you.

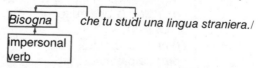

Bisogna che tu studi una lingua straniera./

It's necessary that you study a foreign language.

A superlative expression (review §7.5) that precedes the relative clause also requires the subjunctive.

EXAMPLES

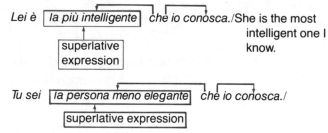

Lei è [*la più intelligente*] *che io conosca.*/She is the most
intelligent one I
know.

superlative
expression

Tu sei [*la persona meno elegante*] *che io conosca.*/

superlative expression

You are the least elegant person I know.

The subjunctive is also used after some conjunctions and
indefinite pronouns.

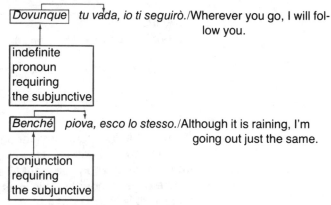

[*Dovunque*] *tu vada, io ti seguirò.*/Wherever you go, I will follow you.

indefinite
pronoun
requiring
the subjunctive

[*Benché*] *piova, esco lo stesso.*/Although it is raining, I'm
going out just the same.

conjunction
requiring
the subjunctive

● The most commonly used indefinite pronouns and conjunctions that require the subjunctive are:

Indefinite Pronouns
chiunque/whoever *dovunque*/wherever *qualsiasi cosa, qualunque cosa*/whatever
Conjunctions
affinché/so that *benché, sebbene*/although *come se*/as if *nel caso che*/in the case (event) that *nonostante che*/despite *senza che*/without *prima che*/before *purché*/provided that

Finally, you will need to use the subjunctive to express
wishes and exhortations. In most cases, the clause is introduced by *che.*

EXAMPLES

Che scriva lui!/Let him write!

Che mangi tutto!/Let him eat everything!

Che piova, se vuole!/Let it rain, if it wants to!
Dio (che Dio) ce la mandi buona!/God help us!

Dio lo voglia./God willing.

As you saw in the conjugation charts at the beginning of this section, the present subjunctive has the same English equivalents as the present indicative. In other words, the present subjunctive expresses a present action with respect to the main verb.

Pare che lui dica la verità./It seems that he is telling the truth.

present action in the indicative	present action in the subjunctive

**§9.5 – 2
Past**

The past subjunctive is also a compound tense (review §9.2–2).

- In this case, the auxiliary verb is in the present subjunctive.

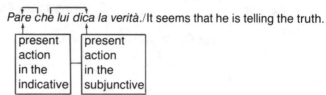

auxiliary = present subjunctive	past participle
che . . . abbia	*mangiato*/that I ate, have eaten, did eat
che . . . sia	*andato* (m.) *andata* (f.)/that I went, have gone

- **For the present subjunctive of the auxiliary verbs, just look them up in the "Verb Charts" section of this book.**

EXAMPLES

Sono contenta lui che abbia capito tutto. / I am happy that he understood everything.

Non è possibile che loro siano già partiti. / **It's not possible that they have already left.**

Benché sia venuto, non era felice. / Although he came, he wasn't happy.

- Notice that the past subjunctive has the same English equivalents as the present perfect (see §9.2–2). In other words, it normally expresses a past action with respect to the main verb:

Sono contenta che lui abbia capito tutto.

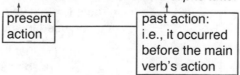

present action	past action: i.e., it occurred before the main verb's action

- In other cases, the action occurred at the same time as the action of the main verb.

Benché sia venuto,   *non era felice.*

- The past subjunctive is used, of course, in all of the constructions described in §9.5–1.

§9.5 – 3
Imperfect

The imperfect subjunctive is formed in the normal way by dropping the infinitive endings and attaching the following endings to the stem:

	Person	Endings to be Added		
		1st Conjugation = are	**2nd Conjugation = ere**	**3rd Conjugation = ire**
S i n g u l a r	1st	-assi	-essi	-issi
	2nd	-assi	-essi	-issi
	3rd	-asse	-esse	-isse
P l u r a l	1st	-assimo	-essimo	-issimo
	2nd	-aste	-este	-iste
	3rd	-assero	-essero	-issero

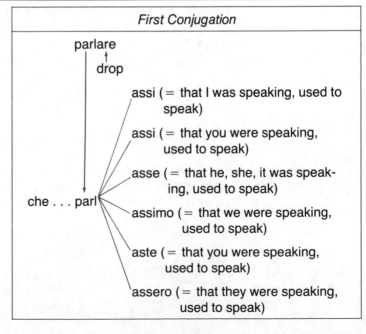

First Conjugation

parlare
↑
drop

che . . . parl

assi (= that I was speaking, used to speak)

assi (= that you were speaking, used to speak)

asse (= that he, she, it was speaking, used to speak)

assimo (= that we were speaking, used to speak)

aste (= that you were speaking, used to speak)

assero (= that they were speaking, used to speak)

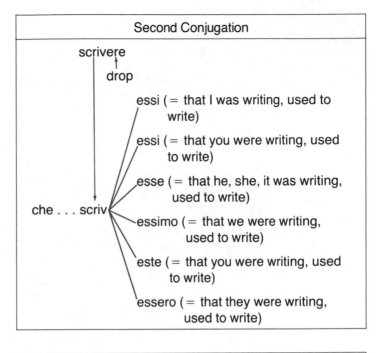

Second Conjugation
scrivere ↑ drop
essi (= that I was writing, used to write)
essi (= that you were writing, used to write)
esse (= that he, she, it was writing, used to write)
essimo (= that we were writing, used to write)
este (= that you were writing, used to write)
essero (= that they were writing, used to write)

che . . . scriv

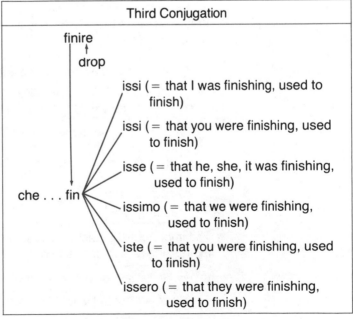

Third Conjugation
finire ↑ drop
issi (= that I was finishing, used to finish)
issi (= that you were finishing, used to finish)
isse (= that he, she, it was finishing, used to finish)
issimo (= that we were finishing, used to finish)
iste (= that you were finishing, used to finish)
issero (= that they were finishing, used to finish)

che . . . fin

As you can see from the charts, the imperfect subjunctive has the exact same English equivalents as the imperfect indicative (see §9.2–3) and is thus used in similar ways. The only difference is that you will find it in the normal subjunctive constructions described above in §9.5–1.

EXAMPLES

Mi è sembrato che lui dicesse la verità. / It seemed to me that he
was telling the truth.

Lei era la persona più intelligente che io conoscessi. / She was
the most intelligent person I knew.

Benché piovesse ieri, sono uscito lo stesso. / Although it was
raining yester-
day, I went out
just the same.

- In other words, it is normally hooked up to a main verb in a
past tense expressing an action that occurred at the same
time:

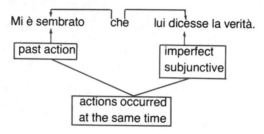

- The imperfect subjunctive is also used after *se* (if) in hypothetical clauses (see §2.3–2) when the main verb is in the
conditional (present or past).

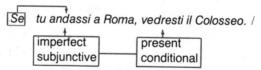

If you were to go to Rome, you would see the Colosseum.

- The imperfect subjunctive is also used in sentences
expressing a wish or desire beginning with *Magari . . . !*

Magari non piovesse!/If only it wouldn't rain!

Magari venissero!/If only they would come!

§9.5 – 4
Pluperfect

The pluperfect subjunctive is a compound tense (see
§9.2–2).

- In this case, the auxiliary verb is in the imperfect
subjunctive.

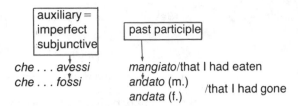

che . . . *avessi*
che . . . *fossi*

mangiato/that I had eaten
andato (m.)
andata (f.) /that I had gone

- You can look up the imperfect subjunctive of *essere* in the "Verb Charts" section of this book.

- This tense corresponds exactly to the pluperfect indicative (see §9.2–5), being used, of course, in the subjunctive constructions discussed in §9.5-1.

EXAMPLES

Mi è sembrato che lui avesse detto la verità. / It seemed to me that he had told the truth.

Eravamo contenti che foste già venuti. / We were glad that you (pl) had already come.

Benché avesse piovuto, sono uscito lo stesso. / Although it had rained, I went out just the same.

- In other words, the pluperfect subjunctive allows you to express a past action that occurred before another past action in the subjunctive mood.

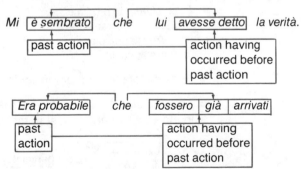

- As in the case of the imperfect subjunctive (see §9.5–3), the pluperfect is used after *se* when the main verb is in the conditional.

EXAMPLES

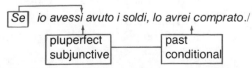

If I had had the money, I would have bought it.

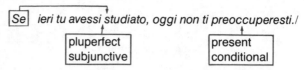

Se ieri tu avessi studiato, oggi non ti preoccuperesti./

pluperfect subjunctive

present conditional

If you had studied yesterday, you wouldn't worry today.

- In most speech situations, the *imperfect subjunctive* is used in conjunction with the *present conditional*, and the *pluperfect subjunctive* with the *past conditional* after *se*.

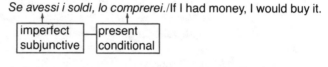

*Se avessi i soldi, lo comprerei./*If I had money, I would buy it.

imperfect subjunctive

present conditional

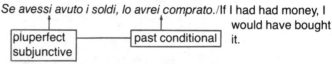

*Se avessi avuto i soldi, lo avrei comprato./*If I had had money, I would have bought it.

pluperfect subjunctive

past conditional

§9.6 THE INDEFINITE TENSES

The indefinite tenses express actions that do not have the usual reference to time relationships (present, past, etc.). The time thus expressed is indefinite.

§9.6 –1 The Infinitive

Recall from §9.1 of this chapter that there are three types of infinitives. Actually, there is a fourth type ending in *-rre*, but there are not too many infinitives of this type:

produrre / to produce
tradurre / to translate
porre / to put, place
trarre / to pull

- All verbs of this type are irregular when conjugated.

- There is also a *past infinitive* consisting of an auxiliary verb in the infinitive and a past participle.

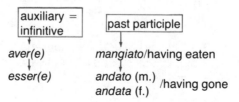

auxiliary = infinitive

past participle

aver(e)

mangiato/having eaten

esser(e)

andato (m.)
andata (f.) /having gone

- The final *-e* is normally dropped in this construction.

EXAMPLES

Dopo aver mangiato, uscirò. / After having eaten, I will go out.
Dopo esser arrivati, sono andati al cinema. / After having arrived, they went to the movies.

- The infinitive is also the only verb form used as the subject *or* the object of a preposition. It is always masculine.

    Il mangiare è necessario per vivere. / Eating is necessary in order to live.
    Invece di mangiare il vitello, ho mangiato il pollo. / Instead of eating veal, I ate chicken.

- Recall that object pronouns are normally attached to infinitives (review §8.3–2):

    Invece di mangiarlo, ho mangiato il pollo. / Instead of eating it (veal), I ate chicken.

- The infinitive is also used with verbs that require the subjunctive, when the subjects of both clauses are the same.

    Lui pensa che io parli bene./He thinks that I speak well.

    Lui pensa che parli bene./He thinks that he speaks well.

    Lui pensa di parlare bene.

- For the use of prepositions in this type of construction see §11.3.

§9.6 – 2 The Gerund

The *gerund* is formed by dropping the infinitive endings and adding the following endings to the stem.

parlare	*scrivere*	*dormire*
drop	drop	drop
parlando/speaking	*scrivendo*/writing	*dormendo*/sleeping

The most important use of the gerund is in the progressive tenses, which are made up of the verb *stare* plus the gerund. The main progressive tenses in Italian are:

Present Progressive

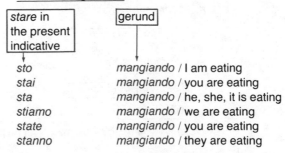

stare in the present indicative	*gerund*	
sto	*mangiando* /	I am eating
stai	*mangiando* /	you are eating
sta	*mangiando* /	he, she, it is eating
stiamo	*mangiando* /	we are eating
state	*mangiando* /	you are eating
stanno	*mangiando* /	they are eating

Imperfect Progressive

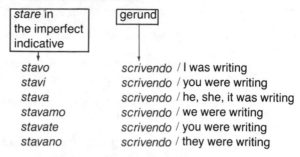

stare in the imperfect indicative	gerund
stavo	scrivendo / I was writing
stavi	scrivendo / you were writing
stava	scrivendo / he, she, it was writing
stavamo	scrivendo / we were writing
stavate	scrivendo / you were writing
stavano	scrivendo / they were writing

- As you can see, these tenses correspond exactly to the English progressive tenses, which, as you may recall, are also covered by the present indicative (see §9.2–1) and the imperfect indicative (see §9.2–3).

```
                    parlo
I speak    | I am speaking |    I do speak
                sto parlando
```

```
                  parlavo
| I was speaking |    I used to speak
            stavo parlando
```

- Although such tenses are equivalent to the present and imperfect indicative referring to progressive action, they do give a more precise rendition of ongoing action.

- There are subjunctive counterparts to these two tenses.
  EXAMPLES

  Penso che Maria stia mangiando. / I think (that) Mary is eating.
  Pensavo che Maria stesse mangiando. / I thought that Mary was eating.

- Look up *stare* in the "Verb Charts" section for its subjunctive forms.

- The gerund can be used alone, as in English, to express an indefinite action, replacing *mentre* + imperfect indicative when the subject of the clauses is the same.
  EXAMPLES

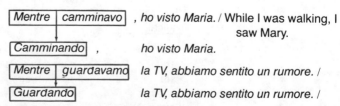

Mentre	camminavo	, ho visto Maria. / While I was walking, I saw Mary.
Camminando	,	ho visto Maria.
Mentre	guardavamo	la TV, abbiamo sentito un rumore. /
Guardando		la TV, abbiamo sentito un rumore. /

While watching TV, we heard a noise.

- Recall that object pronouns are attached to the gerund (review §8.3–2):

  Guardandola, abbiamo sentito un rumore. / Watching it (TV), we heard a noise.

- There is also a *past gerund* consisting of an auxiliary in the gerund and a past participle.

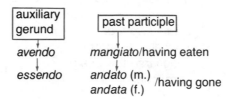

EXAMPLES

Avendo mangiato tutto, siamo usciti per una passeggiata. / Having eaten everything, we went out for a stroll.

Essendo andati in Italia, hanno visto tante belle cose. / Having gone to Italy, they saw many beautiful things.

§9.7 REFLEXIVE VERBS

A *reflexive* verb is simply a verb in any tense or mood that requires reflexive pronouns (review §8.2–3). A reflexive verb is identified in its infinitive form by the ending *-si* (oneself) attached to the infinitive.

> *lavarsi*/to wash oneself, *divertirsi*/to enjoy oneself, etc.

- To conjugate any reflexive verb, drop the *-si* and conjugate it as you would any verb, using, of course, the reflexive pronouns.

EXAMPLES

Mi lavo ogni mattina. / I wash (myself) every morning.

Ci divertiremo in Italia. / We will enjoy ourselves in Italy.

Sembra che tu ti diverta in Italia. / It seems that you enjoy yourself in Italy.

- In compound tenses (see §9.2–2), all reflexive verbs are conjugated with *essere* as the auxiliary.

EXAMPLES

Ci siamo divertiti in Italia. / We enjoyed ourselves in Italy.

Benché si fossero divertiti molto, sono ritornati presto. / Although they had enjoyed themselves a lot, they came back early.

- Here is a list of common reflexive verbs (some of which are not reflexive in English):

> *alzarsi* / to get up, wake up; to stand up
> *annoiarsi* / to become bored
> *arrabbiarsi* / to become angry
> *dimenticarsi* / to forget
> *divertirsi* / to enjoy oneself
> *lamentarsi* / to complain
> *lavarsi* / to wash (oneself)
> *mettersi* (a) / to begin to, set about; to wear
> *prepararsi* / to prepare oneself
> *sentirsi* / to feel
> *sposarsi* / to marry
> *svegliarsi* / to wake up
> *vergognarsi* / to be ashamed

- Recall that, in the imperative, the pronouns are attached to the "nonpolite" forms (see §9.3).

EXAMPLES

Lavati! / Wash yourself!
Sposiamoci! / Let's get married!
Non arrabbiatevi! / Dont get angry!

BUT

Si lavi! / Wash yourself! (pol.)
Non Si arrabbi! / Don't get angry! (pol.)

- In compound tenses, the past participle of reflexive verbs agrees with the direct object pronouns (*lo, la, li, le*), even if otherwise it normally agrees with the subject.

EXAMPLES

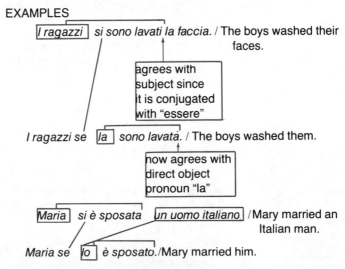

I ragazzi | *si sono lavati la faccia.* / The boys washed their faces.

agrees with subject since it is conjugated with "essere"

I ragazzi se | la | *sono lavata.* / The boys washed them.

now agrees with direct object pronoun "la"

Maria | *si è sposata* | un uomo italiano | / Mary married an Italian man.

Maria se | lo | *è sposato.* / Mary married him.

Some verbs occur in both reflexive and nonreflexive forms.

> *alzare*/to lift up; *alzarsi*/to get up
> *lavare*/to wash something; *lavarsi*/to wash oneself

Many verbs can be made reflexive by simply adding the appropriate pronouns. In such cases, the verbs are called *reciprocal*.

> *Si telefonano ogni sera.* / They phone each other every evening.
> *Ci scriviamo spesso.* / We write to each other often.

In compound tenses, these verbs are treated like any reflexive verb, and are thus conjugated with *essere*.

> *Hanno telefonato ieri sera.* / They phoned last evening.
> BUT
> *Si sono telefonati ogni sera.* / They phoned each other every evening.

§9.8 THE PASSIVE VOICE

Up to this point, all the verbs have been described in their active form. But any verb can be easily turned into its corresponding passive form by the following formula. Review the concepts of *active* and *passive* in §2.2–5:

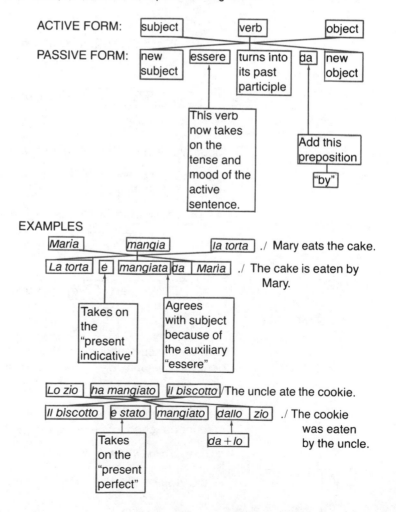

ACTIVE FORM: subject — verb — object

PASSIVE FORM: new subject — essere — turns into its past participle — da — new object

This verb now takes on the tense and mood of the active sentence.

Add this preposition "by"

EXAMPLES

Maria — mangia — la torta ./ Mary eats the cake.

La torta — è — mangiata — da — Maria ./ The cake is eaten by Mary.

Takes on the "present indicative'

Agrees with subject because of the auxiliary "essere"

Lo zio — ha mangiato — il biscotto /The uncle ate the cookie.

Il biscotto — è stato — mangiato — dallo — zio ./ The cookie was eaten by the uncle.

Takes on the "present perfect"

da + lo

- The passive can be found in subjunctive constructions as well.

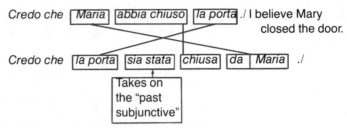

I believe the door was closed by Mary.

§9.9 MODAL VERBS

The main *modal* verbs of Italian are *potere* (to be able to), *dovere* (to have to), and *volere* (to want). You can look up their irregular forms in the "Verb Charts" section. A modal verb is simply one that is normally followed by an infinitive.

EXAMPLES

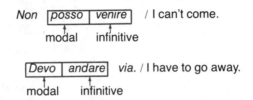

Modal verbs have the following characteristics:

- In compound tenses (§9.2–2), the auxiliary verb is determined by the infinitive.

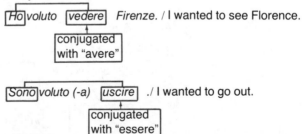

- However, in current conversational Italian, there is a tendency to use only *avere* as the auxiliary.

  Ho voluto uscire./I wanted to go out.

- Recall that object pronouns can be put before the modal verb, or attached to the infinitive (§8.3–2):

  La voglio mangiare. / I want to eat it.

  OR

  Voglio mangiarla.

- Be careful! In compound tenses, the past participle of the modal agrees with the direct object pronoun *if* the object precedes the past participle.

  *Ho voluto mangiarla./*I wanted to eat it.
                          BUT
  La no voluta mangiare.

- In the case of reflexive verbs, used in modal constructions, note the following:

  > If the reflexive pronoun is attached to the infinitive, then the auxiliary is *avere* in compound tenses, and there is no agreement.

  *Maria non ha potuto divertirsi./*Mary was not able to enjoy herself.

  > reflexive
  > pronoun
  > attached to
  > its infinitive

  > But if the reflexive pronoun is put before the modal, then *essere* is used, and there is agreement.

  *Maria non si e potuta divertire./*Mary was not able to enjoy
  herself.

  > reflexive
  > pronoun
  > comes
  > before

- When put into the conditional, these verbs are translated as "could," "would," "should" (present conditional) and as "could have," "would have," "should have" (past conditional).

  Lo potrei fare. / I could do it.
  L'avrei potuto fare. / I could have done it.

  Lo dovrei fare. / I should do it.
  L'avrei dovuto fare. / I should have done it.

  Lo vorrei fare. / I would like to do it.
  L'avrei voluto fare. / I would like to have done it.

§10.

Adverbs

§10.1
WHATARE
ADVERBS?

Adverbs are words that modify verbs, adjectives, or other adverbs. They indicate quantity, time, place, degree of intensity, and manner.

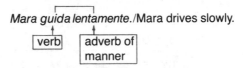

Mara guida lentamente./Mara drives slowly.

| verb | adverb of manner |

Questa casa è molto bella./This house is very beautiful.

| adverb of intensity | adjective |

Giovanni guida troppo lentamente./John drives too slowly.

| adverb of intensity | adverb |

§10.2
ADVERBS OF
MANNER

Adverbs of manner are formed in the following ways. Notice that the ending *-mente* corresponds to the English ending "-ly."

- Change a descriptive adjective ending in *-o* (see §7.2) to *-a*, and add *-mente*.

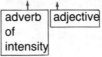

certo/certain

| change to "a" |

certamente/certainly

lento/slow

| change to "a" |

lentamente/slowly

- If the adjective ends in *-e* (see §7.2), then simply add on *-mente*.

  elegante / elegant + *-mente* = *elegantemente* / elegantly
  semplice / simple + *-mente* = *semplicemente* / simply

- However, if the adjective ends in *-le* or *-re* and is preceded by a vowel, then you must drop the *-e*.

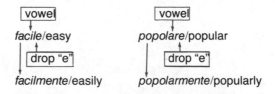

| vowel |

facile/easy

| drop "e" |

facilmente/easily

| vowel |

popolare/popular

| drop "e" |

popolarmente/popularly

176

- The exceptions to these rules are *benevolo* (benevolent) →
benevolmente (benevolently), *leggero* (light) → *leggermente*
(lightly), and *violento* (violent) → *violentemente* (violently).

EXAMPLES

Adjective	Adverb of Manner
raro / rare	*raramente* / rarely
vero / true	*veramente* / truly
preciso / precise	*precisamente* / precisely
felice / happy	*felicemente* / happily
triste / sad	*tristemente* / sadly
enorme / enormous	*enormemente* / enormously
speciale / special	*specialmente* / specially
utile / useful	*utilmente* / usefully
regolare / regular	*regolarmente* / regularly

- These adverbs normally follow the verb, but they may begin
a sentence for emphasis.

EXAMPLES

Lui scrive ai suoi parenti regolarmente. / He writes to his relatives
regularly.

Regolarmente, lui scrive ai suoi parenti. / Regularly, he writes to
his relatives.

§10.3 OTHER KINDS OF ADVERBS

Here are some important adverbs you will need for ordinary
conversation.

abbastanza/enough	*oggi*/today
allora/then	*oggigiorno*/nowadays
anche/also, too	*ormai*/by now
ancora/still, yet	*per caso*/by chance
anzi/as a matter of fact	*piuttosto*/rather
appena/just (have done something)	*poi*/then (eventually)
	presto/early
bene/well	*prima*/first
di nuovo, ancora/again	*purtroppo*/unfortunately
domani/tomorrow	*quasi*/almost
finora/until now	*qui*/here
fra poco/in a little while	*solo*/only
già/already	*stamani*/this morning
in fretta/in a hurry	*stasera*/this evening
insieme/together	*subito*/right away
invece/instead	*tardi*/late
lì, là/there	*vicino*/near(by)
male/bad(ly)	
nel frattempo/in the meanwhile	

EXAMPLES

Noi andiamo spesso al cinema. / We often go to the movies.
Ripeti quello che hai detto ancora una volta. / Repeat what you
have said once
more.

Sono quasi le tre. / It is almost three o'clock.

- As in English, adverbs are normally placed after a verb. In compound tenses (see §9.2–2), many adverbs can be put between the auxiliary verb and the past participle.

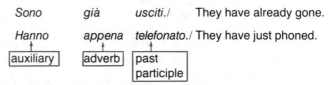

| *Sono* | *già* | *usciti.* / | They have already gone. |

| *Hanno* | *appena* | *telefonato.* / | They have just phoned. |

auxiliary · adverb · past participle

- However, this cannot be done with all adverbs, as is the case in English (which has the same patterns for positioning adverbs).

- The adjectives *molto, tanto, poco, troppo, parecchio* (see §7.4–4) are adverbs as well. In this case, be careful! There is no *noun* for them to agree with!

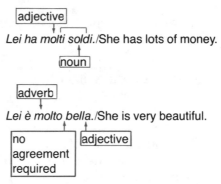

adjective
Lei ha molti soldi./She has lots of money.
noun

adverb
Lei è molto bella./She is very beautiful.
no agreement required · adjective

- You might have trouble with expressions that use nouns in Italian but adjectives in English. These are listed in §14.2.

Italian	English
Lui ha molta fame.	He is very hungry.
noun.	adjective

§10.4 THE COMPARISON OF ADVERBS

Adverbs are compared in exactly the same way as adjectives. So review §7.5.

EXAMPLES

lentamente/slowly ———→ *più lentamente*/more slowly
vicino/near ———→ *meno vicino*/less near
lontano/far ———→ *il più lontano*/the farthest

● Notice the following equivalences:

> *bene*/well →*più bene* = *meglio*/better →*il più bene* =
> *il meglio*/the best
>
> *male*/bad(ly) →*più male* = *peggio*/worse →*il più male*
> = *il peggio*/the worst

● Given that both the adjectives *buono* and *cattivo* and their corresponding adverbs *bene* and *male* are rendered in English by "better" and "worse," respectively, you might become confused about which form to use. Here is a guideline for you:

better = *migliore* or *meglio*?
To figure out which form to use, just go back to the "noncompared" form of the sentence: That wine is better. (compared form) That wine is good. (noncompared form) You can now see that it is an adjective. Therefore, you must use the adjective form *migliore*. *Quel vino è migliore.*/That wine is better.
That watch works better. (compared form) That watch works well. (noncompared form) You can now see that it is an adverb. Therefore, you must use the adverb form *meglio*. *Quell'orologio funziona meglio.*/That watch works better.
Use exactly the same method for *peggiore* and *peggio*.

§11.

Prepositions

§11.1
WHAT ARE
PREPOSI-
TIONS?

Prepositions (literally, "a word that comes before") are words that come before another word or phrase to show its relationship to some other part in the sentence.

La bicicletta | di | Maria | *è nuova.*/Mary's bicycle is new.

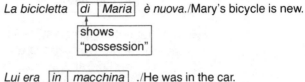

shows "possession"

Lui era | in | macchina | ./He was in the car.

shows "where" he was

§11.2
PREPOSI-
TIONAL
CONTRAC-
TIONS

When the prepositions *a* (to, at), *di* (of), *da* (from), *su* (on), and *in* (in) immediately precede a definite article (review §5.2–1), they contracted with it to form one word.

Questo è il romanzo | del | professore | ./This is the professor's novel.

di + il

C'è una lira | nella | scatola | ./There's a lira in the box.

in + la

Vengo | dall' | Italia | ./I come from Italy.

da + l'

The following chart summarizes the different contractions:

	lo	l'	gli	il	i	la	le
a	allo	all'	agli	al	ai	alla	alle
di	dello	dell'	degli	del	dei	della	delle
da	dallo	dall'	dagli	dal	dai	dalla	dalle
su	sullo	sull'	sugli	sul	sui	sulla	sulle
in	nello	nell	negli	nel	nei	nella	nelle

EXAMPLES

I gioielli sono nel cassetto. / The jewels are in the drawer.
Ecco le matite degli studenti. / Here are the students' pencils.
Le forchette sono sulla tavola. / The forks are on the table.

- The preposition *con* (with) also contracts frequently with the *l'* and *il* forms, although this is not obligatory.

  EXAMPLES

  $$\boxed{con + l' = coll'}$$

  Nadia viene coll'avvocato di Paolo. / Nadia is coming with Paul's lawyer.

  OR

  Nadia viene con l'avvocato di Paolo.

  $$\boxed{con + il = col}$$

  Claudia parla col direttore. / Claudia is speaking with the manager.

  OR

  Claudia parla con il direttore.

- Other prepositions do not contract. Some common ones are *per* (through, on account of), *tra (fra)* (between, among), *sopra* (above), *sotto* (below).

  EXAMPLES

  Lo faccio per il principio. / I'm doing it on (account of) principle.
  L'ho messo tra la tavola e la sedia. / I put it between the table and the chair.

- There are some compound prepositions as well, that is, prepositions made up of two words.

  EXAMPLES

  È vicino alla camera. / It is near the bedroom.
  Sono davanti alla finestra. / I'm in front of the window.

- The prepositions do not contract with the indefinite article.

  EXAMPLES

  L'ho messo in un cassetto. / I put it in a drawer.
  È l'orologio di una donna ricca. / It's the watch of a rich woman.

- The article may be dropped after the preposition in some frequently used expressions.

  EXAMPLES

  Sono a casa. / I'm at home.
  Vado in macchina. / I'm going by car.

- However, when the noun is modified in some way, then the article *must* be used.

  Sono alla casa nuova di Roberto. / I'm at Robert's new house.
  Vado nella macchina verde di Luigi. / I'm going in Louis' green car.

§11.3 SOME PREPOSI- TIONAL USES

Prepositions have many, many uses, and all of them cannot possibly be mentioned here. But here are a few important ones for you to remember:

A is used with a city to express "in."
Abito a Roma./I live in Rome.
Otherwise *in* is used:
Abito in Italia.

Di is used to show possession or relationship:

È l'esame del professore./It is the professor's exam.
È la figlia di Maria./She is Mary's daughter.

Da is used not only to express "from" but also "to" in expressions such as:

to the doctor's	at the pharmacist's	at Mary's
dal dottore	*dal farmacista*	*da Maria*

It translates "since" and "for" in time expressions:

I have been living here	since	Monday.
Abito qui	*da*	*lunedì.*

I have been living here	for	three days.
Abito qui	*da*	*tre giorni.*

It translates the expression "as a . . ."

Te lo dico da amico./I'm telling you as a friend.
Da piccolo, suonavo il flauto./As a young child, I used to play the flute.

It is used in expressions made up of noun + infinitive or noun + noun:

una macchina da vendere/a car to sell
vestito da sera/evening dress

Per is used in time expressions, rather than *da*, when "future duration" is implied:

I will live in this city	for	three years.
Abiterò in questa città	*per*	*tre anni.*

- There are three ways to translate "to" between a conjugated verb and an infinitive.

- Some verbs are followed by *a*.

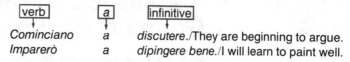

| Cominciano | a | discutere./They are beginning to argue. |
| Imparerò | a | dipingere bene./I will learn to paint well. |

- Some verbs are followed by *di*.

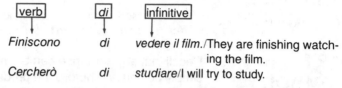

| Finiscono | di | vedere il film./They are finishing watching the film. |
| Cercherò | di | studiare/I will try to study. |

Modal verbs (see §9.9), as well as a few other verbs, do not require a preposition.

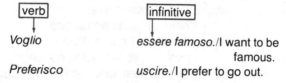

| Voglio | essere famoso./I want to be famous. |
| Preferisco | uscire./I prefer to go out. |

- The only way to learn which preposition (if any) is appropriate in such expressions is to memorize the preposition along with the verb by consulting a dictionary.

§12.

Negatives and Other Grammatical Points

Negatives are words that allow you to say something in the negative.

> *Non conosco nessuno.* / I do not know anyone.
> *Non lo faccio più.* / I won't do it anymore.

Recall that any sentence can be made negative in Italian by simply putting *non* before the predicate (see §2.1–2). The following are some common negative constructions:

---

non . . . mai/never
non . . . nessuno/no one
non . . . niente, nulla/nothing
non . . . più/no more, no longer
non . . . neanche, nemmeno, neppure/not even
non . . . né . . . né/neither . . . nor
non . . . mica/not . . . really

EXAMPLES

Positive	Negative
Canto sempre. / I always sing.	*Non canto mai.* / I never sing.
Qualcuno grida. / Someone is shouting.	*Non grida nessuno.* / No one is shouting.
Lo faccio spesso. / I do it often.	*Non lo faccio più.* / I do not do it anymore.

- You can put a negative at the beginning of a sentence if you wish to be more emphatic. In this case, you drop the *non*.

EXAMPLES

> *Nessuno parla!* / No one is speaking!
> *Mai capirò i verbi!* / Never will I understand verbs!

The conjunctions *e* (and) and *o* (or) allow you to join similar things (two nouns, two verbs, two phrases, etc.).

> *Marco e Carlo sono amici.*/Mark and Charles are friends.
>   ↑   ↑
> noun   noun

> |*Uno studia all'università*| *e*|*l'altro lavora in fabbrica*|/
>   ↑   ↑
>   sentence   sentence

One studies at the university, and the other works in a factory.

- The conjunction *e* and the preposition *a* word can be changed to *ed* and *ad*, respectively, before a noun or adjective beginning with a vowel. This makes the pronunciation smoother.

> *Gina ed Elena sono buone amiche.*/Gina and Helen are good
> ↑   friends.
> vowel

> *Abito ad Atene.*/I live in Athens.
>   ↑
>   vowel

Be careful with the following common expressions!

Singular	Plural
Che cosa è?/What is it?	*Che cosa sono?*/What are they?
È un libro./It is a book.	*Sono dei libri.*/They are books.
Che cosa c'è qui?/What is here?	*Ci sono foto qui?*/Are there photographs here?
C'è una foto qui./There is a photograph here.	*Sì, ci sono alcune foto.*/Yes, there are some photographs here.
Dov'è il ristorante?/Where is the restaurant?	*Dove sono i ristoranti?*/Where are the restaurants?
Ecco l'indirizzo./Here (there) is the address.	*Ecco gli indirizzi.*/Here (there) are the addresses.

- The form *ecco* is invariable; but in the other expressions the verb can, of course, be in any tense and mood:

> *Sarà un ristorante.* / It must be a restaurant.
> *C'erano due foto sulla tavola.* / There were two photographs on the table.

The verb *fare* can be used to render "to have/get something done" and "to have/get someone to do something." Such expressions are called *causative*. The most common form of causative construction is as follows. (Notice how it differs from English).

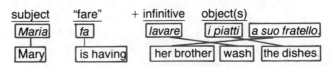

subject	"fare"	+ infinitive	object(s)
Maria	fa	lavare	i piatti · a suo fratello
Mary	is having	her brother · wash · the dishes

- Object pronouns can, of course, be used in a causative construction.

- As with all verbs, the pronouns are attached in the imperative and indefinite tenses.

EXAMPLES

Faglieli lavare! / Have him wash them!
Vuole farglieli lavare. / She wants to have him wash them.

- There are, of course, other ways to form this construction. However, the one above is the most basic. The others are derived from it.

Exercise Set 2

Choose the noun or noun phrase that fits in each slot (§4.1)

1. a. Quella _____ è molto intelligente.
      ☐ Maria   ☐ ragazza

   b. La signora _____ è molto simpatica.
      ☐ Marchi   ☐ donna

   c. _____ è una lingua molto bella.
      ☐ Spagnolo   ☐ Lo spagnolo

   d. _____ fa molto bene alla salute (health).
      ☐ Pane   ☐ Il pane

   e. _____ è una nazione molto grande e bella.
      ☐ Cina   ☐ La Cina

The endings which mark the gender of some of the following nouns are missing. Can you supply them? (§4.2, 4.2–1, 4.2–2, 4.2–3, 4.2–4, 4.2–5, 4.2–6, 4.4, 4.5)

2. a. Quel ragazz___ e quella ragazz___ vivono a Roma.
   b. La signor___ Binni, che si chiama Carl___ Binni, e
      suo marit_____, che si chiama Carl_____ Binni, vivono
      invece a Firenze.
   c. Mio fratell___, Mari___, è un dottor___, e mia
      sorell_____, Mari_____ è anche lei una dottor_____.
   d. Jim è american___, Maria è italian___, e Koichi è
      giappones___.
   e. Betty è ingles___; e anche Bill è ingles_____. Lei è
      infermier_____, e anche lui è infermier_____.
   f. Io mangio sempre una mel___ al giorno, ma non ho
      un mel___ nel mio giardino. Ironicamente (ironically),
      non mangio mai una pesc_____, ma ho un pesc_____
      nel mio giardino.
   g. Mio padr_____ è farmacist_____ e anche mia
      madr_____ è farmacist_____.
   h. Gianni, bevi troppo caff___; dovresti bere più t_____.
   i. Questo è un problem_____ molto difficile. Non capisco
      la tua analis_____ e il tuo diagramm_____.
   j. Marco è un ragazzon___, ma sua sorell___ è una
      ragazzin_____.

> Here's a "pluralization puzzle" for you. Can you fill in the chart with the appropriate singular or plural form of the given noun, if there is one? (§4.3, 4.3–1, 4.3–2, 4.3–3, 4.3–4, 4.3–5, 4.3–6)

3. The "Pluralization Puzzle"

Singular	Plural
acqua	a.
sete	b.
c.	forbici
d.	occhiali
biglietto	e.
f.	aeroporti
attore	g.
attrice	h.
i.	pianisti
j.	pianiste
problema	k.
l.	programmi
crisi	m.
sport	n.
amico	o.
tedesco	p.
q.	amiche
biologo	r.
catalogo	s.

Singular	Plural
bacio	t.
u.	orologi
paio	v.
foto	w.
mano	x.
arcobaleno	y.
uomo	z.

Now, here's an "Article and Demonstrative" puzzle. Can you fill in the chart with the appropriate forms of the definite article (§5.2–1), indefinite article (§5.2–2), the demonstrative indicating nearness, and the demonstrative indicating farness (§5.2–3)?

4. The "Article and Demonstrative" Puzzle

Definite Article	Indefinite Article	Demonstrative of "Nearness"	Demonstrative of "Farness"
…bambino	…giornale	…medico	…finestrino
…bambini	…amico	…medici	…finestrini
…scontro	…psicologo	…studente	…spagnolo
…scontri	…gnocco	…studenti	…spagnoli
…albergo	…amico	…americano	…aeroporto
…alberghi	…amica	…americani	…aeroporti
…fragola	…patata	…ciliegia	…pasticca
…fragole	…zia	…ciliege	…pasticche
…automobile	…allergia	…arancia	…uscita

Definite Article	Indefinite Article	Demonstrative of "Nearness"	Demonstrative of "Farness"
...automobili	...allergia	...arance	...uscite
...altro bambino	...altro giornale	...altro medico	...altro finestrino
...altri bambini	...altro gnocco	...altri medici	...altri finestrini
...brutto scontro	...brutto psicologo	...brutto studente	...brutto zio
...brutti scontri	...brutto amico	...brutti studenti	...brutti zii
...simpatica automobile	...simpatica amica	...simpatica americana	...simpatica amica
...simpatiche automobili	...altra fragola	...simpatiche americane	...simpatiche amiche

> Supply the appropriate forms of the definite article or indefinite article, if necessary, in the spaces (§5.3).

5. Claudia è (a.) _____ ragazza molto simpatica. Quest'anno vuole andare in (b.) _____ Francia, per (c.) _____ seconda volta *(time)* perché ama molto (d.) _____ Francia meridionale. (e.) _____ francesi sono molto simpatici, e allora questa volta ci vuole restare di più. Vuole anche andare a vedere (f.) _____ Parigi, (g.) _____ capitale della Francia. Domani, che è (h.) _____ giovedì, (i.) _____ tre maggio, andrà dal suo agente di viaggi, anche se generalmente, (j.) _____ giovedì, Claudia lavora tutta (k.) _____ giornata. Lei vuole andare in Francia (l.) _____ mese prossimo.

> Rewrite each sentence, changing the partitive given with an equivalent (§6.2, 6.3).

EXAMPLE:

Vuole *della carne*? *Vuole un po' di carne*?

6. *In un negozio di alimentari* (groceries)
   a. Vorrei *dei piselli.*
   b. Ho bisogno di *qualche banana.*
   c. Prendo anche *un po' di frutta.*
   d. Vorrei poi *degli zucchini.*
   e. Prendo, invece, *qualche pomodoro.*
   f. Non voglio *nessuna verdura.*
   g. Vorrei anche *del pesce.*
   h. Mi dia *delle patate.*
   i. E mi dia anche *degli affettati.*

Can you supply the endings missing from the adjectives (§7.2, 7.3, 7.4–1)?

---

7.   *La mia amica*

   La mia amica, Maria, è molto bell___, intelligent____,
   e brav____. Lei ha un fratello. Lui è alt___, ma lei è
   bass____. Tutte le sue amiche sono intelligent___, sim-
   patich____, umil____ e allegr___, ma gli amici del
   fratello sono, invece, maleducat____, antipatic____ e
   pigr____.
   Maria ha anche una buon____ amica che vive in
   Germania, e una buon____ cugina che vive in Olanda.
   Ha due be____ cani e due bell____ gatte. Ha anche un
   be____ pappagallo *(parakeet).* Lei è nata il giorno della
   festa di San____ Stefano.

Form an appropriate question for each of the following statements (§7.4–3). Use polite verb forms throughout.

---

8. a. Ho trentadue anni.
    b. Voglio quattro banane.
    c. Preferisco lo sport del tennis.
    d. Leggo un libro di matematica.
    e. Preferisco quelle persone.

Here's another pluralization puzzle based on possessive and other kinds of adjectives (§7.4–3, 7.4–4). Can you supply the missing singular or plural forms, as the case may be?

9. Another Pluralization Puzzle

Singular	Plural
il mio amico	a.
la tua bicicletta	b.
c.	le sue amiche
d.	i suoi amici
il nostro indirizzo	e.
f.	le vostre case
il loro cane	g.
h.	le loro penne
i.	i miei zii
j.	le nostre cugine
k.	i suoi bravi cugini
l.	le loro zie
mia sorella	m.
il loro fratello	n.
tutta la pagina	o.
l'ultimo posto	p.
q.	le stesse persone
ogni persona	r.

Words that allow you to form the comparative or superlative of adjectives are missing from each sentence (§7.5). Can you complete each sentence in an appropriate manner?

10. a. Giovanni è così intelligente _____ sua sorella.
    b. Mia moglie è _____ brava quanto mia madre.
    c. Mio fratellastro è più furbo _____ me.
    d. La tua amica è più sensibile _____ umile.
    e. Lei è _____ meno simpatica della classe.
    f. Marco è il ragazzo più allegro _____ scuola.
    g. Quel panino è buono, ma questo è _____.
    h. Questo è il _____ ristorante della città.

Write the following italicized noun phrases, replacing them with appropriate demonstrative, possessive, or interrogative pronouns (§8.2).

EXAMPLE:

Questo libro è mio. *Questo* è mio.

11. a. *Quest'orologio* è tuo.
    b. *Quello studente* non è italiano.
    c. Ma *quegli studenti* sono italiani.
    d. *Quell'amico* vive in Brasile.
    e. Chi è *quel bambino?*
    f. Chi sono *quei ragazzi?*
    g. Non conosci *quell'americana?*
    h. *La mia* macchina è una FIAT, ma *la tua* macchina è una Ford.
    i. *Suo fratello* va all'università.
    j. *Vostra cugina* viene domani.
    k. *Che rivista* stai leggendo?
    l. *Quali piatti* preferisci?

Missing from the following sentences are subject personal pronouns (§8.3–1). Can you supply them?

12. a. _____ sono italiano, ma _____ è americana.
    b. Anche _____ sei italiano, non è vero?
    c. Mio fratello abita vicino. _____ ci visita spesso.
    d. _____ non conosciamo quel ristorante, ma _____ lo conoscete, non è vero?
    e. I tuoi cugini sono italiani, e anche _____ vivono a Roma, no?
    f. Scusi, signor Marchi, di dov'è _____?
    g. Maria, anche _____ vai al cinema stasera?

    h. Signori, _____ cosa prendono da mangiare?
    i. Carla, Gina, e _____, cosa prendete da mangiare?
    j. Dante è un grande poeta; _____ è l'autore della
       Divina Commedia.

Rewrite each sentence, substituting the italicized objects with appropriate object pronouns, and making all necessary changes (§8.3–2).

EXAMPLE:

Conosci *mio fratello? Lo* conosci?

13. a. Hai scritto a *tua sorella?*
    b. Ho chiamato *mia madre.*
    c. Claudia ha letto *quella rivista* ieri.
    d. Vedendo *Maria*, l'ho chiamata.
    e. Mi devi dare *il tuo indirizzo.*
    f. Io ti dico sempre *la verità.*
    g. Gianni, paga *il conto*!
    h. Anche Maria va' con *Franco* al cinema.

Missing from the following passage are the pronouns *mi, si, ci, che, cui, quale, quello che, il cui, chi, ne* (§8.3–3, 8.4, 8.5). Can you fill in the blanks correctly with these pronouns?

---

14.   *La mia compagna*

Io (a.) _____ chiamo Cristofero. L'anno scorso ho fatto un viaggio, durante il (b.) _____ ho conosciuto una persona (c.) _____ oggi è diventata una vera compagna. La persona di (d.) _____ sto parlando è mia moglie, (e.) _____ nome è Daniela. (f.) _____ siamo visti per la prima volta in una piazza. (g.) _____ mi ha colpito di lei, da quel primo incontro, è la sua semplicità e onestà. (h.) _____ la conosce come me dirà indubbiamente la stessa cosa. E poi ha una memoria incredibile. Non (i.) _____ dimentica di niente. Per esempio, ieri mi ha comprato alcuni CD del mio compositore favorito—Beethoven. Anzi, me (j.) _____ ha comprati tre, perché era il mio compleanno.

> Verb puzzle! Here's another verb puzzle that tests
> your knowledge of how to conjugate verbs (§9.2,
> 9.3, 9.4, 9.5). Can you supply the corresponding
> singular or plural form?

15. Verb Puzzle

Singular	Plural
io cerco e cercherò	a.
tu mangi e mangerai	b.
c.	loro pagano e pagheranno
d.	noi leggiamo e leggeremmo
tu scrivi e scriveresti	e.
f.	loro finiscono e finirebbero
tu capisci e avrai capito	g.
h.	noi dormiamo e avremmo dormito
i.	abbiamo chiamato e avremmo chiamato
j.	hanno aspettato e aspettarono
k.	siamo usciti e uscimmo
l.	sono andate via e andranno via
volevo e che io volessi	m.
ripetevi e che tu ripetessi	n.
finiva e che lui finisse	o.
Mangia!	p.
q.	Parlino!

Singular	Plural
che io avessi telefonato	r.
che io finisca	s.
che lei scriva	t.
u.	che fossero usciti

There is an error in each sentence. Can you find it and correct the sentence (section §9)?

16. a. Lei non si ha potuto divertire.
    b. Ne ho dovuto comprare tre.
    c. La torta ha stato mangiata da te.
    d. Noi ci siamo telefonato ieri sera.
    e. Ti lava!
    d. Lavisi!
    e. Avendo andato via, non l'ho più visto.
    f. In questo momento io sono mangiato un pezzo di pizza.
    g. Se io potrei non ci andrei.
    h. Se tu avresti conosciuto la mia amica, ti sarebbe piaciuta.
    i. Credevo che sia venuta anche lei alla festa.
    f. Voglio che venisse anche tu alla festa.
    g. Benché pioveva ieri, sono uscito lo stesso.
    h. E' la persona più brava che io conosco.
    i. Mi avevi detto che eri venuto.
    j. Da' mi la tua penna!

To do the following crossword puzzle you will need to review all of §10, 11, 12.

17. A Grammar Crossword Puzzle

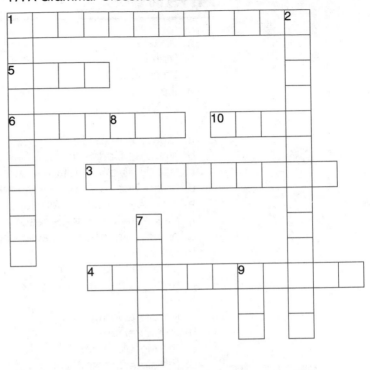

Across
1. adverb form for *allegro*
3. adverb form for *facile*
4. adverb form for *leggero*
5. well
6. this morning
10. toward

Down
1. enough
2. adverb form for *elegante*
7. *più male*
8. *Vado* _____ *casa.*
9. never

Answers

1. a. ragazza
    b. Marchi
    c. Lo spagnolo
    d. Il pane
    e. La Cina

2. a. ragazza - ragazzo
    b. signora - Carla - marito - Carlo
    c. fratello - Mario - dottore - sorella - Maria - dottoressa
    d. americano - italiana - giapponese
    e. inglese - inglese - infermiera - infermiere
    f. mela - melo - pesca - pesco
    g. padre - farmacista - madre - farmacista
    h. caffè - tè
    i. problema - analisi - diagramma
    j. ragazzone - sorella - ragazzina

3. a. (no plural form)
    b. (no plural form)
    c. (no singular form)
    d. (no singular form)
    e. biglietti
    f. aeroporto
    g. attori
    h. attrici
    i. pianista
    j. pianista
    k. problemi
    l. programma
    m. crisi
    n. sport
    o. amici
    p. tedeschi
    q. amica
    r. biologi
    s. cataloghi
    t. baci
    u. orologio
    v. paia
    w. foto
    x. mani
    y. arcobaleni
    z. uomini

4.

il bambino	un giornale	questo medico	quel finestrino
i bambini	un amico	questi medici	quei finestrini
lo scontro	uno psicologo	questo studente	quello spagnolo
gli scontri	uno gnocco	questi studenti	quegli spagnoli
l'albergo	un amico	quest'americano/ questo americano	quell'aeroporto
gli alberghi	un'amica	questi americani	quegli aeroporti
la fragola	una patata	questa ciliegia	quella pasticca
le fragole	una zia	queste ciliege	quelle pasticche
l'automobile	un'allergia	quest'arancia/ questa arancia	quell'uscita
le automobili	un'allergia	queste arance	quelle uscite
l'altro bambino	un altro giornale	quest'altro medico	quell'altro finestrino
gli altri bambini	un altro gnocco	questi altri medici	quegli altri finestrini
il brutto scontro	un brutto psicologo	questo brutto studente	quel brutto zio
i brutti scontri	un brutto amico	questi brutti studenti	quei brutti zii
la simpatica automobile	una simpatica amica	questa simpatica americana	quella simpatica amica
le simpatiche automobili	un'altra fragola	queste simpatiche americane	quelle simpatiche amiche amiche

5.   a. una   b. (no article)   c. una/la   d. la   e. l
     f. (no article)   g. la   h. (no article)   i. il   j. il   k. la
     l. il

6.   a. Vorrei *alcuni piselli/qualche pisello.*
     b. Ho bisogno *di alcune banane/delle banane.*
     c. Prendo anche *della frutta.*
     d. Vorrei poi *alcuni zucchini/qualche zucchino.*
     e. Prendo, invece, *dei pomodori/qualche pomodoro.*
     f. Non voglio *verdura.*
     g. Vorrei anche *un po' di pesce.*
     h. Mi dia *alcune patate/qualche patata.*
     i. E mi dia anche *alcuni affettati/qualche affettato.*

7.   La mia amica, Maria, è molto bella, intelligente e
     brava. Lei ha un fratello. Lui è alto, ma lei è bassa. Tutte
     le sue amiche sono intelligenti, simpatiche, umili e
     allegre, ma gli amici del fratello sono, invece,
     maleducati, antipatici e pigri.
         Maria ha anche una buon' amica che vive in Germania,
     e una buona cugina che vive in Olanda. Ha due bei cani e
     due belle gatte. Ha anche un bel pappagallo *(parakeet).*
     Lei è nata il giorno della festa di Santo Stefano.

8.   a. Quanti anni ha?
     b. Quante banane vuole?
     c. Quali sport preferisce?
     d. Che libro legge?
     e. Quali persone preferisce?

9.   a. i miei amici
     b. le tue biciclette
     c. la sua amica
     d. il suo amico
     e. i nostri indirizzi
     f. la vostra casa
     g. i loro cani
     h. la loro penna
     i. mio zio
     j. nostra cugina
     k. il suo bravo cugino
     l. la loro zia
     m. le mie sorelle
     n. i loro fratelli
     o. tutte le pagine
     p. gli ultimi posti
     q. la stessa persona
     r. (invariable)

10. a. come
    b. tanto
    c. di
    d. che
    e. la
    f. della
    g. migliore/peggiore
    h. miglior(e)/peggior(e)

11. a. Questo
    b. Quello
    c. quelli
    d. Quello
    e. quello
    f. quella
    h. La mia - la tua
    i. Il mio
    j. La vostra
    k. Che
    l. Quali

12. a. To - lei
    b. tu
    c. lui
    d. Noi - voi
    e. loro
    f. Lei
    g. tu
    h. Loro
    i. voi
    j. egli

13. a. Le ho scritto.
    b. La ho (l'ho) chiamata.
    c. Claudia la ha (l'ha) letta ieri.
    d. Vedendola l'ho chiamata.
    e. Me lo devi dare/Devi darmelo.
    f. Io te la dico sempre.
    g. Gianni, pagalo!
    h. Anche Maria va con lui al cinema.

14. a. mi   b. quale   c. che   d. cui   e. il cui   f. ci
    g. Quello che   h. Chi   i. si   j. ne

15.

io cerco e cercherò	a. noi cerchiamo e cercheremo
tu mangi e mangerai	b. voi mangiate e mangerete
c. lui/lei paga e pagherà	loro pagano e pagheranno
d. io leggo e leggerò	noi leggiamo e leggeremmo
tu scrivi e scriveresti	e. voi scrivete e scrivereste
f. lui/lei finisce e finirebbe	loro finiscono e finirebbero
tu capisci e avrai capito	g. voi capite e avrete capito
h. io dormo e avrò dormito	noi dormiamo e avremmo dormito
i. ho chiamato e avrei chiamato	abbiamo chiamato e avremmo chiamato
j. ha aspettato e aspetterà	hanno aspettato e aspettarono
k. sono uscito e uscii	siamo usciti e uscimmo
l. è andata via e andò via	sono andate via e andranno via
volevo e che io volessi	m. volevamo e che noi volessimo
ripetevi e che tu ripetessi	n. ripetevamo e che voi ripeteste
finiva e che lui finisse	o. finivano e che loro finissero
Mangia!	p. Mangiate!
q. Parli!	Parlino!
che io avessi telefonato	r. che noi avessimo telefonato
che io finisca	s. che noi finissimo
che lei scriva	t. che loro scrivano
u. che escano	che fossero usciti

16. a. Lei non si è potuta divertire.
    b. Ne ho dovuti/dovute comprare tre.
    c. La torta è stata mangiata da te.
    d. Noi ci siamo telefonati ieri sera.
    e. Lavati!
    d. Si lavi!
    e. Essendo andato via, non l'ho più visto.
    f. In questo momento io sto mangiato un pezzo di pizza.
    g. Se io potessi non ci andrei.
    h. Se tu avessi conosciuto la mia amica, ti sarebbe piaciuta.
    i. Credevo che fosse venuta anche lei alla festa.
    f. Voglio che venga anche tu alla festa.
    g. Benché piovesse ieri, sono uscito lo stesso.
    h. E' la persona più brava che io conosca.
    i. Mi avevi detto che saresti venuto.
    j. Dammi la tua penna!

17.

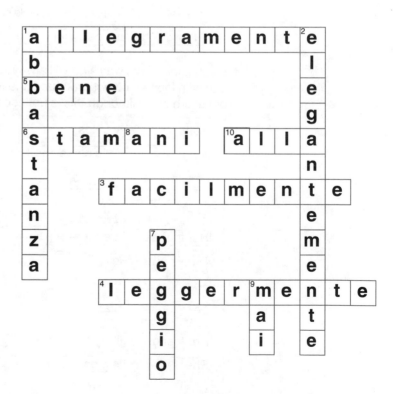

Special Topics

§13.

The Verb *Piacere*

The verb *piacere* allows you to express what you like in Italian. But it is a tricky verb because it really means "to be pleasing to."

Piacere is conjugated irregularly in several tenses. You will find its conjugation in the "Verb Charts" section of this book.

- In order to use this verb correctly, you must always think of what it *really* means.

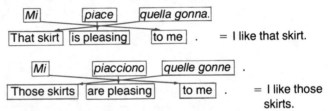

Mi	piace	quella gonna.
That skirt	is pleasing	to me	.	= I like that skirt.

Mi	piacciono	quelle gonne	.
Those skirts	are pleasing	to me	.	= I like those skirts.

- If you think in this way, you will always be correct. Notice that with indirect object pronouns, the real subject is usually put at the end (although this is not necessary).

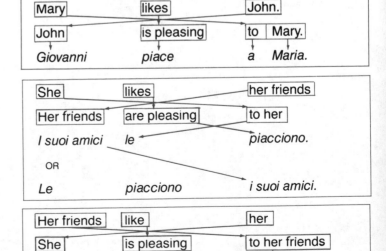

Mary likes John.
John is pleasing to Mary.
Giovanni piace a Maria.

She likes her friends
Her friends are pleasing to her
I suoi amici le piacciono.
OR
Le piacciono i suoi amici.

Her friends like her
She is pleasing to her friends
Lei piace ai suoi amici.

- Be careful using the following expressions!

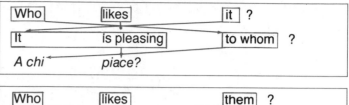

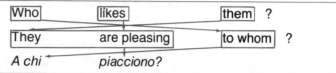

- In compound tenses (see §8.2–2), *piacere* is conjugated with *essere* (to be). This means, of course, that the past participle agrees with the subject—no matter where you put it.

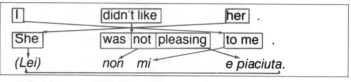

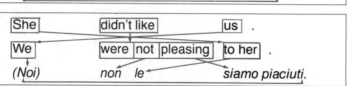

- And do not forget that you might need to use those object pronouns that come after the verb for reasons of emphasis or clarity.

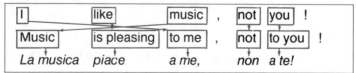

§13.3
A HANDY
RULE OF
THUMB

As you can see, this can be very confusing for anyone accustomed to the English verb "to like." The following rule of thumb might help you use this important verb more readily:

> Since the verb is often used with indirect object pronouns, just think of the pronouns as *subjects*; then make the verb agree with the predicate!

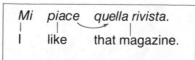

(lit., That magazine is pleasing to me.)

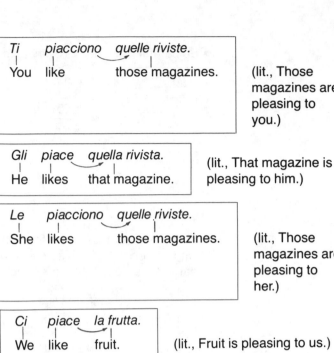

Ti piacciono quelle riviste.
You like those magazines. — (lit., Those magazines are pleasing to you.)

Gli piace quella rivista.
He likes that magazine. — (lit., That magazine is pleasing to him.)

Le piacciono quelle riviste.
She likes those magazines. — (lit., Those magazines are pleasing to her.)

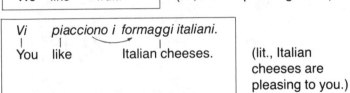

Ci piace la frutta.
We like fruit. — (lit., Fruit is pleasing to us.)

Vi piacciono i formaggi italiani.
You like Italian cheeses. — (lit., Italian cheeses are pleasing to you.)

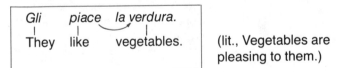

Gli piace la verdura.
They like vegetables. — (lit., Vegetables are pleasing to them.)

- Remember: this is merely a rule of thumb. If you are unsure, you must go through the procedure described in §13.2.

§13.4 EXPRESSING "DISLIKE"

To say that you do not like something, simply put *non* before the predicate in the normal fashion (review §2.2–2).

Non mi piace quella rivista. / I do not like that magazine.
Non le piacciono i ravioli. / She doesn't like ravioli.

- Be careful! The verb *dispiacere* is not used to express the same thing. This verb is used in the following ways, together with an indirect object pronoun.

Mi dispiace./I'm sorry.
Ti dispiace./You are sorry.
Gli dispiace./He is sorry.
etc.

§14

Idiomatic Expressions

**§14.1
WHAT ARE
IDIOMATIC
EXPRES-
SIONS?**

**§14.2
EXPRES-
SIONS WITH
*AVERE***

An idiomatic expression is a phrase that is fixed in form and whose meaning cannot always be determined by the meanings of the particular words in the expression. For example, the English expression "He kicked the bucket" cannot be altered in any way; otherwise, it would lose its meaning.

The following expressions are made up of *avere* + noun, whereas their English equivalents are made up of "to be" + adjective.

	ho	fame.
literally	I have	hunger.
meaning	I am hungry.	

Here is a list of important idioms:

avere fame/to be hungry
avere sete/to be thirsty

avere caldo/to be hot
avere freddo/to be cold

avere sonno/to be sleepy

avere ragione/to be right
avere torto/to be wrong

avere fretta/to be in a hurry

avere paura/to be afraid

avere vergogna/to be ashamed

EXAMPLES
Ieri avevamo fame e allora abbiamo mangiato molto. / Yesterday we were hungry, so we ate a lot.
Scusa, ma ho fretta. / Excuse me, but I'm in a hurry.
Penso che tu abbia torto. / I think you are wrong.

Here are a few other expressions with *avere:*

avere voglia (di)/to feel like
avere bisogno (di)/to need
avercela con qualcuno/to be angry with someone
avere l'occasione (di)/to have the opportunity to

EXAMPLES

Stasera, non ho voglia di uscire. / Tonight, I don't feel like going out.

Gli studenti hanno bisogno di tanta pazienza. / Students need a lot of patience.

Perché ce l'hai con Franca? / Why are you angry with Franca?

§14.3 EXPRES-SIONS WITH *FARE, DARE,* AND *STARE*

If you do not know how to conjugate these irregular verbs, just look them up in the "Verb Charts" section of this book.

Expressions with *Fare*
fare a meno di/to do without
fare attenzione a/to pay attention to
fare finta di/to pretend
fare il biglietto/to buy a (transportation) ticket
farsi la barba/to shave
fare una domanda a/to ask a question
fare una passeggiata/to go for a walk
fare senza/to do without
farsi vivo/to show up
Faccia pure!/Go ahead! (Please do!)
Faccio io!/I'll do it!
Non fa niente!/It doesn't matter!
Non fa per me./It doesn't suit me.

EXAMPLES

Ho fatto il biglietto con Alitalia. / I bought my ticket from Alitalia.
Ogni mattina mi faccio la barba. / Every morning I shave.
Giovanni, perché non ti fai mai vivo? / John, why don't you come (show up) more often?

With *Dare*
darsi da fare/to get busy
dare fastidio a/to bother (someone)
dare la mano a/to shake hands
dare retta a/to heed (pay attention to)

EXAMPLES

Il fumo mi dà fastidio. / Smoke bothers me.
Dare la mano a qualcuno è un segno di cortesia. / Shaking someone's hand is a sign of courtesy.
Da' retta a me! / Heed what I say!

With *Stare*
stare a qualcuno (+ infinitive)/to be up to someone *stare per*/to be about to *stare zitto*/to be quiet *Come sta?* (pol.)/*Come stai* (fam.)?/How are you? *Sto bene.*/I am well.

EXAMPLES

Giorgio, sta' zitto! / George, be quiet!
Sta alla signora Rossi scrivere. / It's up to Mrs. Rossi to write.
Ieri stavo per uscire, quando sono arrivati alcuni amici. / Yesterday I was about to go out, when some friends arrived.

§14.4 MISCELLANEOUS EXPRESSIONS

a destra/to the right *a sinistra*/to the left *nord, sud, est, ovest*/north, south, east, west *Ti piace? Altro che!*/Do you like it? I'll say! *a lungo andare*/in the long run *valere la pena (di)*/to be worthwhile *Auguri!*/All the best! or Congratulations! *in ogni caso*/in any case *Che guaio!*/What a mess! *Non ne posso più!*/I can't stand it anymore! *prendere in giro*/to pull one's leg *Ci vuole molto tempo.*/It will take a long time. *Lo ha fatto apposta!*/He did it on purpose! *Che combinazione!*/What a coincidence! *dipendere da*/to depend on *qualcosa di buono*/something good *niente di buono*/nothing good

EXAMPLES

Quel negozio è qui, a destra. / That store is here, to the right.
Davvero? Non mi prendere in giro! / Really? Don't pull my leg!
Tutto dipende da te. / Everything depends on you.

§15.
Numbers

Cardinal numbers are used for counting (*one, two, three,* etc.) *Ordinal* numbers are used to indicate order (*first, second, third,* etc.).

The numbers from zero to twenty:

Zero to twenty			
0	*zero*	11	*undici*
		12	*dodici*
1	*uno*	13	*tredici*
2	*due*	14	*quattordici*
3	*tre*	15	*quindici*
4	*quattro*	16	*sedici*
5	*cinque*	17	*diciassette*
6	*sei*	18	*diciotto*
7	*sette*	19	*diciannove*
8	*otto*	20	*venti*
9	*nove*		
10	*dieci*		

The numbers from twenty on are formed by adding the first nine numbers to each new category of tens, keeping the following adjustments in mind:

- In front of *uno* and *otto* (the only two that start with a vowel), drop the final vowel of the tens number:

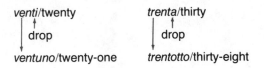

- When *tre* is added on, it must be written with an accent:

venti + tre = venti*trè*
trenta + tre = trenta*trè*

Twenty to a hundred

20	*venti*	30	*trenta*	70	*settanta*
21	*ventuno*	31	*trentuno*	71	*settantuno*
22	*ventidue*	32	*trentadue*	72	*settantadue*
23	*ventitrè*	...		...	
24	*ventiquattro*	40	*quaranta*		
25	*venticinque*	41	*quarantuno*	80	*ottanta*
26	*ventisei*	42	*quarantadue*	81	*ottantuno*
27	*ventisette*	...		82	*ottantadue*
28	*ventotto*	50	*cinquanta*	...	
29	*ventinove*	51	*cinquantuno*	90	*novanta*
		52	*cinquantadue*	91	*novantuno*
		...		92	*novantadue*
		60	*sessanta*	...	
		61	*sessantuno*	100	*cento*
		62	*sessantadue*		
		...			

The same method of construction applies to the remaining numbers:

Numbers above a hundred

101	*centuno*	1000	*mille*	100.000	*centomila*
102	*centodue*	1001	*milleuno*	200.000	*duecentomila*
...			retain the "e"	...	
200	*duecento*			1.000.000	*un milione*
300	*trecento*	1002	*milledue*	2.000.000	*due milioni*
...		...		...	
900	*novecento*	2000	*duemila*	1.000.000.000	*un miliardo*
...		3000	*tremila*		

- Notice that the plural of *mille* is *mila*, whereas *un milione* and *un miliardo* are pluralized in the normal way (see §4.3–1).

EXAMPLES
  due milioni / two million
  tre miliardi / three billion

- The other numbers are invariable, except *uno/una*, as noted below.
- Cardinal numbers normally are placed before a noun.

EXAMPLES
  tre persone / three persons
  cinquantotto minuti / fifty-eight minutes

- When you put *uno* (or any number constructed with it, e.g., *ventuno, trentuno*, etc.) before a noun, then you must treat it exactly like the indefinite article (see §5.2–2).

EXAMPLES
uno zio / one uncle
ventun anni / twenty-one years
trentun giorni / thirty-one days

- *Milione* (*-i*) and *miliardo* (*-i*) are always followed by *di* before a noun.

EXAMPLES
un milione di dollari / a million dollars
due milioni di abitanti / two million inhabitants
tre miliardi di lire / three thousand lira

- The cardinal numbers may be written as one word. But for large numbers, you may need to separate them logically so they can be read easily.

30.256 = trentamila duecento cinquantasei
          (rather than: *trentamiladuecentocinquantasei*!)

§15.3 THE ORDINAL NUMBERS

The first ten ordinal numbers are:

First to tenth			
1st	*primo*	6th	*sesto*
2nd	*secondo*	7th	*settimo*
3rd	*terzo*	8th	*ottavo*
4th	*quarto*	9th	*nono*
5th	*quinto*	10th	*decimo*

The remaining ordinal numbers are easily constructed in the following manner.

- Take the corresponding cardinal number, drop its vowel ending, and then add *-esimo*.

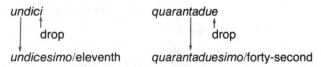

undici   *quarantadue*
        drop   drop

undicesimo/eleventh   *quarantaduesimo*/forty-second

- In the case of numbers ending in *trè*, remove the accent mark (in writing), but keep the final *e*.

ventitrè + *esimo* = *ventitreesimo*/twenty-third
trentatrè + *esimo* = *trentatreesimo*/thirty-third

- Unlike the cardinal numbers, ordinals are adjectives that precede the noun. Therefore, they agree with the noun in the normal fashion (see §7.2).

EXAMPLES
il primo giorno / the first day
la ventesima volta / the twentieth time
gli ottavi capitoli / the eighth chapters

- As any adjective, they can be easily transformed into a pronoun (see §7.2).

  È il quinto che ho fatto. / It's the fifth one I have done.

- As in English, ordinals are used to express the denominator of fractions, whereas the numerator is expressed by cardinals.

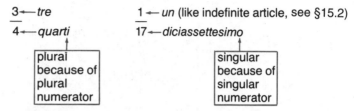

$\dfrac{3 \leftarrow tre}{4 \leftarrow quarti}$

plurai
because of
plural
numerator

$1 \leftarrow un$ (like indefinite article, see §15.2)

$17 \leftarrow diciassettesimo$

singular
because of
singular
numerator

- Be careful! ½ = *mezzo/metà*
- The definite article is not used before an ordinal and a proper name.

  EXAMPLES

  Papa Giovanni XXIII (=ventitreesimo) / Pope John (the) XXIII
  Luigi XIV (=quattordicesimo) / Louis (the) XIV

§15.4 NUMERICAL EXPRESSIONS

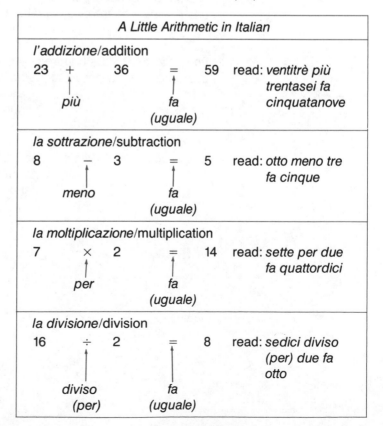

A Little Arithmetic in Italian
l'addizione/addition
23 + 36 = 59 read: *ventitrè più trentasei fa cinquatanove* *più*   *fa*   *(uguale)*
la sottrazione/subtraction
8 − 3 = 5 read: *otto meno tre fa cinque* *meno*   *fa*   *(uguale)*
la moltiplicazione/multiplication
7 × 2 = 14 read: *sette per due fa quattordici* *per*   *fa*   *(uguale)*
la divisione/division
16 ÷ 2 = 8 read: *sedici diviso (per) due fa otto* *diviso (per)*   *fa (uguale)*

How Old Are You?

Quanti anni hai? (fam.)/How old are you?
Quanti anni ha? (pol.)/How old are you?

Ho ventidue anni./I'm twenty-two years old.

> literally,
> "I have 22 years."

Ho trentanove anni./I'm thirty-nine years old.

> literally,
> "I have 39 years."

Some Expressions

il doppio/double
a due a due, a tre a tre . . . /two by two, three by
three . . .

una dozzina/a dozen
una ventina, una trentina . . . /about twenty, about
thirty . . .

un centinaio/about a hundred
due centinaia, tre centinaia . . ./about two hundred,
about three
hundred . . .

un migliaio/about a thousand
due migliaia, tre migliaia . . ./about two thousand,
about three thou-
sand . . .

§16.

Telling Time

You can ask this question either in the singular:

Che ora è?

or in the plural:

Che ore sono?

- The word *ora* literally means "hour." The abstract concept of "time" is expressed by *il tempo*.

  Come passa il tempo! / How time flies!

§16.2
HOURS

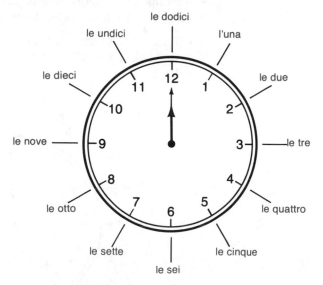

- The hours are all feminine. Therefore, they are preceded by the feminine forms of the definite article (see §5.2–1):

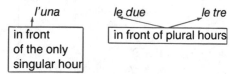

l'una

in front of the only singular hour

le due   *le tre*

in front of plural hours

- Do not forget to make your verbs and prepositions agree!

Che ora è?

È l'una./It's one o'clock.

Sono le due. Sono le tre./It's two o'clock. It's three o'clock.

A che ora arriverai?/At what time are you arriving?
All'una./At one o'clock.
Alle due. Alle tre./At two o'clock. At three o'clock.

215

● In ordinary conversation, morning, afternoon, and evening hours are distinguished by the following expressions:

> *di mattina (della mattina)*/in the morning
> *di sera (della sera)*/in the evening (afternoon)
> *di notte (della notte)*/in the /at night

Sono le otto di mattina. / It's eight o'clock in the morning.
Sono le cinque di sera. / It's five o'clock in the afternoon (evening).

● Although *pomeriggio* means "afternoon," in most parts of Italy, *sera* is used to refer to P.M.

● Officially, Italian time works on the basis of the twenty-four hour clock. Thus, after noon (*le dodici*), official hours are as follows:

EXAMPLES
Sono le quindici. / It's 3 P.M.
Sono le venti. / It's 8 P.M.
Sono le ventiquattro. / It's (twelve) midnight.

§16.3 MINUTES

Minutes (*i minuti*) are simply added to the hour with the conjunction *e* (and).

EXAMPLES
Sono le tre e venti / It's three-twenty.
Sono le quattro e dieci. / It's ten after four.
È l'una e quaranta. / It's one-forty.
Sono le sedici e cinquanta / It's 4:50 P.M.
Sono le ventidue e cinque. / It's 10:05 P.M.

- As the next hour approaches, an alternative way of expressing the minutes is: the next hour *minus* the number of minutes left to go.

  8:58 = *le otto e cinquantotto*

  OR

  le nove meno due (nine minus two)

  10:50 = *le dieci e cinquanta*

  OR

  le undici meno dieci (eleven minus ten)

- The expressions *un quarto* (a quarter), and *mezzo/mezza* also can express the quarter hour and the half hour.

  3:15 = *le tre e quindici*

  OR

  le tre e un quarto

  4:30 = *le quattro e trenta*

  OR

  le quattro e mezzo/mezza

  5:45 = *le sei meno quindici*

  OR

  le sei meno un quarto

  OR

  le cinque e tre quarti (three and three quarters)

§16.4 TIME EXPRESSIONS

Here are some useful time expressions:

noon/midday: *le dodici* OR *mezzogiorno*   midnight: *le ventiquattro* OR *mezzanotte*
EXAMPLES   *È mezzogiorno e venti.*/It's twelve-twenty. (noon)   *È mezzanotte e mezzo.*/It's twelve-thirty. (midnight)

il secondo/second	*l'orologio va avanti*/fast watch
l'orologio/watch or clock	
la sveglia/alarm clock	*l'orologio va indietro*/slow watch
il quadrante/dial	
le lancette/hands (of a clock)	*precisa(-e)*/on the dot
l'orario/schedule	*(l'una precisa* or *le due precise)*

§17.

Days, Months, Seasons, Dates, and the Weather

You can ask this question in one of two main ways:

Che data è (oggi)?
OR
Quanti ne abbiamo oggi?

The latter one literally means "How many of them (= days) do we have?" Thus, you are asking for the "number" of the day, and that is the response you will get.

Che data è?
È il tre maggio. (or È il tre.) / It's May third. (or It's the third.)

OR
Quanti ne abbiamo oggi? / *It's May third.*
(Ne abbiamo) tre.

I giorni della settimana are:

lunedì/Monday	*venerdì*/Friday
martedì/Tuesday	*sabato*/Saturday
mercoledì/Wednesday	*domenica*/Sunday
giovedì/Thursday	

- The days are all masculine, except for *domenica*, which is feminine.

- The expression "On Mondays, Tuesdays," etc., is expressed in Italian with the definite article.

EXAMPLES
il martedì / on Tuesdays
il sabato / on Saturdays
la domenica / on Sundays

- Notice that the days are not capitalized (unless, of course, they are the first word of a sentence).

I mesi dell'anno are:

gennaio/January	*luglio*/July
febbraio/February	*agosto*/August
marzo/March	*settembre*/September
aprile/April	*ottobre*/October
maggio/May	*novembre*/November
giugno/June	*dicembre*/December

- The months are not capitalized (unless they are the first word of a sentence).

- The preposition *di* is often used with a month to indicate something habitual or permanent.

  EXAMPLES

  Di febbraio andiamo spesso al mare. / Every February we often go to the sea (beach).

  Di maggio c'è sempre tanto sole. / Every may there is always lots of sunshine.

  Note: *Ogni* may be used in place of *di*: *ogni febbraio . . .*

- The preposition *a* is used to indicate when something will take place.

  EXAMPLES

  Verrò a giugno. / I will come in June.

  Torneranno a luglio. / They will return in July.

- The preposition *tra (fra)* is used to indicate "in how much time."

  EXAMPLES

  Maria andrà in Italia tra due mesi. / Mary is going to Italy in two months' time.

  Arriveremo fra otto ore. / We will arrive in eight hours' time.

§17.4 SEASONS

Le stagioni dell'anno are as follows:

la primavera/spring	*l'autunno*/fall
l'estate/summer	*l'inverno*/winter

§17.5 RELATED EXPRES- SIONS

Here are some useful expressions:

prossimo (-a)/next: *la settimana prossima*/next week; *il mese prossimo*/next month
scorso (-a)/last: *la settimana scorsa*/last week; *il mese scorso*/last month
due giorni fa, tre mesi fa, un anno fa . . ./two days ago, three months ago, a year ago . . .
a domani, a giovedì . . ./till tomorrow, till Thursday . . .
domani a otto, domenica a otto . . ./a week from tomorrow, a week from Sunday . . .
il giorno/the day: *la giornata*/the whole day (long)
la sera/the evening: *la serata*/the whole evening (long)

> *oggi*/today
> *ieri*/yesterday
> *domani*/tomorrow
> *avantieri*/the day before yesterday
> *dopodomani*/the day after tomorrow

§17.6 DATES

Dates are expressed by the following formula:

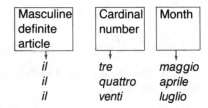

Masculine definite article	Cardinal number	Month
il	*tre*	*maggio*
il	*quattro*	*aprile*
il	*venti*	*luglio*

EXAMPLES

Oggi è il ventinove gennaio. / Today is January 29.
Oggi è il quindici settembre. / Today is September 15.
Oggi è lunedì, il sedici marzo. / Today is Monday, March 16.
Oggi è mercoledì, il due dicembre. / Today is Wednesday, December 2.

- The exception to this is the first day of every month, for which you must use the ordinal number *primo*.

  È il primo ottobre. / It's October 1.
  È il primo giugno. / It's June 1.

Years are always preceded by the definite article.

EXAMPLES

È il 1984./It's 1984.
Sono nato nel 1946./I was born in 1946.

    in + il

- However, in complete dates, the article is omitted before the year.

  Oggi è il cinque febbraio, 1985. / Today is February 5, 1985.

§17.7 THE WEATHER

Che tempo fa? (How's the weather?)
Fa bel tempo./It's beautiful (weather).
Fa brutto (cattivo) tempo./It's bad (awful) weather.
Fa caldo./It's hot.
Fa freddo./It's cold.
Fa molto caldo (freddo)./It's very hot (cold).
Fa un po' caldo (freddo)./It's a bit hot (cold).
Fa fresco./It's cool.
Il caldo è insopportabile./The heat is unbearable.

Le previsioni del tempo (The weather forecast)

Piove./It is raining.
Nevica./It is snowing.
Tira vento./It is windy.
È nuvoloso./It is cloudy.

la pioggia/rain
la neve/snow
il vento/wind
la grandine/hail
l'alba/dawn
il tramonto/twilight
il temporale/storm
il tuono/clap of thunder (verb: *tuonare*)
il lampo/flash of lightning (verb: *lampeggiare*)

● Keep in mind that you can express the weather in the past or in the future.

EXAMPLES

Ieri pioveva. / Yesterday it was raining.
Domani nevicherà. / Tomorrow it will snow.
Ieri faceva molto freddo. / Yesterday it was very cold.
Quest'anno ha fatto bel tempo. / This year the weather has been
beautiful.

● When referring to climate in general, use *essere.*

In Italia il tempo è sempre bello. / The weather is always beautiful in Italy.

§18.

Common Conversation Techniques

§18.1
WHAT ARE
CONVER-
SATION TECH-
NIQUES?

Conversation technique is the manner in which you use a word, phrase, sentence, or expression to communicate within a given situation. Knowing how to start a conversation, how to express politeness, how to ask for something — each is a situation that requires knowledge of appropriate vocabulary and expressions. By knowing how to use the parts of speech, you already know quite a bit about how to communicate: you need interrogative adjectives to ask all kinds of questions; imperative verb forms to give commands; subjunctive tenses to express opinion, doubt, wishes, etc. However, there are some expressions that are not easily classifiable in this way. The following are only a few very common ones.

§18.2
STARTING
AND ENDING
CONVERSA-
TIONS

Saying Hello		
Buon giorno,	signor Verdi,	
	signora Verdi,	come va?
Buona sera,	signorina Verdi,	
Hello,	Mr. Verdi, Mrs. Verdi, Miss Verdi,	how's it going?

- In polite address, "hello" is expressed as *buon giorno* (good morning) until noon, and as *buona sera* (good evening, afternoon) from noon on. These words can also be written as one word: *buongiorno, buonasera.*

Ciao,	Marco,	come va?
Hi,	Mark,	how's it going?

- In familiar address, *ciao* (hi) is used at any time of the day.

Responding		
Bene,	*grazie*	*e Lei?*
Non c'e male,		*e tu?*
Well,	thank you,	and you?
Not bad,		

Making a Phone Call			
Pronto.	*Con chi parlo?*		
	C'e	*il signor . . ./la signora . . ./la signorina . . .?*	
		Marco?	
Hello.	With whom am I speaking?		
	Is	Mr. . . ./Mrs. . . ./Miss . . ./there?	
		Mark there?	

Answering a Phone Call		
Pronto.	*Chi parla?*	*Sì, sono . . .*
Hello.	Who is it?	Yes, this is . . .

Ending Conversations/Phone Calls
Buon giorno.   *Buona sera.*   *Ciao.*
Good-bye.

- The expressions used to start conversations are also used to end them. In addition, you might say *arrivederci* (polite: *arrivederLa*); *buona notte* (good night); *a presto* (see you soon); *a più tardi* (see you later).

● When approached by waiters, store clerks, etc., you will often hear:

Desidera? (sing.)
Desiderano? (pl.)
May I help you?

§18.3 INTRODUC-ING PEOPLE

Come si chiama, Lei? (pol.)	*Mi chiamo . . .*
Come ti chiami? (fam.)	
What is your name?	My name is . . .

Le presento/Permette che Le presenti . . . (pol.)
Ti presento/Permetti che ti presenti . . . (fam.)
Allow me to introduce you to . . .

Piacere di fare	*la Sua conoscenza.* (pol.)
	la tua conoscenza. (fam.)
A pleasure to make	your acquaintance.

§18.4 BEING POLITE

Scusi. (pol.) *Scusa.* (fam.)
Permesso. (used when making one's way through people)
Excuse me.

Grazie.	mille. tante.	Prego.
Thank you	very much.	You're welcome.

Avanti, si accomodi.
Come in, make yourself comfortable.

Buon appetito!	Salute!
used at meals (lit, Have a good appetite!)	Cheers!

§18.5 EXPRESSING YOUR FEELINGS

Surprise
Vero? ─────────────── Really? Davvero? ────────── No! ───────────
Come? ──────────────── How come?
Scherza? (pol.) ────────── Are you joking? Scherzi? (fam.) ──────
Incredibile! ──────────── Unbelievable or Incredible!

Agreement/Disagreement
Buon' idea. ───────────── Good idea.
D'accordo. ────────────── OK. Va bene. ─────────
Non va bene. ─────────── It's not OK.
Non sono d'accordo. ──────── I do not agree.

Pity/Resignation
Peccato. —— Too bad./It's a pity.
Mi dispiace. —— I'm sorry.
Che triste! —— How sad!
Non c'è niente da fare. —— There's nothing to do.
Pazienza! —— Patience!

Indifference/Boredom
Non importa. —— It doesn't matter.
Per me è lo stesso. —— It's all the same thing to me.
Fa lo stesso. —— It's the same thing.
Uffa! —— exclamation similar to "ugh"!
Basta! —— Enough!
Che noia! —— What a bore!

§19.

Synonyms and Antonyms

Synonyms are words that have the same meaning. *Antonyms* are words that have an opposite meaning. Knowing Italian synonyms and antonyms will help you to relate words, thereby enriching your vocabulary.

Synonyms allow you to say the same thing in a different way, thus increasing your communicative abilities. Keep in mind, however, that no two words have the exact meaning.

Meaning	Synonyms	
to ask	chiedere	domandare
crazy	pazzo	matto
dress/suit	abito	vestito
face	faccia	viso
gladly	volentieri	con piacere
much/many/a lot	molto	tanto
near	vicino	presso
nothing	niente	nulla
now	ora	adesso
only	solo	solamente, soltanto
please	per piacere	per favore
quick(ly)	veloce(mente)	svelto
the same	lo stesso	uguale
slowly	lentamente	piano

Meaning	Synonyms	
street/road	*strada*	*via*
therefore	*quindi*	*dunque, perciò*
truly/really	*veramente*	*davvero*
to understand	*capire*	*comprendere*
unfortunately	*purtroppo*	*sfortunatamente*

- The verbs *conoscere* and *sapere* both mean "to know," but are used in different ways.

> "To know someone" is rendered by *conoscere*.

EXAMPLES
> *Maria non conosce quell'avvocatessa.* / Mary doesn't know that lawyer.
> *Chi conosce la dottoressa Verdi?* / Who knows Dr. Verdi?

> "To know how to do something" is rendered by *sapere*.

EXAMPLES
> *Mia sorella non sa pattinare.* / My sister doesn't know how to skate.
> *Sai cucire?* / Do you know how to sew?

> "To know something" is normally rendered by *sapere*.

EXAMPLES
> *Guglielmo non sa la verità.* / William doesn't know the truth.
> *Chi sa come si chiama quella donna?* / Who knows what that woman's name is?

> "To be familiar with something" is rendered by *conoscere*.

EXAMPLES
> *Conosci Roma?* / Are you familiar with Rome?
> *Conosco un bel ristorante qui vicino.* / I know (= I am familiar with) a restaurant nearby.

> When referring to subjects, *sapere* implies complete knowledge, *conoscere* implies partial knowledge.

Lo sai l'italiano? / Do you know Italian?
Lo conosco. / I'm familiar with it.

§19.3 ANTONYMS

Thinking in opposites will also develop your vocabulary.

alba/sunrise	*tramonto*/sunset
alto/tall	*basso*/short
aperto/open	*chiuso*/closed
atterraggio/take-off	*decollo*/landing
bello/beautiful	*brutto*/ugly
bene/well	*male*/bad
bianco/white	*nero*/black
buono/good	*cattivo*/bad
chiaro/light	*scuro*/dark
dentro/inside	*fuori*/outside
entrata/entrance	*uscita*/exit
facile/easy	*difficile*/difficult
magro/thin	*grasso*/fat
presto/early	*tardi*/late
pulito/clean	*sporco*/dirty
piccolo/small	*grande*/big
primo/first	*ultimo*/last
ricco/rich	*povero*/poor
simpatico/nice, pleasant	*antipatico*/unpleasant, disagreeable
spesso/often	*mai*/never
tanto, molto/much	*poco*/little
trovare/to find	*perdere*/to lose
tutto/everything	*niente, nulla*/nothing
vecchio/old	*giovane*/young
vendere/to sell	*comprare*/to buy
venire/to come	*andare*/to go
vicino/near(by)	*lontano*/far
vuoto/empty	*pieno*/full

§20.

Cognates: Good and False Friends

A *cognate* is a word in Italian that looks like a word in English. This is because they have a common origin. They are, so to speak, "friends." But like all friends, they can be "good" or "false."

Cognates that have the *same* meaning are, of course, good friends. Differences between English and Italian occur in the endings of the words. Here are a few related endings that will help you take advantage of language similarities.

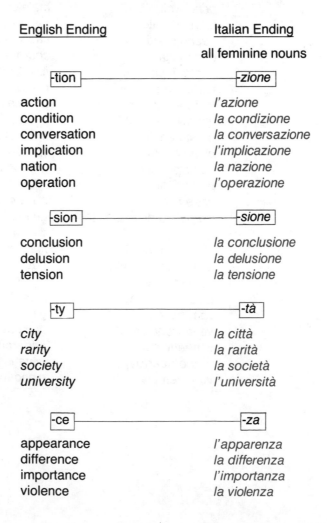

English Ending	Italian Ending
	all feminine nouns
-tion	-zione
action	l'azione
condition	la condizione
conversation	la conversazione
implication	l'implicazione
nation	la nazione
operation	l'operazione
-sion	-sione
conclusion	la conclusione
delusion	la delusione
tension	la tensione
-ty	-tà
city	la città
rarity	la rarità
society	la società
university	l'università
-ce	-za
appearance	l'apparenza
difference	la differenza
importance	l'importanza
violence	la violenza

all masculine nouns

-or	-ore
professor	il professore
doctor	il dottore
actor	l'attore

adjectives ending in -o, or
masculine nouns

-ary	-ario
arbitrary	arbitrario
ordinary	ordinario
vocabulary	il vocabolario

masculine or feminine
nouns (see §3.2–2)

-ist	-ista
dentist	il//la dentista
pianist	il//la pianista
tourist	il//la turista
violinist	il//la violinista

all feminine nouns

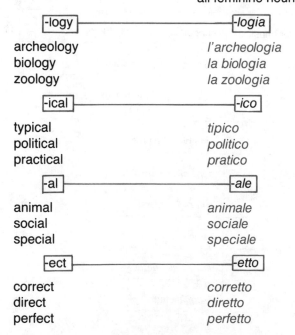

-logy	-logia
archeology	l'archeologia
biology	la biologia
zoology	la zoologia

-ical	-ico
typical	tipico
political	politico
practical	pratico

-al	-ale
animal	animale
social	sociale
special	speciale

-ect	-etto
correct	corretto
direct	diretto
perfect	perfetto

● Of course, you will also find many good friends among verbs.

English Verbs	Italian Verbs
analyze	*analizzare*
complicate	*complicare*
emigrate	*emigrare*
indicate	*indicare*
prefer	*preferire*

§20.3 THE FALSE FRIENDS

Cognates that do not have the same meaning are, needless to say, false friends. Here are a few very common ones:

English Word	False Friend	Correct Word
assist	*assistere* = to be present	*aiutare*
accident	*accidente* = unexpected event	*l'incidente*
brave	*bravo* = good, fine	*coraggioso*
effective	*effettivo* = actual	*efficace*
argument	*argomento* = topic	*la discussione, la lite*
conductor (musical)	*conduttore* = train conductor	*il direttore (d'orchestra)*
complexion	*complessione* = constitution	*la carnagione*
magazine	*magazzino* = warehouse, department store	*la rivista*
stamp	*stampa* = the press	*il francobollo*
sensible	*sensibile* = sensitive	*sensato*
lecture	*lettura* = reading	*la conferenza*
large	*largo* = wide	*grande*
firm	*firma* = signature	*la ditta, l'azienda*
factory	*fattoria* = farm	*la fabbrica*

English Word	False Friend	Correct Word
disgrace	*disgrazia* = misfortune	*la vergogna*
contest	*contesto* = context	*il concorso*
confront	*confrontare* = to compare	*affrontare*
parent	*parente* = relative	*il genitore*
library	*libreria* = bookstore	*la biblioteca*

- Of course, to be sure whether a cognate is a good or false friend, you will have to look it up in a dictionary.

A READING AND WRITING BRUSH-UP

§21.

Reading

§21.1
HOW TO
READ

If you know your basics (§1-3), parts of speech (§4-12), and basic ways of communicating (§13-20), you are now ready to hone your reading skills.

When you have in front of you any written text, there are several strategies that you should be aware of in order to get the most out of your reading. These can be summarized by an acronym: *FOCUS*, for *F*ind—*O*ut—*C*ontextualize—*U*nder*s*tand. The first thing to do is, of course, to *find out* what the text is about by reading it over once or twice in order to get the gist. Then, you should try to infer what you do not know (words, expressions, etc.) from *context*. You should, of course, look up those items that still baffle you.

§21.2
READING
DOCUMENTS

One of the most practical skills you will need to have is how to read documents (checks, forms, questionnaires, etc.). Let us look at a few simple "documents" using the FOCUS approach.

> Sig. G. Ascoli
> Via Garibaldi, 34
> 00124 Roma

You can easily see that this is an envelope and, therefore, that you are reading the name and address of the addressee. Even if you have never seen one before, you can check what you know and can infer what you do not know easily from context. Obviously the letter is addressed to a Mr. *(Sig.)* G. Ascoli. You note that he lives on a street *(Via)* named *Garibaldi*. You can easily infer that the number of his residence is *34*, even if it follows the street name (in contrast to American practice). Finally, you can see that he lives in *Roma* and that in all likelihood his postal code is *00124* (which precedes the city name). Obviously, any word you do not know and cannot infer from context will have to be looked up in a dictionary.

Let us use the FOCUS approach one more time to read the following document.

```
_____ 19 _____ Lit. _____

            Banca Commerciale Italiana
   ROMA, AGENZIA N.9 - CORSO VITTORIO EMANUELE II, 152

                    A vista pagate per questo assegno bancario
   Lire _____

   a _____
      _____

                    firma _____
```

You can easily see that this is a check, and can therefore figure out most of its components from context. You will notice that the top line is where you not only put the date, but also the amount of *lire italiane (= Lit)* in numerical digits. Note the name of the bank, *Banca Commerciale Italiana*, and its address, *Corso Vittorio Emanuele II, 152,* in Rome. You can easily see that you should write out in letters the amount of the check after *Lire* _____, and that the name of the person to whom the check is made out follows *a* _____. Finally, you should have no trouble figuring out where to put your signature: *firma*

_____.

Having "deciphered" these easy parts of the document, you can now attempt to figure out what *A vista* (at sight) *pagate per questo assegno bancario* means. Without understanding the individual words, you should now have no trouble translating it as an instruction to pay the stated amount of lire to the indicated person.

§21.3 READING PROSE

Reading and understanding any kind of prose writing (a letter, a short story, a novel, etc.) involves the same kind of strategies that reading a document implicates. Once again, the FOCUS approach can be used to decipher the meaning of any prose passage.

Consider, for example, the following passage:

> *L'altra sera, mentre stavo dormendo, e sognando tante belle cose, tutto ad un tratto ho sentito un rumore. La prima cosa alla quale ho pensato era che un ladro fosse entrato in casa. Allora mi sono alzato e, quieto quieto, sono andato giù per le scale. Lì, in fondo, ho visto un topo morto!*
>
> *Ho capito subito, che lo aveva ucciso Frufrù, la nostra gatta. Me ne sono ritornato tranquillamente a dormire.*

● **Find out:**

Ask yourself what the story is about? Pick out the key words and phrases: e.g. *stavo dormendo, ho sentito un rumore, un ladro fosse entrato in casa, ho visto un topo morto, lo aveva ucciso Frufrù.* By reading these parts in sequence you get the essential picture that the narrator was sleeping, that he heard a noise, that (he thought) a thief had entered the house, that he saw instead a dead mouse, and that his cat *Frufrù* had killed it.

Most of these parts can be easily figured out. However, you should always look up in a dictionary any word or phrase that baffles you.

● **Contextualize:**

Now you can figure out the remaining details within the story context that you have just established.

It would seem that not only was the narrator sleeping, but also dreaming *(sognando tante belle cose)*, that the noise he heard startled him *(tutto ad un tratto)*, that the first thing he thought about *(La prima cosa alla quale ho pensato)* was that of a thief having entered his house. Now, you can easily reconstruct his movements before he saw the dead mouse: he got up *(Allora mi sono alzato)* and went quietly down the stairs *(qiueto, quieto sono andato giù per le scale)*. After figuring out that *Frufrù* had killed the mouse, he went back to bed *(Me ne sono ritornato tranquillamente a dormire)*.

● **Understand:**

Now you are able to understand the entire passage, filling in the details of vocabulary and grammar by looking them up in the appropriate sections of this book or any reference grammar and dictionary.

§22.

Writing

<table>
<tr>
<td>

§22.1
HOW TO
WRITE

</td>
<td>

Writing is the "other facet" of reading. If you know your basics (§1-3), parts of speech (§4-12), and basic ways of communicating (§13-20), you are ready to use your knowledge and skill to write Italian texts.

When you have to write any text, you can once again incorporate the FOCUS approach. The first thing to do is, of course, to *find out* what you will need to write down in order to reach your intended reader, and/or if there are any "formulas" to follow. Then, you should write your text by keeping all your words, phrases, etc. appropriately *contextualized*, looking up anything you are not sure of. The idea is to make your text as *understandable* as possible to your reader.

</td>
</tr>
<tr>
<td>

§22.2
WRITING
DOCUMENTS

</td>
<td>

The writing of documents (checks, forms, letters, etc.) generally follows pre-established "formulas" or practices. You can easily fill-out checks and forms of all kinds by simply following the instructions.

Here, now, are the conventions for writing letters.

</td>
</tr>
</table>

- **Formal/Business Letters:**

Notice the various components of a formal letter:

Place/Date	Firenze, 3 maggio 1995
Heading	Al signor M. Barni Direttore IBM Italia
Salutation	Gentile signor Barni,
Contents	Le scrivo per ....
Closing	La saluto cordialmente
Signature	*R. Di Santo* (R. Di Santo)

Other possible salutations are:

Spettabile + name of company = "To Whom it May Concern"

Egregio signor/signora + name = very formal version of "Dear Sir"

Other possible closing formulas are:

Con i più cordiali saluti = "With best wishes"

Con ossequi = "With regards"

● **Familiar Letters:**

Now notice the various components of the kind of letter you would write to a friend, a family member, etc.

Place/Date	Napoli, 4 dicembre 1995
Salutation	Caro/Cara ....
Contents	ho saputo che ....
	....
Closing	Tuo/Tua,
Signature	Alessandro/Claudia

Other possible salutations are:

Carissimo/a + name = "Dearest…"

Mio caro/mia cara + name = "My dear…"

Other closing formulas are:

Baci e abbracci = "Hugs and kisses"

A presto = "Talk to you soon"

§22.3 WRITING PROSE

To write a prose piece of any kind (an essay, a story, etc.) you can use the FOCUS approach again. Let's try our hand at writing a brief paragraph on traffic jams.

● **Finding Out**

First, ask yourself what "slant" you want to give your paragraph. Let's say that you think that traffic jams are responsible for an increase in stress. Now, select the key words and phrases that will allow you to write about this. Look up those that you do not know:

traffico, circolazione	= *traffic*
stress, tensione	= *stress*
aumento	= *increase*
aumentare	= *to increase*
ingorgo	= *traffic jam*

- **Contextualizing**

Now, plan out what you are going to say:

You probably will make a statement about the increase in traffic and in traffic jams. You might want to add that in large cities this is becoming unbearable. Then, you will make your point that, in your view, this is probably why more and more people are stressed out.

Now you can figure out the details within the story context that you have just established. So, let's put down our first draft which will show a series of options:

•Increase in traffic and traffic jams.

-*oggi il traffico/la circolazione delle macchine è in aumento/sta aumentando*

-*ci sono molti ingorghi*

•In large cities this is becoming unbearable.

-*nelle grandi città, il traffico è diventato/sta diventando insopportabile*

•This is why you think that stress is on the increase.

-*penso che il traffico/l'aumento del traffico sia responsabile dell'aumento di stress*

-*nell mia opinione l'aumento di stress nella nostra società è dovuto all'aumento del traffico*

- **Understandability**

Now that you have your options laid out before you, you will have to make a selection, employing the grammatical and vocabulary knowledge you have to make understandable, well-formed sentences.

Here's one possible text that can result from the foregoing method:

Oggi il traffico è in aumento. E infatti, ci sono molti ingorghi, specialmente nelle grandi città dove il traffico sta diventando veramente insopportabile. Nella mia opinione l'aumento del traffico è responsabile dell'aumento dello stress nella nostra società.

Exercise Set 3

Say that you or the indicated people both like and do not like the following foods or drinks (§13.3, 13.4).

EXAMPLE: la pizza (io) *Mi piace la pizza/Non mi piace la pizza*

1. a. il gelato (io)
   b. gli spaghetti (tu)
   c. il cappuccino (Lei)
   d. i ravioli (lui)
   e. le lasagne (lei)
   f. l'espresso (noi)
   g. gli gnocchi (loro)
   h. quel succo di frutta (voi)

Say the following (§13.2, 14.2, 14.3, 14.4).

EXAMPLE:

Mary likes him. *Lui piace a Maria.*

2. a. John likes Mary.
   b. Mary likes John.
   c. They like each other.
   d. I like them.
   e. They like me.
   f. My brother likes his girlfriend (*ragazza*).
   g. My brother's girlfriend doesn't like him.
   h. What a coincidence!
   i. I can't stand it anymore!
   j. It's up to you to tell the truth!
   k. John, don't bother me!
   l. It doesn't matter!
   m. I feel like going to the movies.
   n. You're right; I'm wrong.
   o. She's hot, but you're cold.

Write out the answers in letters (§15.2, 15.3, 15.4).

EXAMPLE:

Quanto fa tre per due? *Tre per due fa sei.*

3. Quanto fa…
   a. trentatrè diviso tre?
   b. cento diviso cinque?
   c. ventidue per quattro?
   d. ottanta per undici?
   e. venti meno tre?
   f. cinquanta più ventidue?

4. Marco ha trentatrè anni e Maria ne ha ventidue. Quanti anni hanno insieme?

5. Che numero viene logicamente in sequenza?
   a. undici, dodici, tredici, …
   b. sessanta, settanta, ottanta, …
   c. otto, diciotto, ventotto, …
   d. cento, mille, centomila, …
   e. primo, terzo, quinto, …
   f. undicesimo, ventunesimo, trentunesimo, …
   g. un quarto, due quarti, tre quarti, …

Che ora è? Write out the answer in letters (§16.2, 16.3).

EXAMPLE:

2:00 PM   *Sono le due e trenta del pomeriggio/Sono le quattordici*

6. a. 8:00 AM   b. 8:00 PM   c. 1:30 PM   d. 5:20 PM
   e. 9:55 AM   f. 12:00 (midnight)   g. 4:15 PM

By unscrambling the following letters you will get words referring to time or timepieces (§16.4), to days of the week (§17.2), to months of the year (§17.3), and to the seasons (§17.4).

---

7. a. NDOSECO   _____
    b. CETETNAL   _____
    c. RAOIOR   _____
    d. NULDÌE   _____
    e. MENODICA   _____
    f. GLOIUL   _____
    g. TTBREOO   _____
    h. VERPARIMA   _____

> Match each question with its answer (§17.5, 17.6, 17.7).

8. Match-Ups

> Select the appropriate response (§18.2, 18.3, 18.4, 18.5).

9.   a. You say hello in the morning with…
> ☐ *Buon giorno*   ☐ *Come va?*

Questions	Answers
___1. Quando sei andato in Italia?	a. Tre.
___2. Quando ci vedremo?	b. E' il tre maggio.
___3. Quanti ne abbiamo oggi?	c. Fa freddo.
___4. Che data è oggi?	d. La settimana scorsa.
___5. Che tempo fa?	e. La settimana scorsa.
___6.Che tempo faceva ieri?	f. E' sempre bello.
___7. Com'è il tempo in Italia?	g. Pioveva.

b. You say "hi" to friend with…
> ☐ *Buona sera*   ☐ *Ciao*

c. *Come va?*
> ☐ *Bene, grazie*   ☐ *Grazie*

d. You say good-bye in the evening formally with…
> ☐ *Buona sera*   ☐ *Arrivederci*

e. You say hello over the phone with…
> ☐ *Ciao*   ☐ *Pronto*

f. *Come si chiama Lei?*
> ☐ *Si chiama Gina*   ☐ *Mi chiamo Gina Giusti*

g. *Le presento Gina Giusti.*
> ☐ *Va bene*   ☐ *Piacere di fare la Sua conoscenza*

h. *Grazie.*
> ☐ *Va bene*   ☐ *Prego*

> The Synonym and Antonym Puzzle (§19.2, 19.3). Can you fill in the puzzle chart correctly?

10. Synonyms and Antonyms.

Word	Synonym
domandare	a.
pazzo	b.
viso	c.
presso	d.
per piacere	e.
uguale	f.
perciò	g.
comprendere	h.

Word	Antonym
basso	i.
scuro	j.
fuori	k.
difficile	l.
sporco	m.
comprare	n.
pieno	o.

> Can you supply the appropriate cognates (20.2)?

11. a. action _____
    b. delusion _____
    c. society _____
    d. appearance _____
    e. ordinary _____
    f. tourist _____
    g. archeology _____
    h. practical _____
    i. special _____
    j. perfect _____
    k. prefer _____

> Find the Italian equivalents of the following words in the word-search puzzle (20.3).

12. Word-search puzzle

accident   argument   magazine   stamp   large   factory

a	r	i	v	i	s	t	a	b	c	d	e	f	g
n	m	k	o	l	i	m	l	b	n	m	v	i	r
o	m	o	p	n	m	i	i	c	b	n	m	o	a
i	n	c	i	d	e	n	t	e	n	m	i	o	n
b	h	u	i	o	p	p	e	q	a	e	r	b	d
m	k	o	l	p	o	i	k	i	t	v	i	o	e
f	r	a	n	c	o	b	o	l	l	o	m	i	n
n	m	k	o	i	u	r	t	r	e	s	i	u	t
l	o	i	u	t	r	e	q	n	i	o	m	l	l
f	a	b	b	r	i	c	a	c	d	c	d	c	d

> Read the following document and then check off the appropriate response to each question (§21.1).

13. Che cosa è?

```
AZ 612/22 luglioDORETTI/MINA      AEROPORTI
                                  DI
Volo   Data        Nome           ROMA
                   Passeggero
XYZ                14G   non fumatori
```
Destinazione   Posto

Imbarco
Porta Posteriore

Carta d'imbarco

a. Una carta d'imbarco è necessaria per…
   ☐ salire in aereo   ☐ andare in barca

b. Mina Doretti è…
   ☐ l'agente di viaggi   ☐ il passeggero

c. 14G è…
   ☐ il posto ottenuto   ☐ il numero del volo
     dal passeggero

d. AZ 612 è…
   ☐ il posto ottenuto   ☐ il numero del volo
     dal passeggero

e. Il passeggero è…
   ☐ un fumatore   ☐ un non fumatore

f. la carta d'imbarca è stata rilasciata…
   ☐ in America   ☐ a Roma

g. Qual è, probabilmente, la linea aerea?
   ☐ Alitalia   ☐ TWA

Read the following passage and then indicate if the statements that follow are true *(Vero)* or false *(False)* (§21.2).

14. Vero o falso?

> Niccolò Paganini era non solo uno dei più grandi violinisti del mondo, ma anche, puodarsi, uno dei più grandi compositori di musica strumentale italiani.
> Era così bravo, come virtuoso del violino, che tutti pensavano che il Diavolo lo controllasse! Era un uomo alto, magro, di carnagione scura, con i capelli neri. La sua apparenza destava orrore e paura. Ma la sua musica era divina, una delle più belle musiche che l'Italia ha prodotto. Nella tradizione di Antonio Vivaldi, altro grande compositore italiano del Barocco, Paganini era un genio della melodia. Per indicare che qualcuno è un genio musicale, oggi si dice, infatti, che è "un Paganini"!

_____ a. Vivaldi era controllato dal Diavolo.
_____ b. L'apparenza fisica di Paganini era molto piacevole.
_____ c. Oggi una persona molto brava musicalmente si chiama un Paganini.
_____ d. Paganini era un grande compositore del Barocco.
_____ e. La musica di Paganini era divina.
_____ f. Paganini suonava il violino.

> Now can you match each word/phrase with its meaning or example?

15. Match-Ups

_____ 1. musica strumentale
_____ 2. virtuoso
_____ 3. di carnagione scura
_____ 4. destava orrore
_____ 5. genio

a. i suoni piacevoli di un pezzo di musica
b. una persona molto intelligente
c. faceva venire la paura
d. un periodo musicale e artistico del diciassettesimo secolo (1600–1699)
e. un musicista molto bravo

_____ 6. melodia   f. con la pelle di colore scuro

_____ 7. il Barocco   g. musica senza voci umane

Complete the following letter on the basis of the information given to you (§22.2).

---

16. Una lettera.
    a. You are writing from Venice, on April 4.
    b. Your adressee is Mrs. M. Rossini, Director of Ford Italy.
    c. Tell her that you are writing this letter to inform her that you have changed your address to: 7 Garibaldi Street, Rome 00134.
    d. Your name is C. Di Servo.

Can you put the sentences in order logically to form a coherent text (§22.3)?

---

17. Scrambled Sentences
    -Abbiamo bevuto un cappuccino e parlato per un po'.
    -Abbiamo visto un film di Fellini.
    -Dopo il film siamo andate insieme ad un bar.
    -Era molto bello, ma difficile.
    -Ieri sono andato al cinema con la mia amica.

> Can you find appropriate words to complete the following text (§22.3)?

18. Fill-in

Io mi (a.) _____ Gina Bruni. Vivo (b.) _____
Italia, (c.) _____ Roma. (d.) _____ professoressa
di matematica all' (e.) _____ di Roma. Ho trentasei (f.)
_____; ho i (g.) _____ biondi, e sono alta.

> Write a paragraph as indicated (§22.3).

19. Writing in Italian.
    Say that...
    (a.) Yesterday you went to the airport.   (b.) Your flight,
    AZ 612 for Rome, was on time.   (c.) As soon as you
    received your boarding pass, you went to the gate.
    (d.) This was your first trip to Italy.

Answers

1.   a. Mi piace il gelato/Non mi piace il gelato
     b. Ti piacciono gli spaghetti/Non ti piacciono gli spaghetti
     c. Le piace il cappuccino/Non Le piace il cappuccino
     d. Gli piacciono i ravioli/Non gli piacciono i ravioli
     e. Le piacciono le lasagne/Non le piacciono le lasagne
     f. Ci piace l'espresso/Non ci piace l'espresso
     g. Gli piacciono gli gnocchi/Non gli piacciono gli gnocchi
     h. Vi piace quel succo di frutta/Non vi piace quel succo di frutta

2.   a. Maria piace a Gianni (Giovanni).
     b. Gianni (Giovanni) piace a Maria.
     c. (Loro) si piacciono.
     d. (Loro) mi piacciono.
     e. (Io) gli piaccio/(Io) piaccio loro.
     f. A mio fratello piace la sua ragazza.
     g. Mio fratello non piace alla sua ragazza.
     h. Che combinazione!
     i. Non ne posso più!
     j. Sta a te/Lei dire la verità.
     k. Gianni (Giovanni), non darmi fastidio!/non mi dare fastidio!
     l. Non fa niente!
     m. (Io) ho voglia di andare al cinema.
     n. Tu hai ragione; io ho torto.
     o. Lei ha caldo, ma tu hai freddo.

3.   a. Trentatrè diviso tre fa undici.
     b. Cento diviso cinque fa venticinque.
     c. Ventidue per quattro fa ottantotto.
     d. Ottanta per undici fa ottocento ottantanta.
     e. Venti meno tre fa diciassette.
     f. Cinquanta più ventidue fa settantadue.

4.   Marco e Maria hanno insieme cinquantacinque anni.

5.   a. quattordici
     b. novanta
     c. trentotto
     d. un milione

e. settimo
f. quarantunesimo
g. quattro quarti = uno

6 a. Sono le otto (del mattino/di mattina/della mattina).
   b. Sono le otto di sera/della sera (Sono le venti).
   c. E' l'una e trenta/E' l'una e mezzo (del pomeriggio).
   d. Sono le cinque e venti del pomeriggio/della sera
      (Sono le diciasette e venti).
   e. Sono le nove e cinquantacinque (del mattino/della
      mattina/di mattina)/Sono le dieci meno cinque (del
      mattino/ecc.).
   f. Sono le ventiquattro/E' mezzanotte.
   g. Sono le quattro e un quarto del pomeriggio (di
      sera)/Sono le sedici e quindici.

7. a. secondo
   b. lancette
   c. orario
   d. lunedì
   e. domenica
   f. luglio
   g. domenica
   h. primavera

8. 1-d, 2-e, 3-a, 4-b, 5-c, 6-g, 7-f.

9. a. Buon giorno
   b. Ciao
   c. Bene, grazie
   d. Buona sera
   e. Pronto
   f. Mi chiamo Gina Giusti
   g. Piacere di fare la Sua consocenza
   h. Prego

10.

Word	Synonym
domandare	a. chiedere
pazzo	b. matto
viso	c. faccia
presso	d. vicino

Word	Synonym
per piacere	e. per favore
uguale	f. lo stesso
perciò	g. dunque, quindi
comprendere	h. capire
Word	**Antonym**
basso	i. alto
scuro	j. chiaro
fuori	k. dentro
difficile	l. facile
sporco	m. pulito
comprare	n. vendere
pieno	o. vuoto

11. a. azione
    b. delusione
    c. società
    d. apparenza
    e. ordinario
    f. turista
    g. archeologia
    h. practico
    i. speciale
    j. perfetto
    k. preferire

12.

a	r	i	v	i	s	t	a	b	c	d	e	f	g
n	m	k	o	l	i	m	l	b	n	m	v	i	r
o	m	o	p	n	m	i	i	c	b	n	m	o	a
i	n	c	i	d	e	n	t	e	n	m	i	o	n
b	h	u	i	o	p	p	e	q	a	e	r	b	d
m	k	o	l	p	o	i	k	i	t	v	i	o	e
f	r	a	n	c	o	b	o	l	l	o	m	i	n
n	m	k	o	i	u	r	t	r	e	s	i	u	t
l	o	i	u	t	r	e	q	n	i	o	m	l	l
f	a	b	b	r	i	c	a	c	d	c	d	c	d

13. a. salire in aereo
    b. il passeggero
    c. il posto ottenuto dal passeggero
    d. il numero del volo
    e. un non fumatore
    f. a Roma
    g. Alitalia

14. a. falso
    b. falso
    c. vero
    d. falso
    e. vero
    f. vero

15. 1-g
    2-e
    3-f
    4-c
    5-b
    6-a
    7-d

16.

```
                              Venezia, 4 aprile 1995

Alla gentile Signora M. Rossini,
Direttrice
Ford Italia


Gentile Signora Rossini,
   Le scrivo per informarLa che ho cambiato
indirizzo. Il mio indirizzo nuovo è Via
Garibaldi, 7, 00134 Roma

Con i più cordiali saluti/Cordialmente/ ecc.

                                   C. Di Servo
                                  (C. Di Servo)
```

17. Ieri sono andato al cinema con la mia amica. Abbiamo visto un film di Fellini. Era molto bello, ma difficile. Dopo il film siamo andate insieme ad un bar. Abbiamo bevuto un cappuccino e parlato per un po'.

18. (a) chiamo   (b) in   (c) a   (d) sono   (e) università   (f) anni   (g) capelli

19. (a) Ieri sono andato/a all'aeroporto.   (b) Il mio volo, AZ 612 per Roma, era in orario.   (c) Appena ho ricevuto la mia carta d'imbarco, sono andato/a all'uscita.   (d) Era il mio primo viaggio in Italia.

Verb Charts

The following verbs are irregular in one or more tenses as shown. Their individual conjugations are displayed from left to right (where applicable).

EXAMPLE

Andare in the present indicative:

vado (1st person singular), vai (2nd person singular), va (3rd person singular), andiamo (1st person plural), andate (2nd person plural), vanno (3rd person plural)

andare to go	Present Indicative:	vado, vai, va, andiamo, andate, vanno
	Future:	andrò, andrai, andrà, andremo, andrete, andranno
	Imperative:	—— va', vada, andiamo, andate, vadano
	Present Conditional:	andrei, andresti, andrebbe, andremmo, andreste, andrebbero
	Present Subjunctive:	vada, vada, vada, andiamo, andiate, vadano
avere to have	Present Indicative:	ho, hai, ha, abbiamo, avete, hanno
	Past Absolute:	ebbi, avesti, ebbe, avemmo, aveste, ebbero
	Future:	avrò, avrai, avrà, avremo, avrete, avranno
	Imperative:	—— abbi, abbia, abbiamo, abbiate, abbiano
	Present Conditional:	avrei, avresti, avrebbe, avremmo, avreste, avrebbero
	Present Subjunctive:	abbia, abbia, abbia, abbiamo, abbiate, abbiano
bere to drink	Present Indicative:	bevo, bevi, beve, beviamo, bevete, bevono
	Past Participle:	bevuto
	Imperfect:	bevevo, bevevi, beveva, bevevamo, bevevate, bevevano
	Past Absolute:	bevvi (bevetti), bevesti, bevve (bevvette), bevemmo, beveste, bevvero (bevettero)

	Future:	berrò, berrai, berrà, berremo, berrete, berranno
	Imperative:	—— bevi, beva, beviamo, bevete, bevano
	Present Conditional:	berrei, berresti, berrebbe, berremmo, berreste, berrebbero
	Present Subjunctive:	beva, beva, beva, beviamo, beviate, bevano
	Imperfect Subjunctive:	bevessi, bevessi, bevesse, bevessimo, beveste, bevessero
	Gerund:	bevendo
cadere to fall	Past Absolute:	caddi, cadesti, cadde, cademmo, cadeste, caddero
	Future:	cadrò, cadrai, cadrà, cadremo, cadrete, cadranno
	Present Conditional:	cadrei, cadresti, cadrebbe, cadremmo, cadreste, cadrebbero
	(Conjugated the same way: *accadere*/to happen)	
chiedere to ask	Past Participle:	chiesto
	Past Absolute:	chiesi, chiedesti, chiese, chiedemmo, chiedeste, chiesero
chiudere to close	Past Participle:	chiuso
	Past Absolute:	chiusi, chiudesti, chiuse, chiudemmo, chiudeste, chiusero
conoscere to know, be acquainted with (people, places)	Past Absolute:	conobbi, conoscesti, conobbe, conoscemmo, conosceste, conobbero
dare to give	Present Indicative:	do, dai, dà, diamo, date, danno
	Past Participle:	dato
	Imperfect:	davo, davi, dava, davamo, davate, davano
	Past Absolute:	diedi, desti, diede, demmo, deste, diedero
	Future:	darò, darai, darà, daremo, darete, daranno
	Imperative:	—— da', dia, diamo, date, diano
	Present Conditional:	darei, daresti, darebbe, daremmo, dareste, darebbero
	Present Subjunctive:	dia, dia, dia, diamo, diate, diano
	Imperfect Subjunctive:	dessi, dessi, desse, dessimo, deste, dessero
	Gerund:	dando

dire **to say (tell)**	Present Indicative:	dico, dici, dice, diciamo, dite, dicono
	Past Participle:	detto
	Imperfect:	dicevo, dicevi, diceva, dicevamo, dicevate, dicevano
	Past Absolute:	dissi, dicesti, disse, dicemmo, diceste, dissero
	Future:	dirò, dirai, dirà, diremo, direte, diranno
	Imperative:	—— di', dica, diciamo, dite, dicano
	Present Conditional:	direi, diresti, direbbe, diremmo, direste, direbbero
	Present Subjunctive:	dica, dica, dica, diciamo, diciate, dicano
	Imperfect Subjunctive:	dicessi, dicessi, dicesse, dicessimo, diceste, dicessero
	Gerund:	dicendo
dovere **to have to**	Present Indicative:	devo, devi, deve, dobbiamo, dovete, devono
	Future:	dovrò, dovrai, dovrà, dovremo, dovrete, dovranno
	Present Conditional:	dovrei, dovresti, dovrebbe, dovremmo, dovreste, dovrebbero
	Present Subjunctive:	deva (debba), deva (debba), deva (debba), dobbiamo, dobbiate, devano (debbano)
essere **to be**	Present Indicative:	sono, sei, è, siamo, siete, sono
	Past Participle:	stato
	Imperfect:	ero, eri, era, eravamo, eravate, erano
	Past Absolute:	fui, fosti, fu, fummo, foste, furono
	Future:	sarò, sarai, sarà, saremo, sarete, saranno
	Imperative:	—— sii, sia, siamo, siate, siano
	Present Conditional:	sarei, saresti, sarebbe, saremmo, sareste, sarebbero
	Present Subjunctive:	sia, sia, sia, siamo, siate, siano
	Imperfect Subjunctive:	fossi, fossi, fosse, fossimo, foste, fossero
fare **to do; to make**	Present Indicative:	faccio, fai, fa, facciamo, fate, fanno
	Past Participle:	fatto
	Imperfect:	facevo, facevi, faceva, facevamo, facevate, facevano
	Past Absolute:	feci, facesti, fece, facemmo, faceste, fecero

	Future:	farò, farai, farà, faremo, farete, faranno
	Imperative:	—— fa', faccia, facciamo, fate, facciano
	Present Conditional:	farei, faresti, farebbe, faremmo, fareste, farebbero
	Present Subjunctive:	faccia, faccia, facciamo, facciate, facciano
	Imperfect Subjunctive:	facessi, facessi, facesse, facessimo, faceste, facessero
	Gerund:	facendo

leggere to read	Past Participle:	letto
	Past Absolute	lessi, leggesti, lesse, leggemmo, leggeste, lessero

mettere to put	Past Participle:	messo
	Past Absolute:	misi, mettesti, mise, mettemmo, metteste, misero

(Conjugated the same way: *ammettere*/to admit, *commettere*/to commit, *omettere*/to omit, *permettere*/to permit, *promettere*/to promise)

nascere to be born	Past Participle:	nato
	Past Absolute:	nacqui, nascesti, nacque, nascemmo, nasceste, nacquero

piacere to like (to be pleasing to)	Present Indicative:	piaccio, piaci, piace, piacciamo, piacete, piacciono
	Past Absolute:	piacqui, piacesti, piacque, piacemmo, piaceste, piacquero
	Present Subjunctive:	piaccia, piaccia, piaccia, piacciamo, piacciate, piacciano

potere to be able to	Present Indicative:	posso, puoi, può, possiamo, potete, possono
	Future:	potrò, potrai, potrà, potremo, potrete, potranno
	Present Conditional:	potrei, potresti, potrebbe, potremmo, potreste, potrebbero
	Present Subjunctive:	possa, possa, possa, possiamo, possiate, possano

prendere to take	Past Participle:	preso
	Past Absolute:	presi, prendesti, prese, prendemmo, prendeste, presero

(Conjugated the same way: *comprendere*/to comprehend, *sorprendere*/to surprise)

salire to go up, climb	Present Indicative:	salgo, sali, sale, saliamo, salite, salgono
	Imperative:	—— sali, salga, saliamo, salite, salgano
	Present Subjunctive:	salga, salga, salga, saliamo, saliate, salgano

sapere to know	Present Indicative:	so, sai, sa, sappiamo, sapete, sanno
	Past Absolute:	seppi, sapesti, seppe, sapemmo, sapeste, seppero
	Future:	saprò, saprai, saprà, sapremo, saprete, sapranno
	Present Conditional:	saprei, sapresti, saprebbe, sapremmo, sapreste, saprebbero
	Present Subjunctive:	sappia, sappia, sappia, sappiamo, sappiate, sappiano

scegliere to choose, select	Present Indicative:	scelgo, scegli, sceglie, scegliamo, scegliete, scelgono
	Past Participle:	scelto
	Past Absolute:	scelsi, scegliesti, scelse, scegliemmo, sceglieste, scelsero
	Imperative:	—— scegli, scelga, scegliamo, scegliete, scelgano
	Present Subjunctive:	scelga, scelga, scelga, scegliamo, scegliate, scelgano

scendere to descend, go down	Past Participle:	sceso
	Past Absolute:	scesi, scendesti, scese, scendemmo, scendeste, scesero

scrivere to write	Past Participle:	scritto
	Past Absolute:	scrissi, scrivesti, scrisse, scrivemmo, scriveste, scrissero

(Conjugated the same way: *descrivere*/to describe, *prescrivere*/to prescribe)

stare to stay, remain	Present Indicative:	sto, stai, sta, stiamo, state, stanno
	Past Participle:	stato
	Imperfect:	stavo, stavi, stava, stavamo, stavate, stavano
	Past Absolute:	stetti, stesti, stette, stemmo, steste, stettero
	Future:	starò, starai, starà, staremo, starete, staranno

	Imperative:	——, sta', stia, stiamo, state, stiano
	Present Conditional:	starei, staresti, starebbe, staremmo, stareste, starebbero
	Present Subjunctive:	stia, stia, stia, stiamo, stiate, stiano
	Imperfect Subjunctive:	stessi, stessi, stesse, stessimo, steste, stessero

tenere to keep, to hold	Present Indicative:	tengo, tieni, tiene, teniamo, tenete, tengono
	Past Absolute:	tenni, tenesti, tenne, tenemmo, teneste, tennero
	Future:	terrò, terrai, terrà, terremo, terrete, terranno
	Imperative:	—— tieni, tenga, teniamo, tenete, tengano
	Present Conditional:	terrei, terresti, terrebbe, terremmo, terreste, terrebbero
	Present Subjunctive:	tenga, tenga, tenga, teniamo, tenete, tengano

(Conjugated the same way: *contenere*/to contain, *mantenere*/to support someone, *ritenere*/to retain)

uscire to go out	Present Indicative:	esco, esci, esce, usciamo, uscite, escono
	Imperative:	—— esci, esca, usciamo, uscite, escano
	Present Subjunctive:	esca, esca, esca, usciamo, usciate, escano

vedere to see	Past Participle:	visto (veduto)
	Past Absolute:	vidi, vedesti, vide, vedemmo, vedeste, videro
	Future:	vedrò, vedrai, vedrà, vedremo, vedrete, vedranno
	Present Conditional:	vedrei, vedresti, vedrebbe, vedremmo, vedreste, vedrebbero

venire to come	Present Indicative:	vengo, vieni, viene, veniamo, venite, vengono
	Past Participle:	venuto
	Past Absolute:	venni, venisti, venne, venimmo, veniste, vennero
	Future:	verrò, verrai, verrà, verremo, verrete, verranno
	Imperative:	—— vieni, venga, veniamo, venite, vengano

| | Present Conditional: | verrei, verresti, verrebbe, verremmo, verreste, verrebbero |
| | Present Subjunctive: | venga, venga, venga, veniamo, veniate, vengano |

volere to want	Present Indicative:	voglio, vuoi, vuole, vogliamo, volete, vogliono
	Past Absolute:	volli, volesti, volle, volemmo, voleste, vollero
	Future:	vorrò, vorrai, vorrà, vorremo, vorrete, vorranno
	Present Conditional:	vorrei, vorresti, vorrebbe, vorremmo, vorreste, vorrebbero
	Present Subjunctive:	voglia, voglia, voglia, vogliamo, vogliate, vogliano

LET'S REVIEW

The vocabulary used in the following exercises and activities is found throughout the Grammar Brush-Up section (including the irregular verbs listed in the Verb Charts).

Any new vocabulary needed for the exercises is defined as it is introduced.

The exercises and activities are numbered consecutively, even though they are divided up according to the chapters in the Grammar Brush-Up section.

Test Yourself

1.
ITALIAN SOUNDS AND SPELLING

> The hard *c* and hard *g* sounds represented by *c, ch, g,* and *gh* are missing from the following words. Put the correct letter(s) in each blank.

1. _____ ane ("dog"), _____ ravatta ("tie"), _____ ome ("how"), _____ ola ("throat"), _____ rande ("big"), spa _____etti ("spaghetti"), _____ iesa ("church"), _____iaccio ("ice")

> The soft *c* and soft *g* sounds represented by *c, ci, g,* and *gi* are missing from the following words. Put the correct letter(s) in each blank.

2. _____ ao ("hi, bye"), _____ orno ("day"), _____ ena ("dinner"), _____ iro ("turn"), _____ occolata ("chocolate"), _____ ente ("people"), _____ inema ("movies"), _____ acca ("jacket")

> The following words are misspelled. Correct them.

3. scerzo ("joke") _____ , schena ("scene") _____ , scopero ("labor strike") _____ , anno ("they have") _____ , filio ("son") _____ , songo ("dream") _____ , palla ("shovel") _____ , sono ("sleep") _____ , fato ("fact") _ _ , carro ("dear") _____ .

> Some of the words in the following sentences need accent marks. Add them where appropriate.

4. Oggi e lunedi, non venerdi.
5. Che ora e? E l'una e dieci.
6. Non prendo mai il caffe, perche preferisco il te.

> The following sentences are written without capital letters. Capitalize the appropriate words according to Italian spelling conventions.

7. a primavera fa sempre fresco in italia; ma verso luglio comincia a fare più caldo. _____

8. mercoledì ho conosciuto una persona che veniva dalla spagna, ma che non parlava lo spagnolo. _____

9. la dottoressa martini è italiana, e parla molto bene l'inglese.
_____

10. questo sabato vengo anche io alla festa di san pietro. __
_____

2. SUMMARIES OF WORD ORDER IN AN ITALIAN SENTENCE

> Rearrange each set of words below to form complete sentences.

11. studiano/quegli/troppo/studenti
_____

12. troppa/Giovanni/macchina/di/la/consuma/benzina
_____

13. dice/l'/importante/lingua/una/è/che/professoressa/la/italiano
_____

> Here are four object noun phrases:
>
> | l'autobus | | la radio | | ai suoi studenti | | il pianoforte |
>
> Put them into the blanks. They must, of course, fit "grammatically," completing the thought of each sentence.

14. Ieri sera, la professoressa Martini ha telefonato _____.
15. Ogni sera, Tina ascolta _____.
16. Domani aspetterò _____ davanti a ("in front of") casa tua.
17. Mia sorella suona _____ molto bene.

Answer the following two questions in the negative.

18. Studia l'italiano, tuo fratello?
    No, mio _____

19. Mangi il pane, tu?
    No, io _____

Match each one-word (abbreviated) answer to its question.

20. **Answers**
    - Sì, è vero.
    - Maria.
    - Bene.
    - Al cinema.
    - Ieri.

    Questions
    - Chi aspetta l'autobus?
    - Quando sono andati al cinema?
    - Dove sono andati i tuoi amici?
    - È italiano quell'uomo, vero?
    - Come va, signora?

To the left you will find four main clauses in no particular order. To the right you will find four relative/temporal clauses, also in no particular order. Combine them to make four complex sentences.

21. *Main Clauses*

    | Quella ragazza è mia sorella |
    | È arrivato il professore |
    | Tu dormivi |
    | È necessario |

    Relative/Temporal Clauses

    | che tu dica la verità |
    | mentre io guardavo la TV |
    | appena sei andata via |
    | che legge il giornale |

    Quella ragazza _____ è mia sorella.
    È arrivato il professore, _____.
    Tu dormivi, _____.
    È necessario _____.

The following five sentences make up a story, but they are not in order. Put them in their logical order so as to tell the story correctly.

22. Durante il film hanno comprato il caffè e diverse paste.
    (*durante*/"during," *diverse*/"different," *paste*/"pastries")

Giovanni e Maria sono amici.
Hanno visto un "western" con Clint Eastwood.
Appena è finito il film, sono andati a prendere un gelato.
Ieri sono andati al cinema insieme.

_____ .
_____ .
_____ .
_____ .
_____ .

3.
BASIC
VOCABULARY

Can you find 10 words in the following word-search puzzle which relates to either family members, the body, languages, colors, food, and travel?

23.

g	e	m	e	l	l	o	n	m	o	l	o	e	g
u	b	n	m	e	d	c	t	u	i	o	p	l	r
a	n	m	e	a	u	i	p	z	c	n	m	m	e
n	o	l	p	o	i	u	t	u	r	e	s	c	c
c	i	n	e	s	e	l	p	o	m	e	n	t	o
i	e	g	h	i	l	o	u	i	o	p	c	d	c
a	r	a	n	c	i	o	n	e	d	v	d	c	d
c	c	d	d	e	e	u	i	l	o	o	r	o	e
e	r	c	d	n	c	d	c	d	l	c	d	e
r	t	u	i	a	l	b	e	r	g	o	b	u	i

4.
NOUNS

In the following sentences, the endings of all the nouns have been removed. Can you replace them? The nouns are all singular.

24. In quella citt _____ c'è tanta gent __ __ .
25. Carl _____ , il ragazz _____ che abita qui vicino, oggi non va a scuol _____ .
26. Il padr _____ e la madr _____ di Carl _____ , la ragazz _____ ("girlfriend") di mio fratell _____ , abitano in Itali _____ .
27. La per _____ viene dal per _____ , la mel _____ dal mel _____ , e la pesc _____ dal pesc _____ .

> Give the equivalent feminine nouns for each of the following masculine nouns.

EXAMPLE: *ragazzo ragazza*

28. zio _____ , figlio _____ , cantante _____ , infermiere _____ , cameriere _____ , pittore _____ , attore _____ , dottore _____ , avvocato _____ .

> In the following word-search puzzle there are four nouns ending in *-ista*. Can you find them?

29.

d	e	n	t	i	s	t	a	f	i	s	t
s	d	f	t	u	i	s	t	a	i	s	t
s	t	a	v	i	r	s	y	t	s	t	a
p	i	v	i	o	l	i	n	i	s	t	a
i	o	l	o	i	s	t	s	i	s	t	a
s	u	i	l	i	s	t	a	t	i	s	t
i	s	p	i	a	n	i	s	t	a	i	s

> The answers to the following crossword puzzle are either: (1) nouns ending in an accented vowel; (2) borrowed nouns; (3) nouns ending in *-ema/-amma*; (4) nouns ending in *-si*.

30.

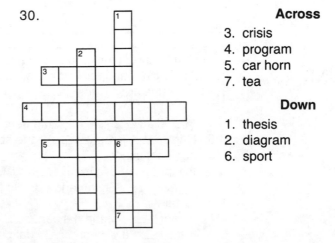

Across

3. crisis
4. program
5. car horn
7. tea

Down

1. thesis
2. diagram
6. sport

Put the following nouns in the plural.

EXAMPLE: *ragazzo/ragazzi*

31. giorno _____ , aeroporto _____ , cameriere _____ , notte
    _____ , mela _____ , avvocatessa _____ , problema
    _____ , programma _____ , citt _____ , computer _____ ,
    ipotesi _____

Now put the following in the plural.

32. il tedesco, i tedes _____
    la tedesca, le tedes _____
    l'amico, gli ami _____
    l'amica, le ami _____
    il medico, i medi _____
    l'albergo, gli alber _____
    lo psicologo, gli psicolo _____
    la psicologa, le psicolo _____
    il dialogo, i dialo _____
    la paga, le pa _____
    la farmacia, le farmac _____
    l'orologio, gli orolo _____
    l'arancia, le aran _____

Try one more pluralization exercise!

33. il figlio, i _____
    la figlia, le _____
    il labbro, le _____
    il miglio, le _____
    il cinema, i _____
    l'uomo, gli _____
    la mano, le _____

Add the name "Rossi" to each of the following titles,
making any appropriate changes if necessary.

EXAMPLE: *il professore*/il professor Rossi

34. il signore _____
    la signora _____
    il dottore _____
    la dottoressa _____
    l'avvocato _____

> The following scrambled words are compound nouns.
> Unscramble them.

35. tenegslava _____
    etiviccaca _____
    rrofeiav _____
    aaoecssfrt _____
    arocbanelo _____

5.
ARTICLES

> Supply the correct definite article for the following
> singular nouns (or adjectives).

EXAMPLE: _____ *ragazzo/il ragazzo*

36. _____ casa, _____ acqua, _____ vino, _____ indirizzo, _____
    piatto, _____ frutta, _____ matita, _____ prezzo, _____
    scuola, _____ scena, _____ specchio, _____ sbaglio, _____
    sogno, _____ zingaro, _____ zio, _____ studente, _____
    altro zio, _____ nuovo studente, _____ altra ragazza, _____
    psicologo, _____ gnocco

> Now supply the definite article for the following plural
> nouns (or adjectives).

EXAMPLE: _____ *ragazzi/i ragazzi*

37. _____ case, _____ amiche, _____ vini, _____ indirizzi, _____
    piatti, _____ frutte, _____ matite, _____ prezzi, _____
    scuole, _____ zingari, _____ scene, _____ specchi, _____
    sbagli, _____ sogni, _____ zii, _____ studenti, _____ altri
    zii, _____ nuovi studenti, _____ altre ragazze, _____
    psicologi, _____ gnocchi

> Supply the indefinite article for the following nouns (or
> adjectives).

EXAMPLE: _____ *ragazzo/un ragazzo*

38. _____ amico, _____ amica, _____ padre, _____ madre,
    _____ italiano, _____ italiana, _____ orologio, _____
    entrata, _____ sorella, _____ zero, _____ zio, _____
    sbaglio, _____ altro studente, _____ gnocco, _____
    buon' amica, _____ psicologo, _____ bravo
    psicologo, _____ stanza

> Supply the correct form of the demonstrative meaning "this" for the following nouns (or adjectives).

EXAMPLE: _____ amico *quest' amico*

39. _____ giorno, _____ valigia, _____ nome, _____ giornale, _____ zio, _____ zia, _____ studente, _____ studentessa, _____ arancio, _____ arancia, _____ psicologo, _____ infermiere, _____ infermiera, _____ altro zio, _____ bravo studente

> Write the correct form of the demonstrative meaning "these" for the following nouns (or adjectives).

EXAMPLE: _____ amici *questi amici*

40. _____ giorni, _____ valige, _____ nomi, _____ giornali, __ zii, _____ zie, _____ studenti, _____ studentesse, _____ aranci, _____ arance, _____ psicologi, _____ infermieri, _____ infermiere, _____ altri zii, _____ bravi studenti

> Now write the correct form of the demonstrative meaning "that" for the following nouns (or adjectives).

EXAMPLE: _____ amico *quell'amico*

41. _____ giorno, _____ valigia, _____ nome, _____ giornale, _____ zio, _____ zia, _____ studente, _____ studentessa, _____ arancio, _____ arancia, _____ psicologo, _____ infermiere, _____ infermiera, _____ altro zio, _____bravo studente

> Now write the correct form of the demonstrative meaning "those" for the following nouns (or adjectives).

EXAMPLE: _____ amici *quegli amici*

42. _____ giorni, _____ valige, _____ nomi, _____ giornali, __ zii, _____ zie, _____ studenti, _____ studentesse, _____ aranci, _____ arance, _____ psicologi, _____ infermieri, _____ infermiere, _____ altri zii, _____ bravi studenti

> Put the following noun phrases in the plural.

EXAMPLE: *quel ragazzo quei ragazzi*

43. la dentista _____, il farmacista _____, lo sport _____, l'entrata _____, il problema _____, l'avvocato _____, questo turista _____, questo medico _____, quest'amica _____, questa farmacia _____, quel figlio _____ , quel bacio_____ , quello zio _____, quello specchio _____, quell'orologio _____ , quell'uscita _____, quella radio _____

> Put the correct form of the definite article, if necessary, in the blanks.

44. _____ pane è un cibo.
45. _____ americani sono simpatici.
46. _____ Roma è la capitale d'Italia.
47. _____ padre e _____ madre di Claudia abitano a Parigi.
48. _____ Italia è bella.
49. Mi fa male _____ dito.
50. _____ signora Binni è molto simpatica.
51. "Buon giorno, _____ signora Binni. Come va?"

6.
PARTITIVES

> Put the following noun phrases into the plural using *di* + the definite article.

EXAMPLE: *un libro dei libri*

52. una forchetta _____ , un bicchiere _____ , uno sbaglio _____ , uno gnocco _____ , un orologio _____ , un telegramma _____ , un'avvocatessa _____ , un'automobile _____ , una sedia _____

> Now put the same nouns into the plural using *alcuni/ alcune*.

53. una forchetta _____ , un bicchiere _____ , uno sbaglio _____ , uno gnocco _____ , un orologio _____ , un telegramma _____ , un'avvocatessa _____ , un'automobile _____ , una sedia _____

> Change each partitive expression to the type with *qualche*, making all necessary changes.

EXAMPLE: *dei libri qualche libro*

54. dei ragazzi _____ , alcune studentesse _____ , delle uscite _____ , dei violinisti _____ , delle violiniste _____ , alcuni problemi _____ , alcuni uomini _____ , delle mani _____

> Rewrite each sentence, replacing the partitive expression with *qualche*, making all necessary changes.

EXAMPLE: *Alcuni studenti non studiano. Qualche studente non studia.*

55. Alcuni italiani sono simpatici. _____
56. Alcune amiche di Paola abitano in Italia. _____
   _____
57. Alcuni amici di Claudio parlano il francese. _____
   _____

> Rewrite the following sentences in the negative by using the *non . . . nessuno* form of the partitive. Don't forget to make all necessary changes.

EXAMPLE: *Claudia compra delle penne. Claudia non compra nessuna penna.*

58. Voglio delle caramelle. _____
   _____
59. Conosco alcuni psicologi. _____
   _____
60. Ho fatto degli sbagli. _____

> Give an equivalent partitive expression.

EXAMPLE: *Mangio della carne. Mangio un po' di carne.*

61. Preferisco del pane. _____
62. Giovanni mangia un po' d'insalata. _____
63. Vogliamo un po' di acqua. _____
64. Lui vuole della carne ed io voglio un po' di caffè. _____
   _____

7. ADJECTIVES

> The adjectives *nero* (black), *verde* (green), *azzurro* (blue), *giallo* (yellow), *rosso* (red), *bianco* (white), *marrone* (brown) (invariable) are used in the following descriptive story, but their endings are missing. Supply them.

65. Maria ha un bel vestito azzurr _____ . Ieri è andata ad un negozio di abbigliamento ("clothing store") per fare alcune spese. Ha comprato un paio di scarpe ner _____, una camicetta ("blouse") verd _____ , e una sciarpa ("scarf") giall _____ . Poi, ha deciso di comprare i guanti marron _____ , un paio di pantaloni ("pants") bianch _____ , e due maglie ross _____ per suo marito. Per sua figlia ha poi comprato una maglia e una borsa verd_____ , e un cappotto e un impermeabile azzurr _____ .

> The following adjectives are already in their correct form, but now you must put them before or after the noun they modify, as the case may be.

66. (quanti) _____ libri _____ hai comprato ieri?
67. (elegante) Quello è veramente un _____ vestito _____.
68. (quale) _____ programma _____ preferisci alla TV?
69. (molto vecchia) La conosco da tanti anni! È una _____ amica ("acquaintance") _____ .

> Put the adjective *buono* in front of the noun, making all necessary changes.

EXAMPLE: *Lei è un'amica buona. Lei è una buon'amica.*

70. Quello è un libro buono. _____
71. Quella è una rivista buona. _____
72. Ho bisogno di un'auto buona. _____

> Now do the same thing with the adjective *bello*.

EXAMPLE: *Sono dei libri belli. Sono dei bei libri.*

73. Mario ha comprato degli orologi belli. _____
74. Maria è veramente una donna bella. _____
75. Mia sorella vuole un'auto bella. _____
76. Giovanni ha delle amiche belle. _____

> Put the proper form of *santo* in front of the following saints' names.

EXAMPLE: _____ Anna *Sant'Anna*

77. _____ Maria, _____ Stefano, _____ Agostino, _____ Paolo, _____ Marco, _____ Agnese

> Using an interrogative adjective, formulate the appropriate question for each of the following.

EXAMPLE: *Ho comprato due libri./Quanti libri hai comprato?*

78. Preferisco quella macchina. _____ ?
79. È un libro interessante. _____ ?
80. Ho mangiato tre panini ("sandwiches"). _____ ?

> Provide the missing parts of the following possessive adjectives.

EXAMPLE: _____ su _____ penna *la sua penna*

81. _____ mi _____ libri, _____ mi _____ giacca, _____ mi _____ amiche, _____ mi _____ quaderno, _____ tu _____ vestito, _____ tu _____ scarpe, _____ tu _____ casa, _____ tu _____ impermeabili, _____ su _____ libro, _____ su _____ libri, _____ su _____ amica, _____ su _____ amiche, _____ nostr _____ dottore, _____ nostr _____ professori, _____ nostr _____ professoressa, _____ nostr _____ professoresse, _____ vostr _____ riviste, _____ vostr _____ amica, _____ vostr _____ sbaglio _____ vostr _____ sbagli, _____ lor _____ problema, _____ _____ lor _____ problemi, _____ lor _____ casa, _____ lor _____ case

> Make the following noun phrases singular. But be careful! There are many "traps" in this exercise.

EXAMPLE: *i nostri zii* *nostro zio*

82. i tuoi cugini _____ , le nostre zie _____ , le vostre cugine _____ , i loro fratelli _____ , le loro sorelle _____ , i suoi zii italiani _____ , le sue cugine americane _____ , i vostri papà _____

Can you figure out the following family relationships?

EXAMPLE: *È la madre di mio padre. È* <u>*mia nonna.*</u>

83. È il figlio di tuo zio. È _____
    È la sorella di nostra madre. È _____
    È il fratello di suo padre. È _____
    È il marito (husband) della loro madre. È _____

Here is a logic puzzle for you.

---

84. Un bambino risponde al telefono. "Pronto. Chi parla?"
    La voce (voice) di un uomo dice: "La madre di tua
    madre è mia suocera (mother-in-law)." Chi è l'uomo?

The following indefinite adjectives are missing from
the passage.
   assai, altre, molti, troppa, stesse, tutti
Put them in their appropriate slots.

---

85. _____ turisti vanno in Italia. Purtroppo, hanno bisogno
    di _____ denaro (money) per andare a vedere _____ i
    bei posti (places) di questo magnifico paese (country).
    Dappertutto (everywhere) c'è _____ gente. Tutti hanno
    le _____ idee. Vogliono vedere Roma, Venezia, Firenze,
    e Napoli. Ma ci sono tante _____ belle città!

Make an appropriate comparison.

EXAMPLE: *Maria è intelligente. Giovanni è meno intelligente.* <u>*Giovanni è meno intelligente di Maria.*</u> OR <u>*Maria è più intelligente di Giovanni.*</u>

86. Mio padre è elegante. Tuo padre è altrettanto elegante
    (as elegant) _____

    _____

87. Gino è simpatico. Mario è più simpatico. _____

    _____

88. Gino è simpatico, ma è più intelligente. _____

    _____

8.
PRONOUNS

Supply the corresponding pronoun for each noun phrase.

EXAMPLE: *Quel ragazzo è italiano.* *Quello è italiano.*

89. Questo negozio è caro. _____ è caro.
    Queste ragazze sono americane. _____ sono americane.
    Quest'orologio è nuovo. _____ è nuovo.
    Quest'auto è bella. _____ è bella.
    Quei francobolli ("stamps") sono belli. _____ sono belli.
    Quello zio abita in Italia. _____ abita in Italia.
    Quegli amici sono bravi. _____ sono bravi.
    Quelle forchette sono sporche. _____ sono sporche.
    Quel vino è molto buono. _____ è molto buono.

Do the same thing for the following.

EXAMPLE: *La sua macchina è bella.* *La sua è bella.*

90. Dove sono i tuoi guanti? Dove sono _____ ?
    Il loro impermeabile è verde. _____ è verde.
    Chi ha le mie scarpe? Chi ha _____ ?
    Nostra sorella abita in Italia. _____ abita in Italia.
    Suo zio è simpatico. _____ è simpatico.

Using interrogative pronouns, formulate the appropriate question for each of the following.

EXAMPLE: *Leggo un libro.* *Che cosa leggi?*

91. Giovanni abita a Roma. _____ ?
92. Questo portafoglio è di Bruno. _____ ?
93. Mi chiamo Giuseppe Perri. _____ ?
94. Abito in via Dante, 24. _____ ?
95. Sono andato in Italia l'anno scorso. _____ ?
96. Mangio i dolci perché mi piacciono. _____ ?

Supply the appropriate subject personal pronouns. These are needed in the passage in order to distinguish all the different persons involved.

97. L'altro giorno, _____ sono andato al cinema con mia sorella, e _____ ha portato con sé un libro da leggere! Quando _____ due siamo arrivati, abbiamo visto due amici nostri. Anche _____ erano venuti al cinema.

"Gianni, Maria, siete proprio _____ ?" ha chiesto mia sorella. "Certo che siamo _____ !" ha risposto Maria. "_____ sono qui per Gianni, e _____ ?" Maria ha chiesto a mia sorella. "Purtroppo anche _____ sono qui per mio fratello!" ha risposto mia sorella.

Replace each of the object pronouns with equivalent ones, rewriting each sentence and making all necessary changes.

EXAMPLE: *Lui dà la penna a me. Lui mi dà la penna.*

98. Giovanni telefonerà a loro domani. _____
99. Penso spesso a te. _____
100. Maria ha chiamato me. _____
101. Chiamerò lui domani. _____
102. Tu telefonerai a lui. _____
103. Maria chiamerà lei. _____
104. E poi telefonerà a lei. _____
105. Maria ha visto noi ieri. _____
106. Il professore parlerà a voi. _____

Now replace each object noun phrase with *lo, la, li, le,* or *gli* as the case may be. Rewrite each sentence, making all necessary changes.

EXAMPLE: *Giovanni ha comprato quelle penne. Giovanni le ha comprate.*

107. Ha già dato *la penna* a quel ragazzo. _____
Ha già dato la penna *a quella ragazza.* _____
Ieri abbiamo mangiato *il pollo.* _____
Ieri abbiamo telefonato *a quel ragazzo.* _____
Giovanni mi ha dato *le sue chiavi.* _____
Mio padre gli ha mandato *i suoi libri.* _____
Il commesso ci ha detto *la verità.* _____
No, non ho dato le mie scarpe *a tua sorella.* _____
Sì, ha mandato *quella lettera al tuo amico.* _____

Use object pronouns to answer each question.

EXAMPLE: *Hai dato la penna a Maria? Sì gliel'ho data.*

108. Mi hai chiamato ieri? Sì, _____
109. Ti hanno telefonato? No, _____

110. Hai ricevuto la lettera? Sì, _____
111. Mi darai il tuo indirizzo? No, _____
112. Ci scriverai una lettera? Sì, _____

Rearrange each set of words below to form complete sentences.

---

113. scritte / gliele / già / ho _____
114. le / mando / ve / domani _____
115. te / dati / li / ieri / ho _____

The relative pronouns are missing from the following passage. Can you supply them?

---

116. Il vestito _____ ho comprato ieri costa poco. Il commesso, dal _____ l'ho comprato, era molto simpatico. Mi ha spiegato ("explained") _____ il verde era il colore d'ultimo grido ("in the latest fashion"). "Questo vestito è per mia figlia, a _____ lo darò domani per il suo compleanno ("birthday"). _____ mi piace in modo particolare è la sua lunghezza ("length")."

The pronouns *ne, ci* (there), and *si* (one) (impersonal form) are missing from the following sentences. Put them in the appropriate slot.

---

117. Non _____ dicono queste cose!
118. Quanta _____ hai mangiata?
119. _____ andremo fra due mesi.
120. Non _____ è mai contenti!
121. _____ sono andati, e poi _____ sono tornati.

9. VERBS

Each one of the following sentences requires that the verb (given to you in its infinitive form) be put into one of the seven indicative tenses. There is enough information in each sentence for you to figure out which tense is appropriate.

EXAMPLE: *Fra una settimana, noi* <u>*andare*</u> *in Italia.* Ans: *andremo*

122. Tu _____ (*uscire*) già, quando sono arrivato io. Che cosa _____ (*comprare*) tu ieri?

Quando ero bambino, i miei genitori _____ (*andare*) spesso in Italia per riposarsi ("to relax").

Dopo che gli ospiti (guests) _____ (*mangiare*) gli spaghetti, allora servirò la carne.

Quanto costa la tua borsa? Non sono sicura. _____ (*costare*) 100.000 lire.

Appena finimmo di lavorare, noi _____ (*cominciare*) a giocare a tennis.

Lo _____ (*pagare*) tu il conto, o lo pago io?

The following exercise is almost the same. This time, however, you must choose the correct verb and then put it in the appropriate indicative tense.

VERBS: cominciare, mangiare, finire, capire, arrivare, scrivere, mettere

123. Anche tu _____ l'insalata? Io l'ho già mangiata. Io _____ a leggere, appena sarà finito quel programma alla TV.

I nostri amici _____ dall'Italia pochi minuti fa.

Quando ha finito? Non sono sicuro. _____ alcune ore fa.

Giovanni non _____ la domanda, perché non la sentì (because he didn't hear it).

Mentre lei _____ una lettera, io dormivo.

Giovanni, dove _____ quella forchetta?

Here's an easy one. Match up the pronouns and verbs.

124.
Pronouns	Verbs
io	finiscono la lezione
tu	è uscita
lui	paghiamo il conto
lei	parlate troppo
noi	non aspetto
voi	è uscito
loro	capisci

Choose the appropriate imperative form.

---

125. Signor Santini, { lo prenda! ☐
{ prendilo! ☐

Marco, { la scriva! ☐
{ scrivila! ☐

Signorina, { me li dia! ☐
{ dammeli! ☐

Gino, { non parli! ☐
{ non parlare! ☐

Ragazzi, { ci andate! ☐
{ andateci! ☐

Now it's time for the conditional tenses. Put each verb
in the present or past conditional, as the case may be.

EXAMPLE: *Anche noi ci saremmo andati (andare), ma non avevamo tempo.*

126. (Io) ti _____ (*scrivere*) volentieri, ma non ho tempo.
(Io) ti _____ (*scrivere*) volentieri, ma non ho avuto
tempo.
Giovanni _____ (*mangiare*) tutto, ma purtroppo non
aveva tempo.
Anche in questo momento ha appetito, e lui _____
(*mangiare*) tutto.

Here's a simple exercise. Choose one of the two verbs
provided. One is in the indicative and the other in the
subjunctive, but only one of the two fits in each
sentence.

127. Maria dice che il { arriverà ☐
professore { arrivi ☐ tra due minuti.

Maria spera che il professore { finisce ☐
{ finisca ☐ presto.

Sebbene { ha piovuto ☐ ieri, sono uscita lo
{ abbia piovuto ☐ stesso.

Se { lavorerai ☐ fino a tardi, non potremo andare al
{ lavorassi ☐ cinema.

Se quella donna { potrà ☐
{ potesse ☐ , ti telefonerebbe.

Era la persona più { avevamo conosciuto ☐ in
simpatica che noi { avessimo conosciuto ☐ Italia.

Supply the missing parts of the following reflexive verbs.

128. Ieri ci _____ divertiti molto in centro (downtown).
A che ora _____ alzi tu ogni mattina?
La dottoressa Visconti non _____ ricorda il nostro indirizzo.
Anche voi ragazze, vi siete divertit _____ , no?
No, non me la sono lavat _____ !
Giovanni, alza _____ subito!
Signora, _____ metta questo cappotto!

Here is Giovanni's love letter to Elena. Since Giovannia does not like to study his verbs, he has left out their endings, or some other parts. Can you complete the verbs?

129. Mia cara Elena,

non ti scriv _____ da tanto tempo, perché _____ stato molto occupato ("busy"). Ieri, benché la giornata _____ stata terribile, sono uscito a compr _____ un regalo. Mentre _____ guardando le vetrine ("store windows"), è venut _____ un uomo vicino a me. Vol _____ parlare, ma io non av _____ tempo. Ma lui _____ cominciato a parlare lo stesso. Mi _____ parlato per un'ora. Io speravo che and _____ via. Finalmente, dopo aver parl _____ a lungo (for a long time), decise di and _____ via.

Quando sar _____ insieme ti dar _____ il regalo. Ti am _____ .

Tuo,

Giovannaccio!

Here's a chance for you to review those irregular verbs, which you can find in the "Verb Charts" section of this book. Each of the following verbs has an irregular past participle hidden in the word-search puzzle. Can you find them?

bere, chiedere, chiudere, dire, essere, fare, leggere, mettere, nascere, prendere, scegliere, scrivere

130.

t	u	i	u	h	n	b	e	v	u	t	o	c	i	o
d	c	l	e	t	t	o	m	e	s	s	o	h	s	n
e	p	h	p	r	e	s	o	d	e	c	t	i	u	a
t	r	r	i	f	t	u	t	i	o	r	t	e	o	t
t	e	i	h	u	u	i	t	b	m	i	n	s	p	o
o	s	g	h	t	s	o	a	h	u	t	k	t	t	o
e	s	t	a	t	o	o	f	o	o	t	o	o	t	o
c	h	i	e	d	s	c	e	l	t	o	d	i	t	t

Change the following sentences into their passive form.

131. Giovanni ha mangiato la torta.
I turisti compreranno molti regali.
Tutti leggono quel libro.
Credo che Sofia Loren abbia interpretato (interpreted) quel film.

10. ADVERBS

Change the following adjectives into adverbs of manner.

EXAMPLE: *lento lentamente*

132. raro _____ , certo _____ , preciso _____ , vero _____ , nuovo _____

Now do the same with these.

EXAMPLE: *facile facilmente*

133. elegante _____ , felice _____ , regolare _____ , difficile _____ , popolare _____ , benevolo _____ , leggero _____

Put each of the following adverbs in the blanks according to the context.

ancora, invece, già, poi, quasi, spesso

134. Sono _____ partiti per l'Italia.
135. So che tu preferisci quella camicia, ma io, _____ , preferisco questa.
136. Non è _____ l'ora di andare a casa.
137. Prima devo studiare, e _____ posso guardare la TV.
138. Noi andiamo _____ al cinema. Infatti, ci andiamo _____ ogni settimana.

> *Molto* is both an adverb and an adjective. Supply the appropriate form of this word.

139. Ieri avevo _____ fame. Allora ho mangiato _____ . Gli spaghetti erano _____ buoni. Anche la carne era _____ _____ buona. A tavola c'erano _____ persone. Tutti hanno mangiato _____ verdure e _____ carne.

> Now add either *migliore* or *meglio*.

140. Quello è un vino _____ .
141. Il mio orologio funziona _____ del tuo.
142. È la _____ cosa che tu abbia potuto fare.
143. Oggi sto _____ (I feel better) di ieri.

11. PREPOSITIONS

> Put *a, di, da, su,* or *in* in the appropriate blanks according to the meaning. Don't forget contractions!

EXAMPLE: Questo è il libro <u>di</u> + <u>il</u> = <u>del</u> professore
(*di* + *il* = *del*) _____ + *il* = _____

144. Ho messo la chiave _____ + *il* = _____ cassetto.
    Il libro è _____ + *il* = _____ tavolo.
    Ieri ho scritto _____ + *gli* = _____ zii di Pina.
    È l'indirizzo _____ + *lo* = _____ studente.
    Sono venuto _____ + *l'* = _____ Italia una settimana fa.
    C'è una caramella _____ + *la* = _____ scatola.

> Put the following sentences in the plural.

145. È il libro dell'amico di Carla. _____
146. Ieri sono andata al negozio di abbigliamento. _____ _____
147. È nello zaino (knapsack). _____
148. Dall'uscita potrai vedere la macchina. _____ _____
149. Ho dato la tua matita alla ragazza. _____

> Put each of the following prepositions in the blanks according to the context.

a, in, da, tra, per

150. Abito in questa città _____ tre anni. Spero, _____ due anni, di andare _____ Francia _____ studiare il francese. Vorrei andare _____ Parigi (Paris).

12.
NEGATIVES AND OTHER GRAMMAT-ICAL POINTS

The negatives in the following sentences are scrambled up. Can you unscramble them?

151. I miei parenti non scrivono "ami" _____ .
Non conosciamo "esnsnou" _____ in quella città.
Alla nostra festa non è venuto "eannhce" _____ Gino.
Non capisco "én" _____ i pronomi "én" _____ i verbi.
Ti prometto (I promise you) che non lo faccio "ipù" _____ .
Sono andato in quel negozio, ma non ho comprato "ieennt" _____ .
Quello che tu dici non è "icma" _____ vero.

Put *è, sono, c'è, ci sono,* or *ecco* in the blanks, as the case may be.

152. Dov'è il mio cappotto? _____ il tuo cappotto!
153. L'ho messo nel cassetto, ma ora non _____ più.
154. Qual _____ il tuo programma preferito?
155. Dove _____ i tuoi libri? In questa stanza non _____ .

Rearrange each set of words below to form a complete sentence. Here is a clue to help you: each sentence contains the "causative" construction.

156. cartolina / zii / fatto / scrivere / ha / agli / madre / la / una

_____

_____

157. comprare / gliela / farò _____
158. suo / a / fratello / Maria / lavare / non / fatto / ha / piatti / i _____

_____

13.
THE VERB
PIACERE

Giovanni has been studying Italian and understands it well. However, he is a little shy about speaking it. In the following dialogue with Maria — who speaks and understands English — Giovanni uses only English because he is afraid to use the verb "piacere." Can you help him out by translating what he says into Italian?

Maria: Ciao, Giovanni. Vedo che vai a lezione (to class). Ti piace il corso d'italiano?

159. *Giovanni*: Yes, I like it very much. _____.
Maria: Ti piace la professoressa?

160. *Giovanni*: Yes, I like her and she likes me. _____
_____ .

Maria: E gli altri studenti?
161. *Giovanni*: I like them, but they do not like me. _____
_____ .

Maria: E io so perché. Tu sei antipatico! Ti è piaciuta la lezione di ieri?
162. *Giovanni*: No, I didn't like it, and the others didn't like it.

_____ .

Maria: E io ti piaccio?
163. *Giovanni*: Yes, I like you. Do you like me? Do we like each other, really? _____ .
Maria: Certamente. Andiamo. La lezione sta per cominciare.

Put either *piace* or *piacciono* in the blanks, as the case may be.

---

164. Sì, mi _____ la tua cravatta, ma non mi _____ i tuoi pantaloni.
165. Ci _____ i tortellini, ma purtroppo non ci _____ il sugo ("sauce").
166. Ti _____ la minestra? A me non _____ , ma mi _____ i ravioli.
167. A lui _____ l'italiano, a me _____ gli sport, a te _____ il cinema, a tutti noi non _____ le barzellette ("jokes").

14. IDIOMATIC EXPRES- SIONS

Give the Italian of the English words in italics.

---

168. Giovanni ed io *are hungry and thirsty* _____.
169. D'estate loro *are always hot* _____ , ma d'inverno *they are always cold* _____.
170. Signora, Lei *are right* _____ ; io, invece, *am wrong* ___.
171. Giovanni, non devi *be ashamed* _____ , e non devi *be afraid*. Vedrai che tutto andrà bene.
172. *I feel like* _____ di andare ad un ristorante stasera.
173. *We need* _____ due cose quando andremo in centro.

Insert *fare, dare,* or *stare* in the right tense and mood, as the case may be.

Commesso: Buongiorno, signora. Desidera?

174. *Signora*: Buongiorno, voglio _____ il biglietto per il treno che parte per Roma tra un'ora.

175. *Commesso*: Va bene. Ma ＿＿ retta a ma! C'è un treno che ＿＿ per partire in questo momento.
176. *Signora*: Per me va bene anche quello. ＿＿ pure il biglietto. Le posso ＿＿ una domanda? Lei si ＿＿ la barba alla mattina?
177. *Commesso*: Lei è impertinente! Farmi la barba, non ＿ per me. Perché mi ＿＿ questa domanda? Le ＿＿ fastidio.
    Signora: No, anzi, a me piacciono gli uomini con la barba!

The following crossword puzzle contains only parts of the expressions defined in the clues. Can you complete it?

178.

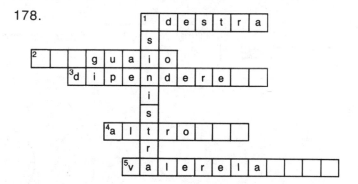

Across
1. to the right
2. What a mess
3. to depend on
4. I'll say!
5. to be worthwhile

Down
1. to the left

15. NUMBERS

Write out each number in words.

---

179. 7 ＿＿ , 9 ＿＿ , 11 ＿＿ , 21 ＿＿ , 42 ＿＿ , 58 ＿＿ , 88 ＿＿ , 123 ＿＿ , 987 ＿＿ , 1.345 ＿＿ , 76.980 ＿＿ , 888.888 ＿＿ , 2.345.678 ＿＿ .

Now do the same for the following ordinal numbers.

---

180. 4th ＿＿ ragazza, 16th ＿＿ lezioni, 23rd ＿＿ sbaglio, 248th ＿＿ giorno, 4,578th ＿＿ pagina

> Now write the following fractions in words.

181. ⅔ _____ , ¹/₂₈ _____ , ¾ _____ , ¹⁵/₁₆ _____ , ³⁴/₈₉ _____

> Are you a math whiz? Try the following.

182. Maria ha due anni più di Gina. Gina ha tre anni meno di Claudia, la quale ha otto anni. Quanti anni ha Maria?

Marco e Gino insieme hanno ventidue anni. Gino ha due anni più di Marco. Quanti anni ha ogni ragazzo?

Giovanni è più alto di Stefano. Stefano è meno alto di Claudio. Chi è il più basso?

16.
TELLING TIME

> Write out the time indicated on each watch. Use the twenty-four-hour-clock, or official time.

183. Che ora è?

17.
DAYS,
MONTHS,
SEASONS,
DATES, AND
THE
WEATHER

Can you find the days of the week hidden in the word-search puzzle?

184.

b	ì	s	t	g	i	o	v	e	d	ì
q	r	y	p	m	e	l	e	w	c	k
a	x	v	o	n	i	z	n	u	d	y
p	n	m	a	b	o	v	e	n	l	r
t	h	a	s	o	l	k	r	t	l	o
m	e	r	c	o	l	e	d	ì	s	a
x	c	t	e	j	u	g	ì	h	a	r
v	w	e	t	o	n	i	k	a	b	l
j	u	d	o	m	e	n	i	c	a	x
p	h	ì	r	e	d	a	s	o	t	g
z	k	a	y	n	ì	n	o	b	o	r

Here are the months of the year all scrambled up. Can you unscramble them?

185. berttoo _____

uoilgl _____

toogsa _____

erbemidc _____

ttseeermb _____

erbmevno _____

oiaegnn _____

uiggon _____

oaibbref _____

ggmmioa _____

leirpa _____

ozrma _____

Fill in the blanks with the appropriate words.

186. La _____ è la prima stagione dell'anno.

Durante l' _____ andiamo sempre a sciare ("to ski").

La settimana _____ sono andato in Italia.

Il mese _____ andremo a Roma.

Tre giorni _____ ho incontrato ("I met") Claudia.

Ciao. _____ domani!

Maria found Giovanni's diary, which she is just dying to read. Everything is written in Italian except the dates. Can you translate them for her?

187. Monday, May 12: "Amo Maria!" _____

Tuesday, January 25: "Amo ancora Maria!" _____

Wednesday, February 1: "Non amo più Maria!" _____
Saturday, December 3: "Amo Claudia!" _____

Match each of the following expressions with the drawings.

EXPRESSIONS: tuona e lampeggia, tira vento, fa molto caldo, fa freddo, fa bel tempo, piove

188.

_____ _____ _____

_____ _____ _____

18.
COMMON
DISCOURSE
STRATEGIES

Fill in the missing parts of the following dialogue.

---

189. *il signor Marchi*: Buon giorno, signora. _____?
la signora Celli: Non _____ , grazie, e _____?
il signor Marchi: Molto bene. Dove va?
la signora Celli: Vado in biblioteca, e ho molto fretta. ArrivederLa.
il signor Marchi: B _____.

Now do the same for the following dialogue.

---

190. *Lucia*: Pronto. ____ parla?
    Gino: Ciao, Lucia. ____ Gino. ____ tua sorella?
    Lucia: No. È uscita per fare delle spese. Hai bisogno di qualcosa?
    Gino: No, grazie. Telefono più tardi. Ciao.
    Lucia: A _____ .

Here's one more for you to do!

---

191. *il professore*: Buona sera, signorina.
    la signorina: ____ , professore.
    il professore: ____ ____ chiama?
    la signorina: Mi ____ Daniela Berti. Professore, permette che ____ presenti un'altra studentessa. ____ presento Dina Armando.
    il professore: ____ di fare la Sua ____ .
    Dina: Grazie, professore.

Check off the appropriate expression for each of the following.

---

192. You're bored. You might say:
    Non importa   ☐
    Che noia!   ☐
    Fa lo stesso.   ☐
193. You might want to tell someone that you are sorry. You might say:
    Mi dispiace.   ☐
    Che triste!   ☐
    Pazienza!   ☐
194. You want to say that you do not agree. You might say:
    D'accordo.   ☐
    Non va bene.   ☐
    Non sono d'accordo.   ☐
195. How would you say: "How come?"
    Davvero?   ☐
    Come?   ☐
    Scherzi?   ☐

19.
SYNONYMS
AND
ANTONYMS

Can you match the synonyms in each column?

196. ora   domandare
      abito   matto
      vicino   viso
      faccia   dunque
      volentieri   adesso
      quindi   vestito
      pazzo   presso
      chiedere   con piacere

Fill in the blanks with either *sapere* or *conoscere*, as the case may be. Don't forget to put them in their appropriate tense and mood.

197. Ieri (io) _____ la professoressa d'italiano.
Quando avrò studiato con lei, allora _____ bene l'italiano.
Quando ero bambino, _____ suonare il pianoforte.
È impossibile che tu non _____ Roma.

Can you match the antonyms in each column?

198. piccolo   chiuso
      magro   tramonto
      dentro   tardi
      aperto   sporco
      pulito   fuori
      alba   decollo
      chiaro   grande
      atterraggio   scuro
      presto   grasso

20.
COGNATES:
GOOD AND
FALSE
FRIENDS

Supply the Italian equivalent for the following English words.

EXAMPLE: nation   *la nazione*

199. condition _____   situation _____
      conclusion _____   society _____
      importance _____   actor _____
      vocabulary _____   violinist _____
      oculist _____   biology _____
      geology _____   typical _____
      social _____   perfect _____
      effect _____   intellect _____

Check off the correct meaning of each word.

200. *la libreria*
 il negozio dove si comprano i libri ☐
 il luogo dove i libri sono a disposizione del
 pubblico ☐

 il parente
 il padre o la madre ☐
 lo zio, la zia, il cugino . . . ☐

 la fattoria
 la casa "in campagna" ☐
 un luogo industriale ☐

 la stampa
 si mette su una busta da lettera ☐
 si "legge" ☐

Translate the italicized words into Italian.

201. Domani, *I will be present* _____ alla riunione
 (meeting).
 Ieri, quell'uomo ha avuto *an accident* _____ brutto.
 Arturo Toscanini era un grande *conductor* _____.
 Non mi piace *that magazine* _____.
 Giovanni lavora per *a big firm* _____.

21.
READING

Read the following text, and then indicate if the statements are true or false.

202.
 *Mi chiamo Maria Celli. Sono dottoressa di pediatria
 presso un ospedale a Roma. Tutti i miei pazienti sono simpatici, perché sono piccoli. Ogni giorno c'è sempre qualche
 crisi medica da risolvere. Quindi, soffro di tensione. Per
 rilassarmi, leggo, guardo un po' la TV, o, ogni tanto, vado al
 cinema con qualche amico. La vita di un medico è veramente difficile!*

a. _____ Celli è un medico.
b. _____ I suoi pazienti sono adulti.
c. _____ E' una persona molto rilassata.
d. _____ Per riposarsi va anche al cinema.
e. _____ Maria è una paziente in un ospedale romano.
f. _____ Ogni giorno Celli risolve qualche crisi medica.
g. _____ Il medico non ha una vita facile.

22. WRITING

Can you put the following elements in their proper places on the letter?

203.

```
-Coca Cola Italia
-Con i più cordiali slauti
-Firenze, 4 dicembre 1995
-Gentile Sig.a Baldini
-Le scrivo per informarLa che potrò venire alla
 riunione del 22 dicembre
-Maria Pulci
-Spett.le Ditta
```

Answers

1. ITALIAN SOUNDS AND SPELLING

1. (*see* §1.3) cane, cravatta, come, gola, grande, spaghetti, chiesa, ghiaccio
2. (*see* §1.3) ciao, giorno, cena, giro, cioccolata, gente, cinema, giacca
3. scherzo, scena, sciopero, hanno, figlio, sogno, pala, sonno, fatto, caro (*see* §1.3)
4. (*see* §1.4) Oggi è lunedì, non venerdì.
5. (*see* §1.4) Che ora è? È l'una e dieci.
6. (*see* §1.4) Non prendo mai il caffè, perché preferisco il tè.
7. (*see* §1.5) A primavera fa sempre fresco in Italia; ma verso luglio comincia a fare più caldo.
8. (*see* §1.5) Mercoledì ho conosciuto una persona che veniva dalla Spagna, ma che non parlava lo spagnolo.
9. (*see* §1.5) La dottoressa Martini è italiana, e parla molto bene l'inglese.
10. (*see* § 1.5) Questo sabato vengo anche io alla festa di San Pietro.

2.
WORD ORDER IN AN ITALIAN SENTENCE

11–13 (§2.1 and general knowledge of word order)
11. Quegli studenti studiano troppo.
12. La macchina di Giovanni consuma troppa benzina.
13. La professoressa dice che l'italiano è una lingua importante.
14–17 (*see* §2.2–1)
14. Ieri sera, la professoressa Martini ha telefonato ai suoi studenti.
15. Ogni sera, Tina ascolta la radio.
16. Domani aspetterò l'autobus davanti a casa tua.
17. Mia sorella suona il pianoforte molto bene.
18, 19 (*see* § 2.2–2 and §2.2–3)
18. No, mio fratello non studia l'italiano.
19. No, io non mangio il pane.
20. (*see* §2.2–3 and §2.4)
    Chi aspetta l'autobus? —Maria.
    Quando sono andati al cinema? —Ieri.
    Dove sono andati i tuoi amici? —Al cinema.
    È italiano quell'uomo, vero? —Sì, è vero.
    Come va, signora? —Bene.
21. (*see* §2.3–1 and §2.3–2)
    Quella ragazza che legge il giornale è mia sorella.
    È arrivato il professore, appena sei andata via.
    Tu dormivi, mentre io guardavo la TV.
    È necessario che tu dica la verità.
22. Giovanni e Maria sono amici. Ieri sono andati al cinema insieme. Hanno visto un "western" con Clint Eastwood. Durante il film hanno comprato il caffè e diverse paste. Appena è finito il film, sono andati a prendere un gelato.

23.

g	e	m	e	l	l	o	n	m	o	l	o	e	g
u	b	n	m	e	d	c	t	u	i	o	p	l	r
a	n	m	e	a	u	i	p	z	c	n	m	m	e
n	o	l	p	o	i	u	t	u	r	e	s	c	c
c	i	n	e	s	e	l	p	o	m	e	n	t	o
i	e	g	h	i	l	o	u	i	o	p	c	d	c
a	r	a	n	c	i	o	n	e	d	v	d	c	d
c	c	d	d	e	e	u	i	l	o	o	r	o	e
e	r	c	d	n	c	d	c	d	d	l	c	d	e
r	t	u	i	a	l	b	e	r	g	o	b	u	i

§4.
Nouns

24–27 (*see* §4.2)

24. In quella città c'è tanta gente.
25. Carlo, il ragazzo che abita qui vicino, oggi non va a scuola.
26. Il padre e la madre di Carla, la ragazza di mio fratello, abitano in Italia.
27. La pera viene dal pero, la mela dal melo, e la pesca dal pesco.
28. (*see* §4.2–1)

zia, figlia, cantante, infermiera, cameriera, pittrice, attrice, dottoressa, avvocatessa

29. (*see* §4.2–2)

d	e	n	t	i	s	t	a	f	i	s	t
s	d	f	t	u	i	s	t	a	i	s	t
s	t	a	v	i	r	s	y	t	s	t	a
p	i	v	i	o	l	i	n	i	s	t	a
i	o	l	o	i	s	t	s	i	s	t	a
s	u	i	l	i	s	t	a	t	i	s	t
i	s	p	i	a	n	i	s	t	a	i	s

30. (*see* §4.2–3 through §4.2–6)

31. (*see* §4.3–1 through §4.3–3)

giorni, aeroporti, camerieri, notti, mele, avvocatesse, problemi, programmi, città, computer, ipotesi

32. (*see* §4.3–4)
i tedeschi
le tedesche
gli amici
le amiche
i medici
gli alberghi
gli psicologi
le psicologhe
i dialoghi
le paghe
le farmacie
gli orologi
le arance

33. (*see* §4.3–5, §4.3–6)
i figli
le figlie
le labbra
le miglia
i cinema
gli uomini
le mani

34. (*see* §4.4)
il signor Rossi
la signora Rossi
il dottor Rossi
la dottoressa Rossi
l'avvocato Rossi

35. (*see* §4.6)
salvagente
cacciavite
ferrovia
cassaforte
arcobaleno

5.
ARTICLES

36. (*see* §5.2–1)
la casa, l'acqua, il vino, l'indirizzo, il piatto, la frutta, la
matita, il prezzo, la scuola, la scena, lo specchio, lo
sbaglio, il sogno, lo zingaro, lo zio, lo studente, l'altro
zio, il nuovo studente, l'altra ragazza, lo psicologo, lo
gnocco

37. (*see* §5.2–1)

le case, le amiche, i vini, gli indirizzi, i piatti, le frutte, le matite, i prezzi, le scuole, le scene, gli specchi, gli sbagli, i sogni, gli zingari, gli zii, gli studenti, gli altri zii, i nuovi studenti, le altre ragazze, gli psicologi, gli gnocchi

38. (*see* §5.2–2)

un amico, un'amica, un padre, una madre, un italiano, un'italiana, un orologio, un'entrata, una sorella, uno zero, uno zio, uno sbaglio, un altro studente, uno gnocco, una buon'amica, uno psicologo, un bravo psicologo, una stanza

39. (*see* §5.2–3)

questo giorno, questa valigia, questo nome, questo giornale, questo zio, questa zia, questo studente, questa studentessa, questo (quest') arancio, questa (quest') arancia, questo psicologo, questo (quest') infermiere, questa (quest') infermiera, questo (quest') altro zio, questo bravo studente

40. (*see* §5.2–3)

questi giorni, queste valige, questi nomi, questi giornali, questi zii, queste zie, questi studenti, queste studentesse, questi aranci, queste arance, questi psicologi, questi infermieri, queste infermiere, questi altri zii, questi bravi studenti

41. (*see* §5.2–3)

quel giorno, quella valigia, quel nome, quel giornale, quello zio, quella zia, quello studente, quella studentessa, quell'arancio, quell'arancia, quello psicologo, quell'infermiere, quell'infermiera, quell'altro zio, quel bravo studente

42. (*see* §5.2–3)

quei giorni, quelle valige, quei nomi, quei giornali, quegli zii, quelle zie, quegli studenti, quelle studentesse, quegli aranci, quelle arance, quegli psicologi, quegli infermieri, quelle infermiere, quegli altri zii, quei bravi studenti

43. (*review* Chapters 4 and 5)

le dentiste, i farmacisti, gli sport, le entrate, i problemi, gli avvocati, questi turisti, questi medici, queste amiche, queste farmacie, quei figli, quei baci, quegli zii, quegli specchi, quegli orologi, quelle uscite, quelle radio

44–51 (*see* 5.3)

44. Il pane è un cibo.

45. Gli americani sono simpatici.

46. Roma è la capitale d'Italia (*no article*).

47. Il padre e la madre di Claudia abitano a Parigi.
48. L'Italia è bella.
49. Mi fa male il dito.
50. La signora Binni è molto simpatica.
51. "Buon giorno, signora Binni. Come va?" (*no article*)

6. PARTITIVES

52–60 (*see* §6.2)
52. delle forchette, dei bicchieri, degli sbagli, **degli gnocchi**, degli orologi, dei telegrammi, delle avvocatesse, **delle automobili, delle sedie**
53. alcune forchette, alcuni bicchieri, alcuni sbagli, alcuni gnocchi, alcuni orologi, alcuni telegrammi, **alcune avvocatesse, alcune automobili, alcune sedie**
54. qualche ragazzo, qualche studentessa, qualche uscita, qualche violinista, qualche violinista, qualche problema, qualche uomo, qualche mano
55. Qualche italiano è simpatico.
56. Qualche amica di Paola abita in Italia.
57. Qualche amico di Claudio parla il francese.
58. Non voglio nessuna caramella.
59. Non conosco nessuno psicologo.
60. Non ho fatto nessuno sbaglio.
61–64 (*see* §6.3)
61. Preferisco un po' di pane.
62. Giovanni mangia dell'insalata.
63. Vogliamo dell'acqua.
64. Lui vuole un po' di carne e io voglio del caffè.

7. ADJECTIVES

65. (*see* §7.2)
    . . . azzurro . . . nere . . . verde . . . gialla . . . marrone . . . bianchi . . . rosse . . . verdi . . . azzurri
66–69 (*see* §7.3)
65. Quanti libri hai comprato ieri?
67. Quello è veramente un vestito elegante.
68. Quale programma preferisci alla TV?
69. La conosco da tanti anni! È una conoscenza molto vecchia.
70–77 (*see* §7.4–1)
70. Quello è un buon libro.
71. Quella è una buona rivista.
72. Ho bisogno di una buon'auto.
73. Mario ha comprato dei begli orologi.
74. Maria è veramente una bella donna.
75. Mia sorella vuole una bell'auto.

76. Giovanni ha delle belle amiche.
77. Santa Maria, Santo Stefano, Sant'Agostino, San Paolo, San Marco, Sant'Agnese

78–80 (*see* §7.4–2)

78. Quale macchina preferisci (preferisce, Lei)?
79. Che (libro) è?
80. Quanti panini hai mangiato?

81–84 (*see* §7.4–3)

81. i miei libri, la mia giacca, le mie amiche, il mio quaderno, il tuo vestito, le tue scarpe, la tua casa, i tuoi impermeabili, il suo libro, i suoi libri, la sua amica, le sue amiche, il nostro dottore, i nostri professori, la nostra professoressa, le nostre professoresse, le vostre riviste, la vostra amica, il vostro sbaglio, i vostri sbagli, il loro problema, i loro problemi, la loro casa, le loro case
82. tuo cugino, nostra zia, vostra cugina, il loro fratello, la loro sorella, il suo zio italiano, la sua cugina americana, il vostro papà
83. È tuo cugino.
    È nostra zia.
    È suo zio.
    È il loro padre.
84. È il padre del bambino.
85. (*see* §7.4–4)
    Molti turisti . . . assai denaro . . . tutti i bei posti . . . troppa gente . . .stesse idee . . . altre belle città

86–88 (*see* §7.5)

86. Tuo padre è (così) elegante come mio padre./Tuo padre è (tanto) elegante quanto mio padre. (Or you can change *tuo padre* and *mio padre* around.)
87. Mario è più simpatico di Gino./Gino è meno simpatico di Mario.
88. Gino è più intelligente che simpatico./Gino è meno simpatico che intelligente.

8.
PRONOUNS

89–96 (*see* §8.2)

89. Questo è caro.
    Queste sono americane.
    Questo è nuovo.
    Questa è bella.
    Quelli sono belli.
    Quello abita in Italia.
    Quelli sono bravi.
    Quelle sono sporche.
    Quello è molto buono.

90. Dove sono i tuoi?
    Il loro è verde.
    Chi ha le mie?
    La nostra abita in Italia.
    Il suo è simpatico.
91. Chi abita a Roma?
92. Di chi è questo portafoglio?
93. Come ti chiami? (Come si chiama?—polite)
94. Dove abiti (abita)?
95. Quando sei/è andato in Italia?
96. Perché mangia (pol) OR mangi (fam) i dolci?
97. (*see* §8.3–1)
    . . . io sono andato . . . lei ha portato . . . noi due . . .
    Anche loro . . . proprio voi . . . siamo noi . . . Io sono qui
    . . . e tu . . . anche io
98–115 (*see* §8.3–2)
98. Giovanni gli telefonerà domani.
99. Ti penso spesso.
100. Maria mi ha chiamato(-a).
101. Lo chiamerò domani.
102. Tu gli telefonerai.
103. Maria la chiamerà.
104. E poi le telefonerà.
105. Maria ci ha visto(-i) ieri.
106. Il professore vi parlerà.
107. L'ha già data a quel ragazzo.
    Le ha già dato la penna.
    Ieri lo abbiamo mangiato.
    Ieri gli abbiamo telefonato.
    Giovanni me le ha date.
    Mio padre glieli ha mandati.
    Il commesso ce l'ha detta.
    No, non gliele ho date.
    Sì, gliela ha mandata.
108. Sì ti ho chiamato (ieri).
109. No, non mi hanno telefonato.
110. Sì, l'ho ricevuta.
111. No, non te lo darò.
112. Sì, ve la scriverò.
113. Gliele ho già scritte./Gliele ho scritte già.
114. Ve le mando domani./Domani ve le mando.
115. Te li ho dati ieri./Ieri te li ho dati.
116. (*see* §8.4)
    . . . che ho comprato . . . dal quale . . . che il verde . . .
    a cui . . . Quello (Quel, Ciò) che mi piace . . .

117–121 (*see* §8.5)
117. Non si dicono queste cose!
118. Quanta ne hai mangiata?
119. Ci andremo fra due mesi.
120. Non si è mai contenti!
121. Ci sono andati, e poi ne sono tornati.

9. Verbs

122–124 (*see* §9.2–1 through 9.2–7)
122. eri uscito già
      hai comprato
      andavano
      avranno mangiato
      Costerà
      cominciammo
      paghi
123. mangi
      comincerò
      sono arrivati
      avrà finito
      capì
      scriveva
      metti/hai messo
124. Io non aspetto.
      Tu capisci.
      Lui è uscito.
      Lei è uscita.
      Noi paghiamo il conto.
      Voi parlate troppo.
      Loro finiscono la lezione.
125. (*see* §9.3)
      Signor Santini, lo prenda!
      Marco, scrivila!
      Signorina, me li dia!
      Gino, non parlare!
      Ragazzi, andateci!
126. (*see* §9.4–1 and §9.4–2)
      scriverei
      avrei scritto
      avrebbe mangiato
      mangerebbe

127. (*see* §9.5–1 through 9.5–4)
arriverà
finisca
abbia piovuto
lavorerai
potesse
avessimo conosciuto

128. (*see* §9.7)
siamo divertiti
ti alzi
si ricorda
vi siete divertite
me la sono lavata
alzati
si metta

129. (*see* §9.6–1, §9.6–2, and 9.9, and review whole chapter)
. . . scrivo . . . sono stato . . . sia stata . . .
a comprare . . . stavo guardando . . . è venuto . . .
Voleva . . . avevo . . . ha cominciato . . . ha parlato . . .
andasse . . . aver parlato . . . decise di andare . . .
saremo . . . darò . . . amo.

130. (see Verb Charts section of this book)

```
t  u  i  u  h  n (b  e  v  u  t  o) c  i  o
d  c (l  e  t  t  o)(m  e  s  s  o) h  s  n
e  p  h (p  r  e  s  o) d  e  c  t  i  u  a
t  r  r  i  t  t  u  t  i  o  r  t  e  o  t
t  e  i  h  u  u  i  t  b  m  i  n  s  p  o
o  s  g  h  t  s  o  a  h  u  t  k  t  t  o
e (s  t  a  t  o) o (f  o  o  t  o) o  t  o
c  h  i  e  d (s  c  e  l  t  o) d  i  t  t
```

131. (*see* §9.8)
La torta è stata mangiata da Giovanni.
Molti regali saranno comprati dai turisti.
Quel libro è letto da tutti.
Credo che quel film sia stato interpretato da Sofia Loren.

10. ADVERBS

132, 133 (*see* §10.2)

132. raramente, certamente, precisamente, veramente, nuovamente
133. elegantemente, felicemente, regolarmente, difficilmente, popolarmente, benevolmente, leggermente

134–139 (*see* §10.3)

134. già
135. invece
136. ancora
137. poi
138. spesso, quasi
139. . . . molta fame . . . mangiato molto . . . molto buoni . . . molto buona . . . molte persone . . . molte verdure . . . molta carne

140–143 (*see* §10.4)

140. migliore
141. meglio
142. miglior(e)
143. meglio

11. PREPOSI-TIONS

144.–149 (*see* §11.2)

144. nel
     sul
     agli
     dello
     dall'
     nella
145. Sono i libri degli amici di Carla.
146. Ieri siamo andati ai negozi di abbigliamento.
147. Sono negli zaini.
148. Dalle uscite potrete vedere le macchine.
149. Abbiamo dato le tue matite alle ragazze.
150. (*see* §11.3).
     . . . da tre anni . . . tra due anni . . . in Francia . . . per studiare . . . a Parigi

12. NEGATIVES AND OTHER GRAMMATICAL POINTS

151. (*see* §12.2)
     mai
     nessuno
     neanche
     né . . . né
     più
     niente
     mica

152–158 (*see* §12.3)
152. Ecco
153. c'è
154. Qual è
155. sono . . . ci sono
156. La madre ha fatto scrivere una cartolina agli zii.
157. Gliela farò comprare
158. Maria non ha fatto lavare i piatti a suo fratello.

13.
THE VERB
"PIACERE"

159–163 (*see* §13.2)
159. Sì, mi piace molto.
160. Sì, mi piace e io piaccio a lei (or io le piaccio).
161. Mi piacciono, ma io non piaccio a loro (ma io non gli piaccio).
162. No, non mi è piaciuta, e agli altri non è piaciuta.
163. Sì, mi piaci. (E io) ti piaccio? Ci piacciamo, veramente?
164–167 (*see* §13.3)
164. Sì, mi piace la tua cravatta, ma non mi piacciono i tuoi pantaloni.
165. Ci piacciono i tortellini, ma purtroppo non ci piace il sugo.
166. Ti piace la minestra? A me non piace, ma mi piacciono i ravioli.
167. A lui piace l'italiano, a me piacciono gli sport, a te piace il cinema, a tutti noi non piacciono le barzellette.

14.
IDIOMATIC
EXPRESSIONS

168–173 (*see* §14.2)
168. Giovanni ed io abbiamo fame e sete.
169. D'estate loro hanno sempre caldo, ma d'inverno hanno sempre freddo.
170. Signora, Lei ha ragione; io, invece, ho torto.
171. Giovanni, non devi avere vergogna, e non devi avere paura.
172. Ho voglia di andare ad un ristorante stasera.
173. Abbiamo bisogno di due cose quando andremo in centro.
174–177 (*see* §14.3)
174. fare
175. dia . . . sta
176. Faccia . . . fare . . . fa
177. fa . . . fa . . . dà

178. (*see* §14.4)

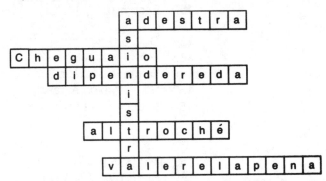

15.
NUMBERS

179. (*see* §15.2)
sette, nove, undici, ventuno, quarantadue, cinquantotto, ottantotto, cento ventitrè, novecento ottantasette, mille trecento quarantacinque, settantasei mila novecento ottanta, ottocento ottantotto mila ottocento ottantotto, due milioni trecento quarantacinque mila seicento settantotto

180. (*see* §15.3)
(la) quarta ragazza, (le) sedicesime lezioni, (il) ventitreesimo sbaglio, (il) duecento quarantottesimo giorno, (la) quattro mila cinquecento settantottesima pagina

181. (*see* §15.3)
due terzi, un ventottesimo, tre quarti, quindici sedicesimi, trentaquattro ottantanovesimi

182. Maria ha sette anni.
Marco ha dieci anni e Gino ha dodici anni.
Stefano è il più basso.

16.
TELLING TIME

183. (*see* §16.2–16.4)
È l'una. Sono le quattro e trenta (mezzo). Sono le due e venti. Sono le sei meno cinque (le cinque e cinquanta).

Sono le quattro e quaranta (le cinque meno venti). Sono le nove meno venti (le otto e quaranta). Sono le sette e quindici (un quarto). Sono le otto e quindici (un quarto).

Sono le venti e trentacinque (le ventuno meno venticinque). Sono le diciannove e trenta (mezzo). Sono le diciotto e quindici (un quarto). Sono le venti e cinque.

Sono le tredici e cinque. Sono le sedici meno venti (le quindici e quaranta). Sono le ventitrè e venticinque. Sono le ventidue e venticinque.

184. (*see* §17.2)

b	ì	s	t	g	i	o	v	e	d	ì
q	r	y	p	m	e	l	e	w	c	k
a	x	v	o	n	i	z	n	u	d	y
p	n	m	a	b	o	v	e	n	l	r
t	h	a	s	o	l	k	r	t	l	o
m	e	r	c	o	l	e	d	ì	s	a
x	c	t	e	j	u	g	ì	h	a	r
v	w	e	t	o	n	i	k	a	b	l
j	u	d	o	m	e	n	i	c	a	x
p	h	ì	r	e	d	a	s	o	t	g
z	k	a	y	n	ì	n	o	b	o	r

185. (*see* §17.3)
ottobre
luglio
agosto
dicembre
settembre
novembre
gennaio
giugno
febbraio
maggio
aprile
marzo

186. (*see* §17.4 and §17.5)
primavera
inverno
scorsa
prossimo
fa
A

187. (*see* §17.6)
lunedì, (il) dodici maggio
martedì, (il) venticinque gennaio
mercoledì, (il) primo febbraio
sabato, (il) tre dicembre

188. (*see* §17.7)

tira vento	tuona e lampeggia	piove
fa molto caldo	fa bel tempo	fa freddo

18.
COMMON DISCOURSE STRATEGIES

189, 190 (see §18.2)
189. Come va?
      Non c'è male, grazie, e Lei?
      Buon giorno.
190. Chi parla?
      Sono Gino. C'è tua sorella?
      Arrivederci.
191. (see §18.3 and §18.4)
      Buona sera, professore.
      Come Si chiama?
      Mi chiamo Daniela Berti. . . . permette che Le presenti
      . . . Le presento Dina Armando.
      Piacere . . . conoscenza
192–195 (see §18.5)
192. Che noia!
193. Mi dispiace.
194. Non sono d'accordo.
195. Come?

19.
SYNONYMS AND ANTONYMS

196, 197 (see §19.2)
196. ora—adesso
      abito—vestito
      vicino—presso
      faccia—viso
      volentieri—con piacere
      quindi—dunque
      pazzo—matto
      chiedere—domandare
197. ho conosciuto

198. piccolo—grande
      magro—grasso
      dentro—fuori
      aperto—chiuso
      pulito—sporco
      alba—tramonto
      chiaro—scuro
      atterraggio—decollo
      presto—tardi

20. COGNATES: GOOD AND FALSE FRIENDS

199. (*see* §20.2)

(la) condizione	(la) situazione
(la) conclusione	la società
(l') importanza	(l')attore
(il) vocabolario	(il/la) violinista
(l') oculista	(la) biologia
(la) geologia	tipico
sociale	perfetto
(l') effetto	(l') intelletto

200, 201 (*see* §20.3)

200. la libreria: Il negozio dove si comprano i libri.
il parente: lo zio, la zia, il cugino . . .
la fattoria: la casa "in campagna"
la stampa: si "legge"

201. assisterò
un incidente
direttore
quella rivista
una ditta grande

21. READING

202. a. vero
b. falso
c. falso
d. vero
e. falso
f. vero
g. vero

22. WRITING

203.

Firenze, 4 dicembre 1995

Spett.le Ditta,
Coca Coca Italia

Gentile Sign.a Baldini,

Le scrivo per informarLa che potrò venire alla riunione del 22 dicembre.

Con i più cordiali saluti,

Maria Pulci
(Maria Pulci)

Index